ICE CAPTAIN

ICE CAPTAIN
THE LIFE OF J.R. STENHOUSE

STEPHEN HADDELSEY

The History Press

Cover images
Front cover, top: The ice-bound *Aurora*; this photograph was probably taken before the ship was driven out to sea in May 1915. *Bottom:* Sir Ernest Shackleton setting out to make a last search for Aeneas Mackintosh and Victor Hayward, Imperial Trans-Antarctic Expedition, January 1917.
Back: A laughing Lieutenant Stenhouse, the officer commanding the Syren Flotilla of armed motor boats, makes his way down the jetty at Lake Onega, probably late spring 1919. (All images courtesy of Patricia and Sarah Mantell)

First published 2008

The History Press
The Mill, Brimscombe Port
Stroud, Gloucestershire, GL5 2QG
www.thehistorypress.co.uk

© Stephen Haddelsey, 2008, 2014

British Library Cataloguing in Publication Data.
A catalogue record for this book is available from the British Library.

isbn 978 0 7524 9779 2

Typesetting and origination by The History Press
Printed in Great Britain

For my nieces, Anna and Rachael

The vast terraqueous Globe I've rambled o'er,
But in myself retir'd discover'd more.

The Life and Errors of John Dunton

CONTENTS

LIST OF ILLUSTRATIONS

All photographs reproduced courtesy of Patricia and Sarah Mantell.

LIST OF MAPS

PREFACE

Ever since news of its astonishing fate broke upon a war-weary world nearly a century ago, Sir Ernest Shackleton's *Endurance* Expedition has been considered one of the supreme examples of polar exploration and survival against the odds. In that incredible story it is generally acknowledged that one of the most dramatic episodes is the epic 800-mile small-boat voyage across the storm-lashed Antarctic Ocean, from Elephant Island to South Georgia. It is less well known, however, that the expedition gave birth to not one but two heroic feats of seamanship, with matters of life and death hinging upon each in equal measure. This book tells, for the first time, the story of the man responsible for that other, less celebrated but equally remarkable odyssey: Joseph Russell Stenhouse.

Shackleton's trial began in the Weddell Sea; but, on the other side of the frozen continent, the expedition's second ship, the *Aurora*, suffered a fate which closely paralleled that of the *Endurance*. Torn from her moorings and driven out to sea by a ferocious gale, she, too, became trapped in pack-ice which, for ten months, sawed relentlessly at her wooden hull. Although the ice lifted the 600-ton ship from the water like a toy and strained her timbers and joints to breaking point, she, unlike the *Endurance*, eventually escaped its grip. With her rudder smashed and water cascading from her seams, under Stenhouse's command, the *Aurora* then embarked upon her own extraordinary and desperate voyage to reach safe harbour. That she survived at all was, in the words of Frank Worsley, entirely due to her captain's 'superb seamanship'. And Worsley knew what he was talking about: as master of the *Endurance*, it was he who had navigated the ship's whaleboat, the *James Caird*, to South Georgia.

But Stenhouse's command of the *Aurora* was just one episode in a career packed with extraordinary adventures. As with so many of his fellows, the Antarctic undoubtedly became the linchpin of his career. Unlike some, however, upon his return from the frozen south in 1917 Stenhouse did not experience any debilitating sense of anti-climax or bathos. In particular, the war offered him an opportunity to excel, both at sea and on land, and to build upon an already firmly established reputation for courage and daring. During its course he earned the Distinguished Service Cross for sinking an enemy submarine and the Distinguished Service Order and the French Croix de Guerre for his part in the Allied struggle with Bolshevism in Murmansk and Archangel. These, when added to the Order of the British Empire and the Polar Medal, which he received for his Antarctic service, made him one of the most highly decorated of all Heroic Age explorers. He also embraced the opportunity to return to Antarctic waters, not with the poorly conceived and goalless *Quest* Expedition which fell apart after the death of Shackleton in 1922, but as master of Captain Scott's *Discovery*, on which he shared responsibility for one of the most detailed and comprehensive surveys of the world's oceans ever undertaken.

In the difficult postwar years, Stenhouse, with so many others, experienced periods of unemployment and he became involved in a variety of money-making schemes. Some, such as his hunt for pirate gold on Robert Louis Stevenson's Treasure Island, smacked of romance and desperation in equal measure; others, such as his attempt to pioneer Antarctic tourism in the 1930s, based upon an altogether more robust premise. But, be they fantastical or rational, he brought to every occupation the same levels of determination and resourcefulness that had enabled him to bring the crippled *Aurora* back to safety.

Almost as extraordinary as the range of Stenhouse's activities is the remarkable survival of the record of his adventures. He was both a diarist and a regular letter-writer and many of these documents have been preserved by his family. Inevitably, some items have been lost or destroyed in the decades since his death, but the residue constitutes what must be one of the most comprehensive archives of any Heroic Age Antarctic explorer in private, or, perhaps, even in public hands. It allows us to observe Stenhouse in a range of circumstances and environments, before, during and after the *Endurance* Expedition. We see him as an apprentice, lashed with spume and spray as his first ship rounded Cape Horn in a tempest; sledging across the Antarctic sea-ice of McMurdo Sound to break into the time capsule of Scott's *Discovery* hut; dodging the bullets of Bolshevik soldiers among the pine forests of the Kola Peninsula; and fighting to salvage ships crucial to the Allied war effort in the Red Sea. These glimpses combine to reveal a man whose courage, resourcefulness and resilience impressed themselves indelibly on those who served with him and earned for him their respect, admiration and enduring affection.

And yet Stenhouse also suffered from prolonged and debilitating bouts of depression and, in certain circumstances, he could demonstrate an inclination to brag, a willingness to strike first and ask questions later and so rigid an adherence to shipboard discipline that he sometimes resembled a martinet of the old school. Operated upon by different pressures and different personalities, the balance of his multifaceted character could shift and change, and the very qualities that enabled him to save the *Aurora* in 1916 led to disastrous discord and disunity on board the *Discovery* in 1927. The fact that these conflicts and inconsistencies can be observed against an ever-changing backdrop of adventure and action, and that they are described in Stenhouse's own words with all the immediacy of felt experience, has made his life fascinating to research and – I can only hope – to read.

ACKNOWLEDGEMENTS

Ifirst became familiar with the career of J.R. Stenhouse when researching that of his friend, the equally daring Heroic Age explorer, Frank Bickerton. The lives and adventures of both men have struck a chord with practically everyone I have contacted during the course of my years of research but, while every facet of Bickerton's life had to be pursued with the tenacity of the most dedicated detective, the vast bulk of the material used in preparing this biography was made available to me after only one or two telephone calls and letters. Practically every document upon which this biography is based, including diaries, letters, notebooks, photographs and memoranda, lies in the hands of Stenhouse's family – in particular, in those of his only daughter, Mrs Patricia Mantell, and his granddaughter, Sarah Mantell. To Mrs Mantell and to Sarah, therefore, I should like to offer my most sincere thanks for all their support, encouragement and hospitality. Without their generosity and enthusiasm this book could never have been written. Furthermore, by preserving such an expansive archive, they have not only ensured that there is hardly a single gap or ambiguity in Stenhouse's remarkable story, they have also done a great service to the history of Antarctic exploration.

I should also like to express my gratitude to the following individuals whose assistance and encouragement have been vital in enabling me to plug the few gaps in the Mantell family archive: Mr and Mrs Charles Stenhouse Martin, for kindly sharing their memories of Stenhouse, as well as for allowing me access to Mr Martin's unpublished biography of his uncle, and to the letters and other documents relating to Stenhouse's career in their possession. Mrs Elisabeth Dowler, daughter of Aeneas and Gladys Mackintosh and stepdaughter of Stenhouse, for once again providing a wealth of anecdotes and stories; and her daughter, Mrs Anne Phillips, for her continued help with and interest in my work. Mr Pat Bamford, for his hospitality and for allowing me access to his archive of material relating to Stenhouse's greatest friend, Commander Frank Worsley. Mr John Thomson, biographer of Worsley, for his valuable help in researching the friendship of Stenhouse and Worsley. Mr John Hooke, for allowing me access to the

Aurora diary of his father, Lionel Hooke. Mr Falcon Scott, for permitting me to quote from the papers of Kathleen Scott held at the Scott Polar Research Institute. The Hon. Alexandra Shackleton, for allowing me to utilise the Shackleton papers in the Scott Polar Research Institute. Mrs Margaret Marshall for kindly copying portions of the diary of her late husband, Dr E.H. Marshall, surgeon on the RRS *Discovery*. Mrs Pippa McNickle for her assistance in tracing the wartime friendship between Stenhouse and her father, Lieutenant-Commander L.M. Bates. Mr Mark Offord for the research undertaken on my behalf at the National Archives in Kew. Mrs Rosalind Marsden and Mrs Ann Savours Shirley for sharing with me their research into the National Oceanographic Expedition. Mrs Jane Seligman, for sharing her memories of Stenhouse's connection with the voyage of the *Cap Pilar*. Mr James Campbell, for information relating to the friendship of his father, Major Walter Campbell, with Stenhouse.

Of course, a variety of institutions and their staff have been of immeasurable help; in particular, I should like to thank the following both for their generous assistance and for permission to quote from materials in their collections: the Scott Polar Research Institute (SPRI), Cambridge, and its archivist, Ms Naomi Boneham; the National Oceanography Centre (NOC), Southampton, and its erstwhile librarian, Ms Pauline Simpson; the Canterbury Museum, Christchurch, New Zealand; Mr Martin Beckett of the State Library of New South Wales, Sydney, Australia; The National Archives (TNA) at Kew in London; the Imperial War Museum (IWM) in London; the Alexander Turnbull Library, New Zealand; and the Bodleian Library (BL) in Oxford. This list is not, indeed cannot, be comprehensive and I hope that those who have not been named individually will not think that their help is any the less appreciated. Every effort has been made to contact copyright holders and I should like to crave the indulgence of any literary executors or copyright holders where these efforts have been unavailing.

Finally, I should like to pay tribute to my wife, Caroline, for her incredible forbearance and for her unflinching support and encouragement, without which this book would never have been completed.

Stephen Haddelsey
Southwell, Nottinghamshire

AUTHOR'S NOTE

Many of the diaries and letters quoted in this book were written in circumstances of extreme stress and hurry which, inevitably, resulted in an array of spelling mistakes and grammatical errors. For purposes of clarity and ease of reading, spelling has been corrected; punctuation has also been adjusted where absolutely necessary. Any words inserted by the author for clarity of meaning are identified by the addition of square brackets.

THE APPRENTICE IN SAIL

O n a late summer's morning in 1904, two figures might have been
seen making their way along the crowded quaysides of South
Shields, on the north-eastern coast of England. Followed by a porter
pushing a conspicuously new-looking trunk on a handcart, they had made
their way from the railway station, negotiating the squalid streets of poor
housing that tumbled down towards the docks and which, for all South
Shields' prosperity, were inhabited by wretched-looking children, filthy and
shoeless. The shorter of the two pedestrians, middle-aged and well-built,
strode with confidence among the cables, crates and assorted impedimenta
of the busy port. He seemed impervious to the stench of the herring fisheries,
wafted by an inshore breeze from North Shields, and cast quick, appraising
glances at the vessels crowding the harbour. The other, for all his powerful,
loose-limbed build and 6ft 1½in, looked altogether less self-assured, as might
be expected of a boy only just approaching the threshold of manhood.
Andrew Stenhouse, engineer for Vickers & Maxim, the great shipbuilder and
armaments manufacturer, and his 16-year-old son, Joe, had just travelled by
train from Barrow-in-Furness, the latter nervously clutching a letter he had
received a fortnight before from the offices of the Andrew Weir Shipping &
Trading Company. The crumpled paper advised him that 'we have arranged
for you to go in our Barque *Springbank*' and that he should hold himself 'in
readiness to join her in the Tyne'.[1]

Only a few weeks earlier, Joseph Russell Stenhouse had been employed
as a clerk in the Barrow offices of Lloyds Register of Shipping. Having left
Barrow's Higher Grade School,[2] aged 14, for two years the muscular and
square-jawed youth had perched upon a high stool in an airless room,
slaving at his duties and proving himself, according to his employer's glowing
reference, 'willing, obliging and attentive'. But he had found it impossible
to settle for a life of pen-pushing drudgery and, with each passing month,
what he would later call the 'strange, strange call' of the sea had sounded
ever more resonantly in his ears. That he should be receptive to this siren
call was not, perhaps, particularly surprising, as his family had a long

established connection with the sea. His grandfather, also called Joseph, had started life, like his father before him, as a ship's carpenter but, by 1875, his ability and drive had resulted in his taking over his employer's shipbuilding yard, and in his founding the firm of Birrell, Stenhouse & Company at Woodyard, Dumbarton.

It was at Woodyard, on 15 November 1887, that the patriarch's namesake had been born. And here also, on 17 May 1889, that he had watched the launching of the firm's last great sailing ship, the *Elginshire*. A near-drowning, which left the child black in the face and full of foul water, failed to instil any fear and the constant proximity of sailing ships, both in Woodyard and in Barrow, where his family moved when he was 2 years old, left an indelible mark on the boy's soul. The culmination of these influences had been a decision to abandon his desk at Lloyd's and to sign on for a four-year apprenticeship with whichever shipping company would have him. Andrew Stenhouse attempted to dissuade his son from the daring step he now seemed determined to take, but his arguments rang rather hollow and, after dutiful consideration, they were ignored. It was, as Andrew himself must have been well aware, a predictable case of 'like father, like son'. For he, too, had once fallen victim to the lure of the ocean, and had served as an apprentice at sea[3] before becoming a manager with the family firm, a position he continued to hold until Birrell's bankruptcy and the decline in demand for sailing vessels forced him to seek employment with Vickers.

Now, the *Springbank* lay before them and her 282ft length and 43ft beam would mark the boundaries of the young Stenhouse's world for many long months to come. She was, as the newest member of her crew later admitted, distinctly unprepossessing in appearance: her iron hull streaked with rust and the water surrounding her made almost metallic by the pollution of fish scales and oil. Originally built for the nitrate trade and launched in Glasgow in September 1894, *Springbank* had spent the last decade ploughing the world's oceans carrying cargoes consisting mostly of timber and coke. Four-masted and jubilee-rigged, she now sat low in the water, her Plimsoll line tickled by the unctuous swell.

Announcing their business, father and son received permission to come aboard and, followed by the shiny trunk, they crossed from shore to ship. A brief tour of inspection followed, during which Andrew Stenhouse cast an expert eye around his son's new berth, taking in her bluff bows and her stump topgallant masts with their square rig, and the fine run aft which gave such promise of excellent sailing qualities. The unexpectedly pungent atmosphere of the claustrophobic afterdeck lavatory, however, brought the tour to a sudden halt – followed by a hasty disembarkation of the retching engineer. His son followed sheepishly, acutely aware of the impression that their rapid departure must have made on his shipmates-to-be. They exchanged farewells on shore; Andrew memorised a last message for Joe's stepmother[4] and 18-year-old sister, Nell, left in Barrow, and then the new apprentice returned to his ship. The *Springbank*'s cargo of coke and general goods had already been loaded and within a few short hours she put to sea, bound for San Francisco via the Cape Verde Islands and Cape Horn. The boy standing on her deck and the anxious parent watching her departure from the shore each knew that a year or more must pass before the Stenhouse family would be reunited.

Under grey skies, the *Springbank* slipped out of the Tyne and into the North Sea, round the coast of East Anglia and down into the English Channel, before pushing her nose out into the deep, open waters of the North Atlantic. Stenhouse had been given his first job within hours of boarding: being sent aloft to reef the jigger-masthead flag halliards, high above the deck. He later recorded that 'although I had no fear, when I hauled myself clear of the futtock rigging and found no ratlines beyond the topmast rigging, I began to feel the strain. . . . Eventually, after a great effort, I reached the masthead pole, and with beating heart, and legs and arms clutching the mast and backstays, I rove the end of the halliards through the truck, overhauled them and started to come down.'[5] He reached the safety of the deck totally exhausted, with his palms flayed by an unintentionally precipitate descent down the backstays but also with a chest expanded with a sense of achievement. His shipmates, however, quickly disabused him of any notion that the minor victories, the opinions or the comfort of a 'first voyager' carried any weight in the ship. Of the seven apprentices aboard, three, including Stenhouse, were complete novices and, as such, the more experienced hands considered them worse than useless. It must have been a galling realisation for a boy who had grown up with sailing ships, whose grandfather had built and launched many vessels such as the *Springbank*, and in whom family pride waxed strongly.

Mercifully, the routine of the ship allowed little time for introspection. The hours were long and the work arduous, particularly for one who, despite his stature and bodily strength, possessed little experience of such intense labour. Of course, the first voyagers were chosen for the least skilled and most tedious tasks. These included all the cleaning duties, from filling the captain's bath to scrubbing the bilge; striking the bell with the regularity of clockwork; and hauling on a sheet or clewline whenever the demands of the moment required unskilled muscle to be applied.

Undertaking these and a hundred other tasks, inevitably Stenhouse found that he was thrown together a good deal with his fellow apprentices. These residents of the half deck proved to be a mixed bunch including three Englishmen, two Scots, one Australian and one Belgian, but they quickly bonded into a tight-knit group. They had little choice, as they found themselves the butt of every joke. Stenhouse proved no exception to the rule and, in his diary, he recorded one trick that a wiseacre among the crew attempted to play on him. 'We are painting our house,' he noted, 'and are consequently sleeping on deck at night and I was awakened by my mattress being drawn from under me as I slept on the main (No. 3) hatch this morning. I didn't know what was the matter at first, but when I saw my mattress going aloft at the end of a rope I made a dive for it and managed to get hold of it and cut it adrift in time to save it from being sent up to the main yard.'[6] With the assumed wisdom and condescension of an old hand, he concluded his entry with the remark that 'This is a common trick at sea and also is [*sic*] the tying of a man to the nearest fixture; Douglas, one of the Port watch being tied to the ring bolts, on the hatch casements.'[7]

Gradually Stenhouse came to know his other shipmates as well, though they seldom allowed him to forget his lowly position in the shipboard hierarchy. The able seamen generally treated the apprentices with a rough kindliness not far removed from contempt. Then came the three mates and, at the apex of the social pyramid, the dour, red-whiskered captain, who saved his smiles for his cabin and for the young wife and baby daughter who sailed with him. But Stenhouse seldom had anything to do with the captain who, so far as the apprentices were concerned, remained as aloof and remote as Ahab. Having agreed to take them, however, the 'old man' felt obliged to make some attempt to educate the boys as seamen and prospective officers and so, sometimes, Stenhouse and his companions would be made to stand on the poop staying the ropes and boxing the compass. But, for the most part, they remained in blissful ignorance as to the ship's course and speed. When writing his diary, Stenhouse often left space to record latitude and longitude but he seldom obtained sufficient information to fill these gaps and the unspoken assumption was that he and his fellows would learn by hard labour, by emulation and by observation – or not at all.

Towards the end of October, the atmosphere on board changed as the crew became engaged in a variety of bizarre activities, apparently more akin to a child's birthday party than to the backbreaking toil of a working merchant vessel. Mature and experienced seamen, usually taciturn and scruffy to the highest degree, now laughed like schoolboys as they dyed their old slops or laboured like fashionable Parisian hairdressers to create wigs and false beards. The cause of their hilarity and industry was the proximity of the Equator. Ancient tradition demanded that 'crossing the line' should be marked with an uproarious ceremonial during which those who had never before passed between the northern and southern hemispheres were subjected to a rough, if usually good-humoured, initiation. And they left

Stenhouse and the other first voyagers in no doubt as to their role in the forthcoming proceedings. The older sailors winked at them and laughed among themselves, while the second voyagers taunted them with stories of rough handling, near-drowning and humiliation before the assembled crew.

The preparations, which provided a welcome break from the routine of shipboard life, continued for three weeks until, on the morning of 19 November, thirty-three days out from South Shields, the *Springbank* crossed the line. At 8.30 a.m., as Stenhouse swallowed his last mouthful of breakfast, a whistle sounded, 'that being the Sergeant's signal to his four policemen to come and lay hold on some first-voyager'. Stenhouse had already decided on his course of action:

> As soon as I heard the whistle I put some biscuits in my pockets and made a dash for the poop, meaning to go down the sail locker and hide from the policemen, but I met the Mate and he sent me down on deck again. Running into the half-deck again I jumped into the clothes locker and one of the second-voyagers shut [the] door on me. After about a quarter of an hour one of the policemen came into the half-deck and searched everywhere, clothes locker as well, even putting his hand on my shoulder, but did not see me. After another short lapse of time another sergeant came, this time he got me and blowing a whistle in rushed four men in blue, armed with belaying pins, the sergeant himself having a wooden dagger, with which he probed me when I refused to come out of the locker. After about five minutes struggling, during which I got a few cuffs on the head and other parts with the pins, they got me out and carried me forrard, kicking all the while, and dumped me head first into the port WC ... [8]

Half an hour later, as he waited to be dragged before his judge, another first voyager opened the door – and he made a second bid for freedom. This time the unwilling neophyte climbed up into the rigging. He smiled to himself at the surprise of his jailers when they found that 'the bird had flown', but his escape was only temporary. Soon his pursuers spotted him on the topgallant yard and, when he refused to descend, the Mate who throughout the proceedings had evidenced his firm belief in tradition, ordered him to return to the deck. Immediately his feet touched the planking, the policemen blindfolded him and then dragged him, still struggling, before Neptune who sat in state on a box covered with a Union Jack. Asked his age, Stenhouse forgot himself so far as to attempt a reply:

> I opened my mouth to speak, when the Soap Boy, who was rigged with a fancy head piece of rope yarns and reddened on his face with red lead,

shoved in some pills, which the Doctor had made of soap, etc. Then came
the tarring, after being stripped to my waist, I was tarred with a brush
and then scrubbed with a broom. This was repeated again and again and
then I was shaved with a wooden razor, the blade of which was about two
feet long. Then they dumped me in the bath and kept my head under long
enough to make me think I was drowning.[9]

Still undaunted, as soon as he surfaced, Stenhouse grabbed a tar brush
and tried to belabour one of the policemen, but his tormentors quickly
overpowered him and made him submit to another shave, before finally
handing him his hard-earned certificate for crossing the line.

Although he resisted such indignities with all his might, and received
a sound cuffing in reply, Stenhouse's strength and courage earned him
the respect of many of his shipmates. Unfortunately, these qualities, his
unwillingness to suffer in silence beneath a slight, whether real or perceived,
and his refusal to 'turn the other cheek' also led him into direct conflict with
his superiors. But, as he would later state, 'a man without pride is no man
at all'[10] and, despite his avowed respect for authority, any offer of violence
would be instantly and vigorously reciprocated. Still only 16 years old and
on his first voyage, this bullish attitude resulted in a bout of fisticuffs with
the belligerent second mate. One watch, this Irishman, 'hefty as a bullock'
and impatient of any impertinence or slackness, took exception to the
unusually musical manner in which the young apprentice struck six bells
[at 11 p.m.]. When he asked Stenhouse to explain himself, he took further
umbrage at what he took to be the boy's insolent response and, rather than
debate the issue further, he resorted to his fists. Fortunately for Stenhouse,
his own length of reach made him a match for the mate's greater bulk, and
within seconds they were locked in a clinch which only the appearance of
the enraged captain brought to a close. An act of insubordination which,
on a ship of the Royal Navy would have ended in the direst consequences,
resulted in nothing worse than the loss of an hour's sleep in each watch
below, during which Stenhouse paced the flying-bridge between the poop
and the after deck-house, with a heavy capstan-bar balanced on each
shoulder. Such lessons proved salutary and an unbending demand for
discipline at sea, gradually and unconsciously imbibed, would become
second nature. In later life, indeed, and in conditions of both war and peace,
men under his command would learn that Stenhouse would have no truck
with indiscipline, that he could be a martinet altogether more exacting
even than the *Springbank*'s officers.

He learned other lessons as well: the most potent of all being love of the
ocean and of the sailing ships that plied their trade across its ever-changing
surface. Even before taking to the sea, Stenhouse possessed a strong feeling

of family pride: pride in the three – now four – generations who had made the sea their trade; pride also in the vessels which his family had launched and which he occasionally recognised in the ports and harbours visited by the *Springbank*. Now he added to these feelings a deep and enduring love of the ships' grace and beauty under sail, qualities made all the more poignant by his realisation that he was witnessing the nadir of the sailing ships' fortunes, as steam and the internal combustion engine pushed them ever closer to extinction. Even in the carelessness of youth, he knew that, by serving his apprenticeship on such a ship, he had become forever bound to a way of life that stood on the brink of annihilation. His appreciation of the beauty that he saw about him, and which made his heart beat perceptibly faster every time a similar vessel came over the horizon, was already tinged with nostalgia and regret. This love and this wistfulness would mark him for life.

As the *Springbank* plunged ever southwards, he saw the Atlantic Ocean in all its moods: from smiling serenity to wave-whipped fury. South of the line, she picked up the south-east Trade winds and made steady progress. Dolphins leapt and danced in the ship's bow-wave, seemingly in constant danger of being run down but miraculously avoiding harm. Flying fish, too, broke the surface at regular intervals, skimming the waves for perhaps a hundred yards, the sun glinting on their silver scales and outstretched bony fins, before they returned to their natural element. Sometimes, they would land flapping on the deck and the crew dived upon them, as a welcome and God-given supplement to their otherwise monotonous diet. And once, in the stillness of the night, when the mastheads whirled like skaters in skies dotted with a thousand stars, Stenhouse witnessed a more unusual phenomenon: the fiery passage of a comet, 'its tail which was like a streak of lightning' remaining visible for nearly 10 minutes after its passing.

As they entered the South Atlantic, conditions changed for the worse. He remembered that 'Off the River Plate we were struck by a Pampero; lightning, thunder, cold driving rain, and a howling gale of wind broken by squalls that would have lifted the sticks out of her if she had not been shortened down in time.'[11] As they approached Cape Horn, where the waters of the Atlantic and the Pacific tumble and churn in violent confusion, the weather grew colder and more uncertain. On 12 December, he noted that:

When we turned out, at 12 midnight, found the ship scudding along on fore and main topsails and mizzen lower topsail and foresail. Blowing hard today and the vessel, tho' she rides the water like a duck, is shipping a lot of water, so much so that, when at 12 o'clock noon, all hands were forward pulling on the weather fore brace a sea came over and washed us away from the brace. Before I knew what was happening I found myself on my back, full of water, and with two other chaps on top of me. However we went to the brace again, and again got filled. After another sea came, which washed two men into the scuppers, the Captain sent us to haul the braces tight to leeward.[12]

The crew rigged lifelines fore and aft, both port and starboard, to prevent men being washed overboard and everyone prepared to do battle with some of the most turbulent waters on the face of the earth. The sky turned leaden and black clouds, caught in the wind's gripe, swept past at seemingly impossible speeds.

With high seas, biting winds and snow flurries, conditions on board rapidly deteriorated. The seawater, as it broke over the rail, proved no respecter of people, bunks or possessions and it seemed that the crew would never again be dry or warm. Such conditions took a physical toll, particularly on Stenhouse and his fellows, whose flesh had never before been subjected to such a penetrating dampness. Oilskins chafed their gooseflesh and saltwater boils swelled on their wrists and necks; while between their fingers and in the palms of their hands cuts and abrasions, opened wide and made excruciatingly sore by cold and saltwater, refused to heal. In this misery, the crew celebrated Christmas off the Horn, with 'Currant Bread for breakfast and Duff for dinner'. The captain's wife also gave the apprentices 'a large plateful of sweets and nuts and in the evening the mate brought in his guitar and we sang a few carols.'[13]

The *Springbank* rounded the Horn in a howling gale, her decks awash and the sea around her a swirling, deadly maelstrom. She ran the gauntlet with two stout men handling the bucking wheel and every member of the crew stretched to breaking point in their desperate attempts to avoid being blown too far south. Having once negotiated South America's rocky tip, however, the ship and her exhausted crew could at last head north into the blue waters of the Pacific. Passing through the Roaring Forties, each mile covered took them further from the blear, gunmetal skies of the South Atlantic and closer to warmth and sunshine. They entered the tropics again and, exchanging pea jackets for bare torsos, allowed the sun to play on their pallid skin, while their thoughts raced ahead to the pleasures of 'Frisco.

The captain and his mates, meanwhile, turned their attention to the condition of their battered vessel. Under their watchful eyes, the crew repaired rigging, buffed dull brasswork to a splendid lustre and gradually patched up the wounds inflicted by weeks of unremitting storm. Stenhouse, as befitted a first-year apprentice, found himself responsible for a particularly unpleasant job: cleaning the freshwater tank. It was a foul task, demanding no skill but considerable powers of endurance, and to be completed in stifling heat and in a dark, claustrophobic space, soon made even more unpalatable by the stink of two sweating men. 'To get at the tank bottom,' he noted in his diary, 'we have to crawl in thro' a small hole, onto the timber hatches and lay on our backs as the space between the tank's bottom and the limber hatches is only about 2ft deep. This is hot work for the Tropics, especially as there are two lamps burning near to us.'[14] But, between watches, he quickly forgot the unpleasantness of such duties, as the whole crew, young and old, veteran and novice, talked excitedly of their coming landfall.

With the bitterness of long experience, Stenhouse later claimed that the soaring expectations entertained by every deep-water man regarding his next port were inevitably dashed by the reality they found ashore. But, to a youth of seventeen who had not set foot on dry land for 155 days, San Francisco offered no such disappointment. In his mind's eye, indeed, the Golden Gates were not far removed from the gates of Paradise itself: they promised new faces, a break from the routine and drudgery of shipboard life, fresh food and drink and, not least in the catalogue of desired objects, new adventures.

This was San Francisco before the great earthquake and fire of 1906, well acquainted with crime, licentiousness and violence and nowhere more so than on the city's waterfront, known ominously as the Barbary Coast. Here a confusion of cheap saloons, brothels, theatres and opium dens pandered to the needs and tastes of sailors who, after voyages of many months, found themselves cast ashore with a handful of dollars in their pockets and a finely honed desire for alcohol, amusement and fornication. Led by a couple of second voyagers, who had visited 'Frisco once before, and therefore considered themselves expert guides, Stenhouse and his peers launched themselves into the tawdry streets and alleyways, bent on pleasure, the single dollar allowed to first voyagers burning a hole in their pockets. They dined on chocolate and cakes, and then paid 10 cents to enter a vaudeville theatre, with sawdust-strewn floors and an atmosphere thick with tobacco smoke, sweat and the fumes of cheap beer and whisky. The product of a middle-class Scottish upbringing, Stenhouse found the show disgusting: full of obscenity and innuendo, and his discomfort was made even more acute by the insistent ribaldry of the prostitutes in the audience, keen to ply their trade among the fresh-faced and gullible young sailors.

But the night was still young and, having once extricated themselves from the increasingly strident attentions of the drunken whores, Stenhouse and his fellows sought refreshment at one of the many noisy and crowded saloons. Made conspicuous by their swaggering, if skin-deep, assumption of self-confidence and their fastidiously clean shore-going rig, the *Springbank*'s apprentices soon found themselves attracting more unwanted attention: this time from a set of pugnacious Scandinavian sailors or, as Stenhouse called them, 'yah-for-yes men'. Jests were directed firstly at the boys themselves and then, more dangerously, at their country of origin. Stenhouse had little of the pacifist in his make-up; an insult should be resented, a slight must be rebuffed: 'As a spark to the tinder so is an insult to an Englishman or so it should be, and so the fight began. In a moment the saloon was a mass of flying glasses, arms and legs. The wise ones made for the door. In the midst of that wild fighting mob our little party of five surged to and fro across the saloon floor, fighting our way to the door. We stuck together, which cramped our style but gave us weight, and as we burst out into the night air we heard the cry of cops. That did not sound so good.'[15] And so, after five months at sea, Stenhouse's first night on dry land ended in a police cell, in company with cut-throats, thieves and pimps, followed, after hours of intense uncertainty, by a judge's caution and merciful release. It could have been far worse. They had got off with some cuts and bruises, a ticking-off from a worldly judge and, when they returned to their ship, a sound berating from an irate captain.

Having unshipped her cargo of coke, the *Springbank*'s hold was partly filled with Oregon pine. She then made her way rapidly northwards to complete her loading of timber in Vancouver. After the febrile atmosphere of San Francisco, ostensibly at least, Vancouver had little to offer in the way of excitement or adventure. Writing to his father, Stenhouse described the town as 'just like a big mining camp, wooden houses and badly made roads, but [it] is a far nicer place than 'Frisco. We are laying opposite to N. Vancouver. It is composed of a few Siwash Indians' huts surrounded by hills and lumber but it is still going to be the residential place of future Vancouverites.'[16] Nicer than San Francisco, perhaps, but still prone to the noise, disruption and danger seemingly inseparable from waterfront life. If murder and assaults were commonplace in old 'Frisco, violence often lurked just beneath the surface even in ports altogether less notorious.

One morning, in the most ragged of his ocean-going slops, Stenhouse stood on a platform swung out over the ship's side, adding a fresh coat of paint to the *Springbank*'s weather-stained hull. His work was disturbed by the activity on board another rather scruffier vessel, the Liverpool-registered *Senator*. The barking of orders and the rapid movement of sailors about her decks revealed that she was preparing to weigh anchor, bound for home. From his precarious perch, Stenhouse could see in the *Senator*'s shadow a small dinghy, its owner seemingly bent on nothing more than some idle sightseeing. And then, quite suddenly, the scene burst into unexpected and violent action. In quick succession, and without a cry, two men threw themselves, or fell, from the rails of the *Senator* straight into the dinghy below, nearly causing it to capsize. As the boat rocked, the sounds of a heated altercation drifted across the waters of the bay and one of the jumpers could be seen wresting the oars from the dinghy's owner. As the *Vancouver Daily Province* reported:

> 'Here you – gimme those oars and be d—d quick about it,' sang out one of the unexpected and unwelcome visitors just as the owner of the boat collected his wits sufficiently to gather that the visitors were escaping sailors. He gave up the oars.
>
> Then commenced a race for the shore. The man at the oars had not taken two strokes before a head was poked over the rail of the ship, followed by a rifle on which the sun glinted in a way that was most disconcerting to the owner of the boat. A hoarse command that the boat should return went unheeded by the escaping sailors.
>
> 'Phug—szip.'
>
> It was the rifle that spoke, and the shot hit the water near the rowboat and then glanced and skipped over the water. . . . It was followed by half a dozen in quick succession. None of them hit the mark, but they were at last becoming sufficiently close to scare the deserters. They gave up, and rowing back to the ship, clambered aboard.[17]

Not so very long before, the wharves and jetties of Vancouver had resounded to the footsteps of gold prospectors hopefully making their way to the Klondike, and the town was no stranger to brawling and even murder. In reporting the incident that Stenhouse witnessed, the *Daily Province* reminded its readers that a similar incident had occurred only eighteen months earlier and one man had been shot and wounded. Suitably impressed by this exhibition of bloodthirsty lawlessness, Stenhouse cut the account of the fracas out of the newspaper and sent it home, so that his father might 'see from the enclosed that there are bears, whales and fights around here'.[18]

In fact, desertion was commonplace, though the lengths to which the *Senator*'s officers were prepared to go to prevent it were rather less so. The *Springbank* enjoyed no immunity and she had lost a large portion of her crew among the brothels and rookeries of San Francisco, with the result that Stenhouse found 'that the work comes on us pretty heavily'. For the apprentices, however, the desertion of the more experienced members of the crew brought some compensations. For long months they had been regarded as little more than supercargo, hardly trusted to undertake the most menial job without supervision; now the reduction in the numbers of able seamen meant that, as well as more work, more responsibility came their way. This recognition proved something of a watershed in Stenhouse's career. Still less than a year into his four-year articles, he had taken the crucial first step towards being acknowledged as a capable and useful sailor. He had also proved himself to be tough, strong-willed and independent: qualities essential to any budding officer.

Over the next few months, the *Springbank* sailed into the South Seas, hurried on her way by the north-east Trades. She anchored briefly at Penrhyn Island, where the islanders wandered all over the ship selling coconuts, corals and cod and then danced and sang to the accompaniment of the captain's gramophone. She fought with a sail-splitting hurricane among the south-east Trades, skimmed across the Tasman Sea in fine style and, on the approach to Melbourne, all but grazed the basaltic rocks at the entrance to the Bass Strait, narrowly avoiding catastrophe. If Stenhouse thought British Columbia 'a man's country', he found Australia the 'happiest of all places',[19] a veritable home from home, where dances, picnics and 'beautiful' fights could be enjoyed in equal numbers. He also met for the first time his great-uncle Andrew, who had left Scotland's shores a quarter of a century before to make his fortune. After a sojourn which breathed new life into the crew, the *Springbank* headed back towards northern waters and home. On reaching Cardiff, in a drizzling rain, the capstan span and the cargo was discharged and then, paid off, the crew dispersed towards their homes: to London, Dublin, Belfast and Barrow.

If Barrow had not changed in the many months of Stenhouse's absence, he had – almost beyond recognition. He had parted from his family a gawky if determined youth; he returned a man, bronzed and hardened by months of punishing physical exertion and by fights on ship and shore. His experience of mankind had been widened by contact with every species of humanity: from veteran whalers and deep-water men to semi-naked South Sea islanders; from foul-mouthed whores to knife-wielding toughs in 'Frisco's 'Barbary Coast'. A youthful and perhaps naïve passion for the sea had also been transformed into an abiding, deep-seated love, underpinned by a detailed knowledge of every rope and every sail necessary to a ship's propulsion and her safety. But beneath the changed exterior and in spite of this new depth of knowledge and understanding, his affections remained unaltered. In Vancouver, he had pined for his family, 'wondering how it is that I have received no letters from home' and anxious that the photographs he had taken during his cruise 'must have gone astray'.[20] Now, once again, he dwelled, albeit briefly, in the bosom of his family: the centre of their attention and the hero of the hour. Andrew Stenhouse tried to dissuade his only son from returning to his ship, hoping perhaps that one round trip would have sated his appetite for seafaring, as it had his own, nearly thirty years earlier. But here, father and son differed. Stenhouse junior had determined that the sea was to be his profession, and he remained, if not unmoved, then unswayed by the arguments of his father and of his sister. When the call came to rejoin the *Springbank*, he answered.

This time, with a hold full of coal, the ship sailed from Cardiff to Antofagasta in Chile. She completed a speedy and trouble-free passage to Cape Horn, with Stenhouse even enjoying sufficient leisure to learn the art of wrestling from one of the Russian Finns on board. Rounding the Horn was a different matter entirely. For weeks, the boiling ocean tossed the 2,398-ton ship like a cork. Huge seas swept the decks and icy water foamed through hatches and doorways, soaking everything that stood in their way. The exhausted and drenched men floundered about the decks, struggling grimly with canvas that whipped and beat them as though possessed of a malign will of its own. Called from his bucking crib at 3 a.m. on the morning of 13 August 1906, Stenhouse noted that the ship was 'Rolling heavily and shipping big seas to leeward.'[21] As the *Springbank* lurched, one man 'was taken by a sea against the galley and then under the spar. Had his head smashed in.' Another 'damaged his foot and two or three others mauled a bit. Deck full of water; galley fo'c'sle after-house, lamp locker and cabin flooded. Ventilator hatch on the forecastle head smashed, hen coop . . . broke adrift and was flying around the deck before it went to pieces.'[22] He was, however, too busy to observe the fate of the unfortunate hens.

After seventeen days of bruising labour, the *Springbank* at last rounded the Horn but, his ship still beset by tempests, the captain had little choice but to run to the south. Stenhouse recorded that, by 10 September, they had been blown down almost to the parallel of 61°S, and still there was no respite:

The ship looked as if she were on a polar expedition, from truck to deck she was covered with snow and ice. The forecastle head was covered with ice; from all the rigging 18in icicles hung and to let go a rope from a pin, the ice had first to be knocked off it.

When wearing ship, which we did about twice every day, she would go under like a submarine boat and all hands would cruise round the decks under water making frantic efforts to grab something, even tho' it were the leg of some fortunate who had managed [to] get on his feet . . .

To add to [the] joys of life all the houses were full of water. Our half-deck was as bad as on deck. The chests burst their lashings and while cruising round, capsized the table. All our gear, go-ashore clothes, etc, were full of salt water, ashes, and everything else which happened to be floating round.[23]

Having undergone such misery to reach Antofagasta, the crew must have been disappointed at what they found: a dreary, ramshackle frontier town, perched dolefully between arid hills on the one hand and, on the other, the sea. For all its grim appearance, however, arrival at this small Chilean town marked a turning point in Stenhouse's career. The third mate, having completed his articles and anxious to forward his career, left the ship in Antofagasta, creating a vacancy. Stenhouse had grown in stature: having made one more voyage than any of his current cabin mates, he ranked as senior apprentice and his seamanship, courage and physical prowess all commanded the respect of his fellows. These facts had not gone unnoticed by the captain and, in need of an officer, he asked Stenhouse if he would 'run a watch'. The answer, of course, was yes, and Stenhouse, though still within the period of his articles, became acting third mate.

Promotion meant that he moved out of the half-deck and said goodbye to his messmates. From now on he would eat with the other officers and berth with the second mate in their own cabin: an unheard-of luxury, but also a rather lonely one when compared with the rough and tumble companionship of the apprentices. But Stenhouse had no time now for nostalgia and, in the pride of his new rank, perhaps, little inclination for it either. If the loneliness of command beckoned him, it beckoned with a smiling face and he later remembered that, sometimes, 'when the dignity of such sudden promotion became too much for me, I slipped into my cabin and laughed like a fool'.[24] His current voyage would last for many more months yet, despite the fair winds that sent the *Springbank* flying on her way to Australia. And there would be years more of hard, grinding work and many thousands of miles of ocean to be crossed and recrossed before he clawed his way to the coveted posts of second mate, mate and master. But now, with dusty, flyblown Antofagasta receding into the distance, and the coast of Chile mingling with the loom of the land, Stenhouse knew that he had placed his foot firmly on the ladder. His apprenticeship in sail, if not his apprenticeship to Andrew Weir, was over.

SOUTH WITH SHACKLETON

For eight long years Stenhouse stuck manfully to his profession, not simply enduring but actually relishing the physical punishment and dangers inseparable from shipboard existence. And with every passing watch he added to his hard-won store of knowledge and experience: of men, of navigation and the age-old lore of the sea. His tall, thickset body grew harder and tougher, tested by the rigours of his chosen life; by a string of minor injuries, including a broken nose and cracked ribs; and by occasional illnesses caused by his exposure to the elements, from the constant drenching and icy cold of the Horn, to the broiling torpor of the doldrums.

But pleasure in his life at sea was alloyed with ambition, and promotion to third mate fixed him in his determination that he would one day take his rightful place as captain upon the bridge of his own ship. To become captain he must possess his Master's Certificate in Sail and, in July 1909, he took a temporary leave of absence from the *Springbank* to study for his examinations. Captain Royal encouraged his junior officer's ambition and, hoping to remove any lingering anxiety that Stenhouse might have been feeling, confirmed that 'Should he pass in this post I shall be only too pleased to take him back with me as second mate.'[1] Perhaps out of gratitude for this encouragement, having duly passed his examinations, Stenhouse took up his captain's offer and chose to stay with the *Springbank* until June 1910. But he had also decided that the time had come for a change. Though he loved sail passionately, he could also see that to safeguard his future prospects he must obtain sufficient experience to enable him to sit for his Master's Certificate in Steam.

With this aim in mind, in July 1910 Stenhouse parted company with the Andrew Weir Line after nearly six years' service and, on the 27th of the month, he sailed on the African Steamship Company's *Zungeru* as third officer. Only two months later, he transferred again, this time to the Battle Line's SS *Sellasia*, as second and navigating officer. He stayed with the *Sellasia* for eighteen months, sailing to St Thomas, St Lucia, San Francisco, Buenos

Aires, Las Palmas and Aden, and by July 1912 he felt sufficiently confident to sit for his second Master's Certificate, which he succeeded in obtaining on 7 September. With this further qualification under his belt, he joined the British India Steam Navigation Company and, in October 1912, sailed in the *Mombassa* for Calcutta, where he took up duties as third and then second officer with their Coastal Service.

Aged 24, Stenhouse had completed his apprenticeship, secured his place on the bridge and gained both of his Master's Certificates. By most people's standards, his life had already been one of endless adventure, filled with variety and voyages to distant lands. But, from another perspective, his horizons had been strictly limited: his experience of Africa, Australasia and the Americas was restricted to the hinterlands of the ports where his ships briefly touched to load and replenish their stores. And his entire adult life had been circumscribed by the routine of shipboard life: his existence portioned by the striking of the ship's bell. Now, without departing wholly from his chosen profession, he wanted new experiences and fresh adventures. Fortunately, new opportunities lay just over the horizon and, in grasping them, he would change the course of his life forever.

As a boy, Stenhouse had been enthralled by Fridtjof Nansen's *Farthest North* and, more recently, by the exploits of William Speirs Bruce and Captain Scott in the Antarctic. Then, during his maiden voyage on the *Springbank*, he had been enraptured by his first glimpse of the snow-clad hills of Staten Island: 'I longed to go ashore there', he later remembered. 'I imagined the joy of the seaman on sighting new land and, fancy free, I thought of the "dawn lands, for youth to reap; dim lands where empires sleep . . . and all that dolphined deep – where the ships swing".'[2] Then and there he had decided that, one day, he would become an explorer. His first chance to fulfil that dream came in the latter part of 1913: when Joseph Foster Stackhouse advertised for men to join his planned expedition to Antarctica. Stenhouse wrote to Stackhouse to express his interest and was rewarded with the appointment of second officer on the expedition ship.

Stackhouse intended to undertake a detailed exploration of the coast of King Edward VII Land. 'In so doing,' he told Kathleen Scott, 'I am carrying into effect arrangements which were fully discussed early in 1910 with Captain Scott.'[3] Unfortunately, Scott had not shared the import of these supposed discussions with any member of his inner circle and, through his indiscriminate use of the dead hero's name to gain publicity and funding for his own expedition, Stackhouse succeeded in alienating the entire polar establishment. Frank Debenham, geologist on Scott's last expedition, doubted his sincerity; Commander Harry Pennell, captain of the *Terra Nova*, found him 'most objectionable'; and Dr Edward Atkinson, the surgeon who had discovered the frozen corpses of Scott and his polar party, thought him 'a rogue in more ways than one'.[4] The Royal Society also refused to have anything to do with Stackhouse and, snubbed on every front, his expedition quickly fizzled out. Given the distrust and dislike which Stackhouse engendered, the expedition's collapse might have been a lucky escape for a young man keen to make his way in the tight-knit world of exploration.

Stenhouse hardly had time to swallow his disappointment before another opportunity presented itself. It came at an unexpected time, when illness had forced him away from the heat and humidity of Calcutta to the more salubrious climate of his great-uncle's house near Melbourne. The illness, described by his employer's doctors as a nervous breakdown, was almost certainly a prolonged and serious bout of depression – the first recorded instance of a malady that would dog Stenhouse throughout his career. Desperate for distraction and occupation, the new opportunity could not have come at a better moment, and this time it came from the hands of a man with a fully established reputation for heroic endeavour in the Antarctic wastes: a veteran of Scott's *Discovery* Expedition of 1902 and leader of the British Antarctic Expedition (BAE) of 1907–9, Sir Ernest Shackleton.

Shackleton, like Stackhouse, was considered something of a maverick by the deeply conservative bigwigs of the Royal Geographical Society (RGS), but no one could doubt his credentials. In December 1902, he had joined Scott and Dr Edward Wilson on their South Polar journey, eventually attaining latitude 82° 15' South – the furthest south that any man had reached to that date. Then, in January 1909, he and three companions had bettered that achievement by some 366 miles, pushing to within 97 miles of the pole itself. These feats had made Shackleton's name a household word and had brought him a knighthood – but his failure to reach the pole remained a bitter disappointment. Then, in the Antarctic summer of 1911–12, the achievements and sacrifice of Amundsen and Scott denied him forever the longed-for accolade of being the first man to the pole. It seemed to Shackleton that he might simply pass into history as an 'also ran' and for a time he drifted, uncertain what to do now that his particular grail had been dashed from his hands.

But the lure of the south remained as strong as ever. Douglas Mawson, a fellow BAE veteran and leader of the Australasian Antarctic Expedition (AAE) of 1911–14, later remembered a time when 'once more a man in the world of men, lulled in the easy repose of routine, and performing the ordinary duties of a workaday world, old emotions awakened, the grand sweet days returned in irresistible glamour, far away "voices" called'.[5] Those voices never sounded louder or more insistent than in the ears of

Ernest Shackleton and before long he realised that, despite the conquest of the South Pole by others, the Antarctic could still present him with new challenges. Soon, one in particular began to dominate his thoughts.

At the end of 1913, he made the nature of that new challenge public for the first time. 'It has been an open secret for some time past,' he wrote in *The Times* on 29 December, 'that I have been desirous of leading another expedition to the South Polar regions. I am glad now to be able to state that, through the generosity of a friend, I can announce that an expedition will start next year with the object of crossing the South Polar continent from sea to sea. I have taken the liberty of calling the expedition "The Imperial Trans-Antarctic Expedition".' He also claimed in his expedition prospectus that 'from a sentimental point of view, it is the last great Polar journey that can be made'.

In fact, the idea of an Antarctic crossing was not a new one: the Scottish explorer, W.S. Bruce, had first proposed the scheme in 1908, but he had been unable to attract sufficient capital for its consummation. Bruce and Shackleton, however, were very different men, with very different attitudes towards fund-raising. Bruce, a self-effacing and committed scientist, made no allowance for the British public's appetite for sensationalism and he balked at the idea of publicity-driven gamesmanship. Shackleton, on the other hand, was a born publicist, dedicated to the pursuit of headlines and laurels; he was also by far the most entrepreneurial of all Heroic Age explorers when it came to charming the pounds, shillings and pence from the pockets of wealthy benefactors.

Despite his nonconformity, Shackleton also recognised the importance of furthering the cause of science (not least because the scientific community had disposable funds) and his plans included a comprehensive programme of magnetic and meteorological observations to be made by the six men who would make the crossing. The party remaining at the expedition's main base would also include a number of scientists who would spend their time collecting and analysing samples of flora, fauna and minerals. Geographically, the expedition's greatest object would be to prove or disprove the theory that the great Victoria Land mountain range stretched across the whole of the continent.

Shackleton's plans were hugely ambitious; so ambitious indeed that many in the geographical establishment gravely doubted his chances of success. They also questioned the benefits of the expedition's main goal: to cross the continent. Lord Curzon, the President of the RGS, even went so far as to tell him that 'I should not say too much about that. No doubt the public likes it and admires the British spirit, but the scepticism that exists among scientific bodies will be most satisfactorily met by the scientific work you may be able to do, or the geographical discoveries you make.'[6]

Whatever the establishment's reservations, Curzon was right about the attitude of the general public, who certainly did 'like it'. In talking of the expedition to *The Times*, Shackleton had asserted that 'I feel that not only the people of these islands, but also our kinsmen in all the lands under the Union Jack will be willing to assist towards the carrying out of the full programme of exploration to which my comrades and myself are pledged.' The national and colonial press rapidly picked up this clarion call and soon the idea of a crossing of Antarctica became the matter for discussions at breakfast tables across the empire: from London to Ottawa; from Delhi to Cape Town; and from Nairobi to Melbourne. It was one such newspaper report that first alerted Stenhouse to the existence of the Imperial Trans-Antarctic Expedition (ITAE). Sixteen years later, in an interview with the *Daily Mail*, he remembered his initial reaction, and that of his great-uncle Andrew, to the news of Shackleton's bold new venture: '"I must go with him," said Commander Stenhouse, but his uncle did not encourage him very much, for he knew there would be hundreds of applications for such an adventure.'[7]

In spite of his uncle's views, Stenhouse remained undaunted. He hastily packed his battered seaman's chest, said a fond farewell to his relative, purchased a second-class ticket to England and immediately boarded the first available ship bound for home. The vessel he joined was the P&O steamship *Medina* and, by a strange quirk of fate, she carried among her passengers a group of men whose recent experiences could not have accorded better with his current determination. These men were veterans of Mawson's AAE, many of them just returned from the frozen south, still full of their recent exploits and happy to share them with any willing audience. On the month-long voyage from Melbourne to England, the ardent young sailor and would-be volunteer enjoyed ample opportunities to hear their tales of life and death in the Antarctic: tales which lacked nothing in drama, heroism and excitement.

The AAE had set out from Hobart in December 1911 on board a veteran Dundee whaler called the *Aurora*. By sheer fluke, the expedition had landed, a month later, at the windiest place at sea level on the face of the planet: Cape Denison in Adélie Land. For two years, Mawson and his men survived in conditions of almost unimaginable ferocity. The average wind speed for the first year had been 50mph, with gusts of nearly 300mph, and the almost incessant drift snow had often been so blinding that a man might actually stand on the roof of his shelter and not know it. Some of the expeditionaries had never mastered the technique of walking against the wind and, despite two years of practice, they had been reduced to crawling on hands and knees or slithering on their stomachs like snakes whenever they left their flimsy hut. Despite these atrocious conditions, Mawson's team had done extraordinary work. They had undertaken pioneering experiments with wireless telegraphy; sledging parties had explored 2,600 miles of previously unknown territory; and an exhaustive study of the area's flora, fauna, geology and meteorology would eventually produce thousands of pages of scientific reports, which were still being published more than three decades after the expedition's return to civilisation. But, like Scott's *Terra Nova* Expedition, the AAE had also suffered tragedy. On his Far Eastern Sledging Expedition of November 1912 to February 1913, Mawson had lost both of his companions: an Englishman, Belgrave Ninnis, had fallen to his death when he and his supply-laden sledge broke through the concealed lid of a crevasse and the Swiss ski-champion, Xavier Mertz, had died of malnutrition as he and Mawson attempted to trudge the 300 miles back to their base. Mawson's own solitary trek and ultimate survival were already well on their way to becoming the stuff of Antarctic legend.

Sitting in the *Medina*'s saloon, Stenhouse listened spellbound to the stories of his new friends and, with every tale of hardship endured and obstacles heroically overcome, his desire to join Shackleton became more deeply rooted. But how could he turn his hopes into reality? The Antarctic fraternity was close knit, with most explorers being known to each other, if not personally, then at least by name and reputation: breaking into this charmed circle would not be easy. Moreover, Andrew Stenhouse had been right in predicting that Shackleton would be inundated with applications: over the succeeding months, more than 5,000 fell through the letter-box of the ITAE's office, all of them to be sifted into pigeon-holes designated 'Mad', 'Hopeless' and 'Possible'. Fortunately for Stenhouse, the man responsible for the filing was Shackleton's trusted lieutenant, Frank Wild, who had served on Scott's *Discovery* and on the BAE. More importantly, Wild had also led Mawson's Western Base Party and, as a result, he knew all of Stenhouse's friends on the *Medina*. In the first flush of rekindled camaraderie, Wild allowed himself to be persuaded to file Stenhouse's application under 'Possible' – and this constituted the first step towards the fulfilment of the young Scot's ambition. The second, altogether more daunting, step would be to impress the man known to all his Antarctic companions as, quite simply, 'The Boss'.

Stenhouse's interview took place at the ITAE's offices in New Burlington Street in early August 1914. On 1 January, a *Daily Mail* reporter had suggested that 'If any medical student wishes to study a case of "go fever", in its finest stage of development, he should visit Sir Ernest Shackleton.' The passage of seven months had done nothing to reduce the atmosphere of urgency and bustle and, up to his eyes in the work of preparing for the expedition, Shackleton allowed applicants very little time to impress him – sometimes as little as 5 minutes. For an assessment of a man's professional or scientific qualifications the explorer willingly applied to experts in that particular field, whether it be geology, mineralogy or meteorology. But, in reality, Shackleton considered such qualifications to be of secondary importance. In discussing the members of his team with the officers of the RGS, he had told them that 'in the main their function is to get through' and, in judging a man's character and overall fitness for the achievement of that goal, he relied exclusively upon his own shrewdness and insight. So far they had served him well.

As Stenhouse stood before him in the small, paper-strewn room, Shackleton, broad-shouldered and grim-faced, paced up and down, listening to the young sailor's earnest plea, occasionally interrupting to fire a quick, direct question. It was an unnerving experience but Stenhouse seemed to pass through the ordeal satisfactorily because Shackleton offered him a post on the spot and the interview ended with a handshake. When, a couple of days later, Stenhouse received a letter on the headed notepaper of the ITAE, he naturally assumed it to be a confirmation of his appointment. Instead, the formally couched letter advised him that his application had been unsuccessful. Reeling from this unexpected blow and feeling 'almost broken-hearted', Stenhouse again presented himself at the ITAE's offices and requested a further audience. Shackleton was not usually known for his fickleness but for whatever reason, perhaps because Stenhouse's eloquence and passionate desire to join the expedition moved him, or because the letter of refusal had been the result of a mistake in the paperwork, he again changed his mind: Stenhouse would be allowed to join the expedition after all.

Over the preceding months, Shackleton's plans had been gradually evolving. Originally, he had intended to take just one ship to the Antarctic. This vessel would land the members of the transcontinental party on the coast of the Weddell Sea and then proceed to the Ross Sea where it would pick them up once they had completed their journey. Now he proposed two ships: the first would carry the Weddell Sea Party, including Shackleton; the second would sail to the Ross Sea, where it would land a party in McMurdo Sound, somewhere in the vicinity of Scott's huts from the *Discovery* and *Terra Nova* expeditions. The primary function of this second party would be to lay supply depots deep into the Great Ice Barrier in the direction of the Beardmore Glacier. These cached supplies could then be picked up by Shackleton and his team on the second half of their epic journey. The great advantage of this approach was that the transcontinental party would have to carry only 50 per cent of the rations and fuel needed to complete the crossing.

By the time of Stenhouse's recruitment, both ships had been purchased. The Weddell Sea Party would be carried in a Norwegian whaler originally called the *Polaris* but now renamed the *Endurance* and commanded by a New

Zealander named Frank Worsley. The Ross Sea Party, meanwhile, would sail in Mawson's old AAE expedition ship, the Steam Yacht *Aurora*, which Shackleton had bought for £14,000 and which now lay in dock at Hobart, Tasmania. Initially, Shackleton hoped that John King Davis would command the *Aurora*. A veteran of both the BAE and AAE, Shackleton thought Davis 'the best navigator and sailor that ever went into the Antarctic'. But Davis declined the job and it went instead to Aeneas Mackintosh, an aristocratic and mercurial Scotsman who had served as second officer on the BAE's *Nimrod*, until the loss of his right eye in an accident had forced him to retire from the expedition. On 18 August, finally reassured that his position with the expedition was secure, Stenhouse could at last write to his father and tell him of the role that he would fill: 'I am a lucky chap,' he enthused, 'I am chief officer of the *Aurora* and second-in-command of the Ross Sea Party which will "Winter" in the ice.'[8]

Even events on the wider world stage did not appear to threaten Stenhouse's new career as an Antarctic explorer. Ever since the assassination of the Austro-Hungarian Archduke Franz Ferdinand at Sarajevo on 28 June 1914, Europe had been moving inexorably towards war. In the days leading up to Britain's declaration on 4 August, the War Office recalled most of the professional soldiers who had volunteered for the ITAE, but the gaps they left were easily plugged. Moreover, the government demonstrated very little inclination to interfere with the expedition. In response to the rapidly worsening international situation, Shackleton volunteered the *Endurance*, himself and his men to aid the war effort, but Winston Churchill, as First Lord of the Admiralty, and then George V himself, ordered him to continue with his plans. As a highly experienced mariner, Stenhouse joined the Royal Naval Reserve and offered his services independently, but he received the same response. He told his father that 'The RNR people, whom I saw on Monday, gave me my commission, and said they would not call me up for service, as Sir E. Shackleton had offered our services and the King had commanded him to proceed with the expedition; my seniority dates from 01.07.14.'[9]

Having been advised that the Royal Navy could dispense with his services, for the time being at least, Stenhouse felt free to throw himself headlong into the final preparations for the expedition. At a meeting with Shackleton on 4 March, Lord Curzon had expressed the opinion that the Ross Sea Party would 'require to be well commanded, properly equipped, and sufficiently organised, much in the same way as if it were an independent expedition going to the Pole'.[10] Inevitably, this meant that, as second-in-command, Stenhouse's list of responsibilities was a long one. On 26 August, he again wrote to his father, this time somewhat breathlessly: 'I don't know when I shall be home; Captain Mackintosh (my commander) leaves on Friday, by

the Orient Line's *Osterley*, and I and about 10 of the *Aurora*'s party leave on
Sept. 18th, by the *Ionic*. You will find the key of my chest on my dressing-
table, I think; please leave all my things out, so that I can take what I want,
in a hurry.'[11]

By 16 September the preparations were nearly complete. With all of the
Ross Sea Party's baggage and equipment loaded on to the steamship *Ionic* at
London's Royal Albert Docks, the time had come to transfer the huskies that
would provide the motive power of the depot-laying parties. 'The dogs are
in crates (used previously for the same purpose from Canada to England),'
Stenhouse wrote in his diary, '. . . and have been placed on the Boat Deck;
three larger crates have been put on board for special purposes (Sick Bay,
etc.) . . . Mauger, the carpenter of the *Aurora*, is on board to attend to the
dogs.'[12] Once the animals had been safely embarked, the ship slipped down
the Thames to Tilbury. Then, at 10.30 a.m. on 18 September, Stenhouse
and ten other members of the Ross Sea Party said farewell to Shackleton at
St Pancras station before catching the train for Tilbury Docks. If their plans
worked out, they would next meet when Shackleton and his five companions
trudged down to the Ross Sea Party base at McMurdo Sound. Two and a
half hours after this hopeful and historic valediction, the *Ionic*'s windlasses
turned and her anchors thudded against her sides. Stenhouse's life as an
explorer had officially begun.

As the *Ionic* passed down the river and entered the Channel, Stenhouse
saw everywhere the signs of war. 'The lower reaches of the Thames and
Southend and Sheerness are much altered in appearance,' he noted, '. .
. warships to be seen everywhere, several passed close to us including a
submarine . . . Passed Dover about 8 p.m. Searchlights playing on ship.'[13]
On board, however, peace continued to reign – disturbed only by the
incessant howling of the dogs in their crates. As the expedition's senior
officer on board, over the coming days Stenhouse established a strict
routine. This included instruction for the novices in such subjects as
signalling, seamanship and first aid but much of it revolved around caring
for the animals. 'Bear in mind', he wrote, 'that success of the Southern
Party depends, to a great deal, upon the good health of our dogs. Without
good healthy dogs the plans of the Southern Party will be seriously
handicapped; it is therefore desirable that . . . they should be exercised
whenever possible.'[14] As well as being exercised, the dogs also needed to
be fed, watered, doctored and their makeshift kennels regularly cleaned.
Unfortunately, since Mauger had badly twisted his hip in a fall, most of this
work fell to the other expedition members.

As well as the staff of the ITAE, the *Ionic* carried additional fare-paying passengers, and both they and the crew took a keen interest in the expedition's plans. Sometimes, indeed, their curiosity overtook their caution and Stenhouse eventually found it necessary to pin up a notice in the saloon, advising them to keep a safe distance from the sometimes ferocious dogs. But he and his companions also sought to respond to the passengers' obvious enthusiasm, and issued an open invitation to a series of lectures on various aspects of the expedition. Over the coming days, John Lachlan Cope, the biologist, lectured on 'the value of foodstuffs'; Alfred Larkman, the second engineer, talked about electricity and magnetism; and Alexander Stevens, geologist and chief scientist, delivered what Stenhouse thought 'a most enjoyable and instructive discourse' on the wide-ranging subject of 'Polar Problems'.

But there were limits to the fraternisation of the expeditionaries and the other passengers. On 24 September, Stenhouse commented rather scornfully that 'The committee, for the ship's sports, was formed today . . . our party will have little time to spare so will have no need for pastimes and I think few have the inclination . . . most of our party realise that we are bound on a voyage in which we hope to do *big things* scientifically and geographically and we can spend our time more profitably than by heaving quoits about the decks . . . deck quoits is a game for old men, women and children.' The correspondence between the two groups also became a catalyst for dissension among some of the explorers. In a report he later wrote for Shackleton, Stevens noted that Henry Leonard, 'the second mate of the *Aurora*, was in a sense the focus of the trouble. He was not considered to be keeping himself sufficiently aloof from the other passengers, and was imagined to be too communicative of the doings of the Expedition on board. This was proved to be in large measure due to the malice of another individual in the party. In any case, on this poor foundation were built up differences between Leonard and the chief officer, Stenhouse.'[15] Stevens forbore to name the malicious scandalmonger, but he clearly attributed at least some of the blame for the discord to Stenhouse, if only for being too gullible. Another individual who gave cause for concern was Mason, the chief engineer, who quickly revealed an inability to hold his drink.

Despite these anxieties, when, after a voyage of forty-three days, the *Ionic* dropped anchor off Ocean Pier, Hobart, on Saturday 31 October, Stenhouse noted in his diary that he felt glad to be alive and ready for the real work of the expedition. And the work began immediately. Mackintosh had sailed for Sydney a fortnight earlier in the *Aurora*, but he had left detailed instructions for his second-in-command. First, he must see to the debarkation of the dogs. Despite occasional fights and diarrhoea, all the animals had survived the passage and now they were to be transported to the Quarantine Station at Taroona, about 7 miles distant. 'We had little difficulty in getting them down the steep ladders from the boat deck to the launch,' Stenhouse recorded gratefully, 'and as everyone worked with a will we had them all in the boats at 12.45 a.m. Several scraps ensued between the dogs but, as they were muzzled no damage was done.'[16]

Next came the unloading of the expedition's stores: a task which the stevedores of Hobart made more complicated than necessary by mixing them with packages, trunks and crates which had nothing to do with the expedition. Such irritations aside, the work progressed well, with all the expeditionaries lending a willing hand despite the rain which drenched them as they laboured. With the stores and equipment secured in a local warehouse, on the morning of 3 November Stenhouse and all but two of his Ross Sea contingent boarded the *Moeraki* bound for Sydney. They left the dogs in Hobart, in the care of Aubrey Ninnis, a cousin of Belgrave Ninnis who had died on the AAE, and Ernest Wild, a younger brother of the more famous Frank. The *Moeraki* arrived at Sydney two days later and Stenhouse and his companions immediately booked themselves into the Wentworth Hotel. Shortly afterwards, Captain Mackintosh arrived to greet them.

If, so far, things had gone relatively well for the chief officer, the same could not be said for Mackintosh, whom Stenhouse found tired and anxious. His story was quickly told: having arrived in Sydney, Mackintosh had learned that, despite Shackleton's promises, no money had been sent out from England to meet the expedition's expenses. He had also discovered that, while the 600-ton *Aurora* had already proved her suitability for work in the Antarctic, nine months in dock had left her in much poorer condition than anyone had supposed and she needed a great deal of work before she could again be taken south. Lastly, when he attempted to mortgage the ship in order to pay for her refit, he found not only that he had no power of attorney but that the necessary paperwork had not been completed and the vessel was still registered in Mawson's name. Combined, these factors meant that, through no fault of his own, Mackintosh had been effectively hamstrung even before the expedition had begun. Angry and frustrated, he had cabled Shackleton's agents in London to acquaint them with his predicament. 'Made every endeavour to raise money;' he told them, 'absolutely unable. Ship cannot leave unless you remit. You must realise Shackleton's danger. As last resort consult his friends.' Instead of relieving him of his anxiety, the agents' reply pushed all responsibility on to his shoulders: 'Ship must leave according Shackleton's instructions,' Messrs Perris & Hutchison admonished him, 'Obligation yours to see starts proper time. . . . Have confidence [in] you personally. Rely your honour get ship away on minimum cash.' Mackintosh was incensed, particularly by the references to his honour. 'It would have been better if they had not wasted words in any insinuations regarding it,' he grumbled. 'I wish I were satisfied with that of Sir Ernest's attorneys.'[17]

With his customary activity, Stenhouse immediately threw himself into relieving the burden which weighed down his harassed captain. He even attempted to persuade Andrew Stenhouse to assist with mortgaging the *Aurora* but the old man, who had consistently expressed his disapproval of his great-nephew's new career, refused. Eventually, Professor Edgeworth David, a fêted Australian veteran of the BAE, exerted his influence and managed to persuade the Australian government to guarantee a loan of £1,000. As Stevens later told Shackleton, the government also 'extended to the *Aurora* the harbour and other privileges of a King's Ship. They also agreed to dock her free, and refit her to the extent, I have heard, of £500.'[18] Having accepted this generous offer, Mackintosh docked the *Aurora* at Sydney's Cockatoo Island and an extensive overhaul of rigging, top hamper, engines and crew quarters began. 'We are having a busy time refitting at Cockatoo Island Dockyard,' Stenhouse told his father a few weeks later. 'It has been hard work and rush since we arrived in Hobart. . . . My time has been absolutely taken up . . . on board ship in the day-time and at store and equipment lists during the evening. With carpenters, caulkers, joiners, blacksmiths, plumbers, fitters and others aboard the old *Aurora*, big alterations are being made.'[19] In fact, the alterations turned out to be much too big: the programme of refurbishment far exceeded what had been envisaged by the Australian authorities and the cost eventually reached a figure in the region of £4,000. Having been given an inch, in his extremity, Mackintosh had grasped a yard and thereby stored up a great deal of future trouble for his chief officer.

For the time being, however, there was more than enough trouble to keep everyone occupied. Besides irritations and delays caused by striking dockhands, problems regarding the expedition's staff had become acute. Among the ship's crew, Mason's drinking had now reached such proportions that Mackintosh decided to sack him and to promote Alfred Larkman from second to chief engineer. The post of second engineer thereby became vacant and, after a fruitless recruitment drive, Mackintosh had little option but to fill it with Adrian Donnelly – an engineer, admittedly, but one entirely lacking in sea experience. The poisoned relations between Stenhouse and the second officer, Leonard, had also soured even further and, about half way through the *Aurora*'s stay in Sydney, Stenhouse announced that either he or Leonard must leave the ship. 'Notwithstanding attempts made on his behalf,' Stevens remembered, 'Leonard was discharged, nominally on account of his health', and it looked as though the *Aurora* must sail without a second officer.

So far as scientists were concerned, Shackleton had advised Mackintosh to consult with Edgeworth David when filling the still vacant posts of physicist and surgeon. But, perhaps still smarting from having been left in the lurch by the expedition's poor organisation, Mackintosh determinedly exceeded his brief. His first new recruit was Irvine Gaze. Ostensibly on a visit to Sydney to wave off his cousin, the expedition's photographer and chaplain, Arnold Spencer-Smith, Gaze had been so impressed by all that he had seen that he had volunteered for the role of commissariat officer, (or 'lamp-and-oil man', as Stevens scathingly referred to the job). Dick Richards, a keen sportsman and teacher, became the expedition physicist, while Lionel Hooke would operate the wireless equipment acquired, second-hand, from Douglas Mawson. Finally, Keith Jack would serve as Assistant Biologist. Despite this wholesale recruitment, the post of surgeon remained vacant and, with a dearth of candidates to choose from, Mackintosh eventually had little option but to appoint Cope as make-do surgeon, as well as biologist.

With all but one of the expedition posts now filled and with the ship's refurbishment complete, the Ross Sea Party could at last think of heading south – weeks late and seriously overspent. At 1.35 p.m. on 15 December, the *Aurora* put out to sea, bound once again for Hobart where stores and equipment would be loaded and Ninnis, Wild and the dogs embarked. 'Thank Heaven!' sighed Stenhouse to his diary, 'we are started on the Lone Trail.' Now, too, he could learn something of the sea-going qualities of the vessel that would be his home for the next sixteen months. He found the experience far from satisfying: 'the old packet rolls like a log', he wrote towards the end of the five-day voyage. 'The Chief Engineer came to me one night, after a particularly lively display of rolling, with a very lugubrious countenance and the remark "This isn't a ship, she's a bally pendulum".' Perhaps determined to put the best face possible on a situation that he could do nothing to remedy at this late stage, he concluded his diary entry with the more sanguine assertion that 'pendulum or no, she is a splendid sea vessel'.[20]

Once alongside the King's Wharf at Hobart the frenzy of final preparations reached a crescendo. 'There is little rest for any of us now . . . ,' the exhausted chief officer recorded on 21 December, 'stores arriving alongside the ship at all hours keep us busy stowing. Joyce has been my right hand man in this trying time of hustle and hurry and with me has just done a 48-hour stretch of work.' In addition to Ernest Joyce, a veteran of both the *Discovery* and *Nimrod* (BAE) expeditions, and the Ross Sea Party's most experienced member, the whole crew worked well in these last anxious hours; and Stenhouse couldn't begrudge them the alcoholic 'blow-out' that they all enjoyed onshore that night – it would be their last for a very long time. He felt rather less sympathetic when the crew rolled on board late in the afternoon of the 23rd, reeking of drink and unsteady in their gait. Fortunately, his aggravation was somewhat alleviated by the news that, at zero-hour, Mackintosh had managed to fill Leonard's vacant berth by recruiting Leslie Thomson, an Australian, who left his post on the Union Line's SS *Kakapo* to join the expedition. At least the *Aurora* would sail with a full complement of officers.

At 5.15 p.m. on 23 December, as Thomson manhandled his trunk down to his cabin, Mackintosh gave the order to cast off. The lazy wisps of smoke issuing from the *Aurora*'s single funnel gave way to a more determined thick black plume, pulsing in time to the beat of her engine, and the oily green water at her stern foamed as her reinforced, four-bladed propeller started to spin. On the departure of Mawson's expedition in December 1911, the wharves of Hobart had been crowded with enthusiastic well-wishers, cheering and waving as the *Aurora* prepared to steam south. Now, in an atmosphere dominated by war fever, the departure of the veteran Antarctic expedition ship hardly raised an eyebrow. 'No one cares a hang about this Expedition,' Stenhouse grumbled, ' . . . a few loafers and others were the only people on the wharf when we left.' A few minutes later, he might have been glad of the absence of spectators. Thomson noted in his diary that, as the *Aurora* backed out to clear the wharf, the whole crew 'Had rather an exciting few minutes getting her head turned round and nearly took a piece off the end of the New Wharf, Hobart.'[21]

The feelings of bathos that Stenhouse experienced when the *Aurora* slipped anonymously and rather clumsily from Hobart's King's Wharf were underpinned the following day. After a night spent at anchor in Sandy Bay, Mackintosh had intended that they should make an early start, beginning with the embarkation of the dogs at the Taroona Quarantine Station. In the event, engine trouble meant that, instead, the *Aurora* spent most of the day hove to, as Larkman and Donnelly struggled to remove a cylinder cover to make essential repairs. Eventually, however, the impatient, howling animals, along with an equally impatient Ninnis and Wild, were brought on board and, at 5.10 p.m. on Christmas Eve 1914, the *Aurora*'s weed-strewn anchor clattered against her side and the ship's bows turned towards the open sea. By 9.15 that evening, she had passed the Tasman Island lighthouse bound for Macquarie Island and then on to the Antarctic. All in all, as everyone on board was painfully aware, the events of the last two days could hardly be considered the most auspicious start to the expedition. The Ross Sea Party had a lot of catching up to do if Shackleton was to have any hope of succeeding in his historic bid for transcontinental glory.

ARRIVALS AND DEPARTURES

Afert her hesitant start southwards, on Christmas Day 1914 the *Aurora* made a steady, if rather unimpressive, 6 knots under sail before a moderate east-north-easterly breeze. The ship rolled in a heavy swell beneath a dull and cloudy sky, but the mood on board remained buoyant. Conditions continued much the same for the next few days but, on the night of 29 December, the glass fell ominously and the moderate winds began to increase in violence. With a full westerly gale in the offing, at 11.45 p.m. Mackintosh gave the order to heave to under fore-lower-topsail and wait for dawn. Hidden somewhere in the gloaming lay the grim spectre of Macquarie Island: 20 miles long by 4 wide, with an interior consisting of nothing but tussock grass, swamp and black volcanic mountains, and a coastline like the blade of a double-edged saw. Most dangerous of all, a submarine reef runs out from either end of the island, appearing above the waves in the form of isolated rocky islets: the Bishop and Clerk to the south and, 8 miles to the north, the Judge and Clerk. All round Macquarie Island's barren shores lay the wrecks of ships that had been taken in too close or whose anchors had dragged on the rocky bottom. In late December 1911, the *Aurora* herself had come close to disaster here when en route to Antarctica, and only the prompt action of her master, J.K. Davis, had saved her from being holed.

In pitch blackness and stormy seas, Mackintosh knew that pressing on regardless would place his small ship in imminent peril of blundering on to the rocks that had so nearly ended her career three years earlier. Instead, the *Aurora* spent the next few hours holding her position, her lookouts straining their eyes as they scanned the black ocean, watching for any flash of white water that might indicate the presence of submerged rocks. Later that morning, a relieved Stenhouse noted that 'the splendid sea qualities of our little ship showed up well . . . seas tumbling along threatening to swamp us were danced over and every alteration in the seas during the heavy squalls seemed to be anticipated by the *Aurora*'.[1] Not all the crew shared his admiration, however, and Alfred Larkman commented that 'she's a damned oscillating farmyard and what with the dogs, sheep and poultry and oil on deck, is the queerest vessel I was ever on. Things below are far from comfortable . . . one has to have a keen sense of humour to survive a watch.'[2] As dawn glimmered on the eastern horizon, Stenhouse could see the surf breaking on the Judge and Clerk rocks on the starboard bow and, looming to port, the dark, inhospitable mass of Macquarie Island. Despite the crew's best efforts, the *Aurora* had drifted during the night but now, with dawn breaking, the men of the Ross Sea Party could congratulate themselves on having passed their first ordeal unscathed.

During its brief stop in the closing days of 1911, Mawson's AAE had set up a five-man wireless and meteorological station on Macquarie Island. The Australian expedition had been the first to carry wireless to Antarctica but its Telefunken apparatus had insufficient power to transmit all the way back to Australia; the Macquarie Island base, therefore, had been set up to act as a relay station. After the return of the expedition in February 1914, the Australian government had maintained the station on the island but its operators needed to be regularly supplied with foodstuffs and other essentials. Since it must, perforce, pass within a hair's breadth of the island, the Ross Sea Party had offered to undertake one of these supply trips and the *Aurora* carried a menagerie consisting of hens and ducks and fifty sheep for the meteorologists. At 4 a.m. on 30 December, in a violent hailstorm, Mackintosh ordered the engineers to raise steam and the *Aurora* made her way cautiously into the island's north-east harbour to shelter under the lee of the land.

By 5.40 a.m. the ship lay anchored in the bay. The weather, however, remained foul and a choppy sea meant that there could be no question of trying to land. Despite an ardent desire to dispense their charity and to then turn their backs on the jagged island, the crew had little option but to stand idle while they waited for the seas to subside. Only at 5 p.m. could they lower a whaleboat safely and begin the process of unloading. Throughout that evening and the next morning, the small craft plied to and fro, cautiously navigating the countless submerged rocks and the streaming brown ribbons of kelp, to land the livestock. At the same time, a small party of hunters clambered across the rocky beaches and through the spiky tussock grass to shoot sea-elephants so that the dogs, and the men themselves, might enjoy more variety in their diet.

In the late morning of the 31st, Stenhouse and his companions waved farewell to Tulloch, Ferguson and Henderson, the men who staffed the wireless station, and left them once again to their lonely vigil, monitoring their meteorological instruments and listening to the intermittent crackle of the Morse transmissions of unseen shipping. Mackintosh recorded that 'after giving three lusty cheers to the islanders, [we] shoved off, repaired to the old *Aurora*, weighed anchor and proceeded on our voyage – and at last really for the Southlands – adieux to Macquarie. This has been a pleasant break to the crew – we now are prepared to meet the powers that be, and what they grant us. . . . The old year is treating us kindly – may the New Year be as good.'[3]

As might have been expected of a ship commanded by Scots, Hogmanay was marked in traditional fashion with what Thomson called a 'gentleman's concert and a wee drop of something hot to keep the chill out of our hearts'. The weather of New Year's Day, however, allowed very little respite to anyone suffering from a hangover. Beneath a deceptively bright and clear sky, fresh north-easterly winds whipped the sea into spume and spray and the *Aurora* repeatedly plunged into troughs so deep that they threatened to swallow her whole. As the weather worsened, Stenhouse recorded that 'The old ship is beginning now to take seas on board and, as she occasionally stands on her head and threatens to somersault, life is rather uncomfortable.'[4] Uncomfortable, in particular, for the dogs whose jerry-built kennels on the deck gave them little protection from the seas constantly breaking over the *Aurora*'s bows. Mackintosh observed that the animals 'look objects of abject pity, and look appealingly at us for consolation in their discomfort'. But, as they dashed about the decks to haul upon a flying sheet or tighten a lashing with their frozen fingers, neither crew nor scientists had much time to sympathise.

With their nostrils twitching with the stink of sodden fur and their boots sliding in the dog faeces slopping about the decks, Thomson noted ruefully that the men's plight hardly bettered that of the wretched animals:

> There is not much comfort to be found anywhere, even in our bunks, we could hardly keep from pitching out onto the floor and some of our gentlemen passengers looked very displeased with their little lot and should have very much liked to argue it out with the Clerk of the Weather. There was never any risk of being knocked over by anybody rushing to the weather braces when it was required to check them in a point or two, during the time the rough weather lasted.[5]

The brief honeymoon period following the departure from Hobart had come to an abrupt end and, like Thomson, Alexander Stevens observed that the scientists demonstrated a great reluctance to lend a hand in the running of the ship. 'The imposition of these duties,' he later told Shackleton, 'was badly received, and they were, in general, badly performed . . . and there was continual grumbling. . . . No one seemed to remember that they had joined anxious to "do anything".'[6] Unusually, Stenhouse, who generally had very little patience with landlubbers, felt more sympathetic. He recorded that the men were divided into three watches, Red, White and Blue, and that, in addition to a standard working day of 7 hours, each man would be expected to keep a watch of 4 hours at night: 'eleven altogether, easy hours for those who are used to such but jolly hard on men who have never before done manual work and have not yet found their sea legs'.

The air had grown gradually colder since the departure from Macquarie Island; warm clothes had been issued to all hands and, in answer to their constant questioning, Mackintosh told the impatient landsmen that they might expect to see their first iceberg at any time. Sure enough, at 8 p.m. on 3 January, at latitude 59° South, Stenhouse reported ice ahead. He and the other officers exhorted the lookouts to keep a particularly careful watch and, over the next few days, the *Aurora* passed berg after berg while the scientists, open-mouthed and wide-eyed, leant over the rails to gape at their eerie beauty. Even Thomson, despite the pragmatism of the professional mariner, thought them remarkable. 'Some of these bergs were very pretty,' he noted in his diary, 'and had lovely shadings of blue and green colour about the caverns in them that had been hollowed out by the action of the sea water. They were of numerous shapes and one would at one moment liken one to The White City Sydney and another to a large loaf of bread and so on; you could almost imagine them to be like anything you could think of.'[7] But, for all their splendour, the bergs had to be treated with the greatest caution. In later life, Stenhouse would remark that 'though a seaman may become familiar with icebergs, he will always treat them with the respect due to potential foes, and in bad weather or snow fog their room is usually to be preferred to their company'.[8] He knew only too well that any fault in navigation might lead to the ship drawing too close and result in her being disembowelled and sent, with all hands, to an icy grave. With the water temperature hardly a degree above freezing and with the *Aurora* now well outside the shipping lanes, a man in the water could expect to survive no more than a few, numbing minutes.

To add to their difficulties, by 4 January 1915 the ship was being struck by heavy snow squalls, while a moderate south-westerly gale caused her to buck and lurch in what Stenhouse described as 'an imbecile's tango'; all in all, he admitted, it made for 'fascinating navigation!' Not that he enjoyed much opportunity to consider his circumstances. Ten days later he would record that, despite a significant improvement in the weather, 'I have kept no notes of the many interesting happenings on the passage down nor do I remember them; I took no note of when we saw the last Albatross and the first Antarctic Petrel etc. and I feel rather sick about it. I have been much too busy for such things and in my short watches below my bunk called too strongly.'[9] He was not too busy, however, to record the first sighting of South Victoria Land's Mount Sabine at 9 a.m. on 7 January, the day upon which the *Aurora* crossed the Antarctic Circle. 'Our first view of the Antarctic Continent was most impressive,' he enthused, ' . . . far away to starboard the snow-covered range with Mt Sabine 10,000ft high standing out in prominence like an immense sentinel to the South; an untrodden piece of the Earth . . . what a place for alpinists; I think most of us felt the wanderlust magnet, which takes men into the Wild, more strongly after viewing this noble work of Nature.'[10] He and his companions all felt the sighting to be symbolic: estimating that the mountain lay only 75 miles distant, they recognised that they stood on the very brink of their historic enterprise.

Two days later, on 9 January, Beaufort Island and then Ross Island, with the twin volcanoes Erebus and Terror, came into view on the starboard bow while, a mile ahead, the great ice barrier stretched from the eastern horizon to the high cliffs of Cape Crozier. 'Marvellous!' cried an ecstatic Lionel Hooke, 'One simply gasps and stares astounded at the enormous sharp rising snow-clad mounts, swarming with bird life.'[11] A nostalgic Mackintosh, meanwhile, wrote that 'to me it seemed just as if I had left it a day or so ago, there was still the stream of smoke from the crater, the same graceful snow covered slopes, and rock protrusions, then the steep perpendicular cliffs at the sea edge . . . with the beautiful clear water the whole scene was majestic'.[12] That afternoon, with the sea as smooth as oil, Stenhouse had grasped the opportunity to take a well-deserved nap; now he clambered from his cabin into a scene filled with light and beauty. He was thrilled, firstly by the awe-inspiring view and then by the news that Mackintosh wanted him to take a boat and see whether a landing might be possible at Cape Crozier. Along with Cope, Ninnis, Joyce, Mauger and Able Seaman Sydney Atkin, he would be one of the first among the Ross Sea Party to set foot on the frozen continent.

As part of his programme of scientific investigations, Shackleton intended that the Ross Sea Party should build a hut at Cape Crozier to undertake a study of the emperor penguins known to live there. At 5.30 p.m., therefore, the six men left the ship's side and headed for the junction of the cliffs and the barrier in order to identify a suitable location for the proposed settlement. Almost immediately they found an opening which led into a large bight cutting into the towering face of the ice cliff. Having failed in their attempt to scale the steep foot at the base of the cliffs, they proceeded further up the bay to try again. 'Hundreds of Adélie penguins were on and about the ice,' Stenhouse observed, 'all apparently very much surprised at the new arrivals.' With the men rowing hard, the boat nosed into another bay which turned out to be a cul-de-sac with a kind of grotto at its extremity. All around them the ice glimmered in a kaleidoscope of blues and greens, giving the scene the unreality of a stage-set while, from a series of snow-bridges, the bands of small but highly vocal Adélie penguins squawked an uncertain welcome. In the opposite direction, meanwhile, a mist had descended and, by the time Stenhouse and his companions regained the mouth of the bay, the *Aurora* was almost completely hidden from view.

At the entrance to the bay, Stenhouse and Joyce at last managed to make a landing by cutting steps into the ice slope, which then allowed them to scramble on to the scree separating the rocky cliffs from the ice. Having found a somewhat tenuous foothold on the continent, Stenhouse ordered the boat back to the ship to report their failure to find a suitable spot to depot stores and build a hut. While the boatmen delivered this message, he and Joyce continued to explore the narrow ledge in the shadow of the cliffs in the hope of locating the emperor penguins' rookery:

> We walked for about a mile along the foot of the cliffs, over undulating paths, sometimes crawling carefully down a gully and then over rocks and debris, which had fallen from the stupendous, steep cliffs, which we skirted and which towered above us . . . seeing an apparent turn in the cliffs ahead, which we thought might lead to better prospects, we trudged on and were rewarded by a sight which Joyce admitted as being the grandest he had ever witnessed . . . the Barrier had come into contact with the cliffs and from where we viewed it looked as if icebergs had fallen into a tremendous cavern and lay jumbled together in wild disorder. Looking down into that wonderful picture one realised, a little, the 'Eternalness' of things.[13]

While Stenhouse and Joyce relished their moment of quiet contemplation, back on board the *Aurora*, Mackintosh was having an altogether less tranquil time. After the departure of the boat crew, he had decided to bring the ship close in to the barrier, where she would be more sheltered. At a critical juncture during the manoeuvres, however, the engines failed to switch into reverse with the result that the 600-ton vessel collided with the 40ft wall of ice looming above her. She struck head-on, so that the jib-boom, a spar running out from the bowsprit, first bent and then snapped like a matchstick. 'This was regrettable,' Mackintosh confided in his diary, 'but the responsibility lay on my shoulders.' Fortunately, the impact caused no damage aloft and the crew immediately set about clearing the wreckage.

When, at last, Stenhouse regained the ship and reported that he had been unable to identify any suitable spot where a base might be established, Mackintosh ordered that they should abandon any further attempt in that area and instead shape a course for Beaufort Island and McMurdo Sound. 'Cape Crozier has been unfortunate,' he admitted, 'but we must take the rough with the smooth.' Looking at the shattered spar, Stenhouse couldn't help agreeing that they had encountered 'Rather a bad introduction to the Antarctic' but he buoyed himself up with the reflection that, all things being equal, a bad start might lead to a good finish. When he and Joyce climbed aloft to the crow's nest, however, neither could see any leads which might allow the ship to push further south. Things were beginning to look bleak.

The following day, as the *Aurora* once again attempted to force her way into the pack-ice, Mackintosh rather gloomily considered his position and the delays which prevented the Ross Sea Party from starting its crucial depot laying. 'I see Scott on the 10th January, was snugly installed in his hut at Cape Evans,' he mused, looking over the accounts of previous expeditions. 'In the *Nimrod*, though, we were held up about this same place. As we could see no lanes or open water there was nothing left to do but shove her nose up to it and lay out the ice anchor.' Early in 1914, Shackleton had told the officials of the RGS that a failure to begin his transcontinental bid in the Antarctic summer of 1914–15 would not be disastrous. But, as he later admitted in his famous account of the expedition, he had also 'told Captain Mackintosh that it was possible the transcontinental journey would be attempted in the 1914–15 season in the event of the landing on the Weddell Sea coast proving unexpectedly easy, and it would be his duty, therefore, to lay out depots to the south immediately after his arrival at his base'.[14] In essence, this meant that while Shackleton could begin his expedition whenever he chose, Mackintosh must consider the timeliness of his own departure to be absolutely critical. Since he had no way of knowing when Shackleton and his companions would set off, he must assume that they had started at the earliest opportunity. Even now, they might be en route to the pole, confident in the knowledge that, once that landmark had been passed, they would be able to pick up the fuel and food left for them on the barrier. He therefore had no choice but to believe that every delay in his own departure could be jeopardising the lives of the Weddell Sea Party.

For the next week, the *Aurora*'s course remained blocked by the loose pack. Each day, with Larkman and Donnelly often working 12- to 18-hour shifts, she steamed up and down the pack edge seeking a suitable opening and then, if a promising opportunity presented itself, she would spend hours ramming the ice. With each impact the whole ship shivered, knocking over cups and glasses, waking men tired after their last watch and causing the wretched dogs to howl in their distress. Despite the inevitable frustration, by and large, the mood on board remained remarkably cheerful as the men passed the time in preparing for sledging and, when the ship had been secured by ice-anchors, practising their skiing on the floes. Of course, there were some exceptions. Mackintosh was concerned and annoyed in equal measure when one of the firemen, Harry Shaw, fell into a fit. 'This fellow has always been rather a nuisance,' he noted in his diary, 'and this makes matters worse. Of course he ought never to have come, but here he is so we must put up with him.'[15] And on the same day, he found it necessary to deliver a lecture to Cope, who 'thinks he is here for a picnic'. For Stenhouse, though, Mackintosh had nothing but praise: 'He is doing excellently,' he wrote on 13 January, 'he is a good fellow, always ready in any contingency, keen and an enthusiast of the highest order – it's such a comfort to have him.'

By the close of 14 January, the expedition had managed to push to within 3 miles of Cape Royds but the following day they immediately lost much of what they had gained. 'After lunch today', Mackintosh noted, 'made an effort to get out; it's a most tantalising position, open water within 300 yards of us, and all around; we manoeuvred for over an hour trying to release ourselves from the floes, but in vain; we then tried warping with lines on the port quarter and starboard bows, this also proved futile – so now we are remaining at the mercy of the floes which surround us, and have drifted 10 miles to the northward!'[16]

At last, on 16 January, their luck changed. At 1 a.m. Thomson, the officer of the watch, woke the captain with the news that the ship lay very close to open water. Mackintosh immediately issued the order to raise steam and, within a short time, the *Aurora* had managed to break her bonds and force her way into clear water. After some anxious moments, during which it became necessary to steer north-east to avoid the pack, Larkman received the order to increase revolutions until the ship charged towards her goal at full speed. By 5.45 a.m. she lay off the ice foot at Cape Evans buffeted by a force 6 gale. From the bridge, Mackintosh and Stenhouse could see quite clearly the dark, squat shape of the hut that Scott had built there in January 1911 during the early days of the *Terra Nova* Expedition. Mackintosh tried to take the *Aurora* in close to the hut, but the thickness of the ice foiled his efforts and instead, at 9 a.m., he decided to make an attempt to reach it by skis in the company of Joyce, Spencer-Smith and Stevens.

Although their recent practice had shown that few members of the expedition could boast any great proficiency on skis, the four men crossed the 3 miles of ice separating the ship from the hut without any serious mishap. Scott's men had abandoned the base two years earlier, but they had left it well stocked. Having forced their way in, Mackintosh and his companions examined its contents by candlelight and found an assortment of items that might be of use as well as a sounding tube containing a record of the life and work of the previous inhabitants. They made a rapid inventory of the contents and then, bundling up the most immediately useful, loaded them on to one of the discarded sledges that lay outside. By lunchtime, the party had regained the ship and was being bombarded with questions regarding its discoveries. That evening, after a cheerful dinner during which the officers and scientists toasted wives and sweethearts as well as the day's historic landing, an enthusiastic Mackintosh confided in his diary: 'It is all extremely interesting, and really good to be here on the primary scene of our own work; unfortunately it has been blizzing all day; so we have been unable to make a start: but on the first sign of the weather improving we are all prepared to commence.'

They devoted the next day to unloading supplies and equipment in preparation for the departure of the first of the sledging parties; then, on 18 January, Mackintosh gave Stenhouse his first chance to take part in a sledging excursion. Eleven miles across the bay at Hut Point stood the building constructed by Scott's *Discovery* Expedition. As with the hut at Cape Evans, Mackintosh wanted to ascertain the condition of the building and to make an inventory of any useful stores that might have been left behind. As well as Stenhouse, the party included Joyce, by far the most experienced in sledge-hauling, Stevens, Wild, Gaze and Victor Hayward, an office clerk whose experience as a ranch-hand in Canada had persuaded Shackleton to recruit him as a general assistant to the expedition. Although the party didn't leave until 9.30 p.m., they expected to be back at the ship by the following morning. As they started, Spencer-Smith cranked the handle of the cinematograph camera and recorded the event for posterity.

Meanwhile, the remaining members of the expedition began the process of unloading the weird, Heath-Robinson 'motor-crawler' or mechanised sledge which Shackleton hoped would alleviate some of the burden placed on the dogs and on the men during the forthcoming sledging season. All of the recent British expeditions to Antarctica had experimented with different forms of transport: the *Discovery* had sailed with a hot-air balloon; the BAE had taken a motor-car; members of the AAE had piloted an 'air-tractor sledge' along the coast of Commonwealth Bay; and Scott's *Terra Nova* had carried three tracked motor-sledges. The machine now debarked from the *Aurora* was just one of three different designs that had been developed for the ITAE by Albert Girling and the Motor Despatch Company of Southwark Bridge Road in London. The Weddell Sea Party had taken a propeller-driven sledge powered by an aeroplane engine. The Ross Sea Party's machine, however, looked like a more conventional type of tractor with a 9hp Coventry Simplex engine delivering power to a Swedish-designed paddle wheel. The blades of the paddle wheel were intended to grip the ice, enabling the machine to pull a train of sledges laden with fuel, food and equipment.[17] When questioned by officers of the RGS, Shackleton had been forced to admit that the machines were designed as much for the attraction of publicity as for their practicality but he still believed that they would prove 'a tremendous asset'.

Having unloaded the tractor, those left with the *Aurora* then relaxed with a game of football on the floe. 'In this latter,' Mackintosh recorded, 'the penguins brought out a team and we had a tough match with them.' Stenhouse and his companions, meanwhile, continued to slog their way towards Hut Point. Conditions when they set off had been ideal; the following morning, however, the situation had changed for the worse. At 2 a.m., some 4½ hours after Stenhouse's departure, Mackintosh awoke to the sound of violent thuds along the ship's side:

[O]n going on deck, I discovered a host of loose ice, brash, and large blocks hurtling themselves unmercifully alongside the ship; a fresh North West wind was blowing which made matters worse, as our stern was to the wind, and the loose ice was just swishing up against the flow and rebounding back on the ship's side, much of it would soon begin to tell on the hull, so I decided to vacate our position and steam to a safer harbour – steam was soon in the engines – ten minutes – and we cleared off, the hands poling off the larger lumps, to give the propeller clearance, also the rudder; after an hour's steaming we got round to the west of Tent Island, where the ice was so soft that the ice anchor would not hold. . . . The anxiety now is for the fellows who are away – I do hope they will not attempt to cross on this ice, as there are pools forming all over the place: but I distinctly told them not to attempt to make a passage, unless all was clear . . . [18]

His anxiety continued unabated until noon on 21 January, when lookouts at last spotted the sledging party making its way back to the ship. Mackintosh and Jack went out on skis to greet them and, by mid-afternoon, all were safe on board. As the grimy and unshaven adventurers clambered over the ship's rail, a rather fastidious Thomson noted that 'The sledging party arrived at ship looking very much the worse of wear, as if an application of soap and hot water would do them a lot of good.'[19]

Stenhouse's tale was soon told. Mackintosh's concerns regarding the weight-bearing capacities of the bay ice had proved well founded. Midway between the ship and Hut Point, one by one, Joyce, Stenhouse and Gaze all plunged through cracks into the bitterly cold water beneath. Fortunately, their companions had managed to pull them to safety and they had staggered the last few miles chilled to the bone. When they reached the sanctuary of the hut in the early hours of 19 January they found that it, unlike its counterpart at Cape Evans, had not withstood the elements unscathed: a large quantity of drift snow had found its way through the doors and windows, filling a large part of the interior. Anticipating a swift return to the *Aurora*, the expedition had set off ill prepared but, rummaging among the assorted detritus of the *Discovery* Expedition, they had located a stove and soon had it, and their sledging primus, spitting and crackling with a portion of the half-ton of evil-smelling seal blubber that lay scattered about the hut. They also pulled two sleeping bags from the wreckage and, for the next few hours, they rested and kept watch, by turns.

Finding that the bay ice had largely disintegrated the following day, they spent their time making a tally of the hut's contents in the half-light and in clearing the interior of some of the accumulated snow and ice. Scott's men had left the hut well supplied and Stenhouse's inventory included foodstuffs ranging from thirty tins of Lipton's tea to 294lb of self-raising flour. By the morning of the 21st, tired of their troglodyte existence and sick of the stench of hot blubber, which also left their skin and clothes black and greasy, they decided that conditions had improved sufficiently for them to attempt a return journey. Over the next few hours they navigated a circuitous course back to the ship, all the time dodging treacherous-looking stretches of thin ice and the numerous pools forming in the warm sunlight, and grateful at last to see a group of their shipmates waving them on.

Although Mackintosh admitted to feeling pleased to find that the sledgers had 'all enjoyed the first experience of sledging and all are anxious to be off again', Stenhouse's enthusiasm would end in disappointment. 'We officers of the ship will have very little opportunity of going sledging,' Thomson complained a few days later, 'as there is only the Chief Officer and myself in the deck staff of officers left on board to look after the ship, and look for a good place to berth her for the winter.'

Although Stevens later told Shackleton that 'There was much confusion about starting, and I for one lost grasp of the scheme as a whole,'[20] throughout the preceding weeks, much attention had been paid to the arrangements for sledging, particularly the weighing and distributing of food and fuel. Many hours, too, had been devoted to stitching sledge harnesses which might help prevent a man from plunging to his death, should he accidentally break through the rotten lid of a crevasse. Now, with the sledging season actually upon them, the men of the land parties concentrated on the final preparations, including the division of the dogs into teams. 'Joyce has been considered to have selected the best,' Mackintosh confided to his diary, 'but I am not so sure that he has, as most of his dogs are fighters, which is not at all a blessing.' His doubts seemed justified when, on 24 January, Joyce's party got under way:

At 3 p.m. the first sledge party, consisting of Joyce in charge, Jack and Gaze were all ready to make a start; their sledge equipment and stores had been weighed. . . . The dogs were all keen with excitement to be off . . . but when once the order was given to start they made a wild dash, ran into each other and furiously bit their partners which brought the sledge

to a standstill. Another try was then made after adjusting the tangle they
had put themselves into. The method was tried then of each man leading
a dog, which went well at first: but again a bundle of dogs fighting in
their keenness to be off again occurred; a third and a fourth try and then
at last with 3 men sitting on the sledge they went off fairly respectably.
A parting shout and three cheers, and then they gradually [dwindled to]
specks in the distance . . . [21]

That evening, looking back on the day's momentous, if somewhat chaotic,
events Thomson noted that 'I am rather sorry to see Joyce leave us as he
is such a jolly good sort, but the work we came down here for is important
so it must be done as soon as possible. . . . There was no show of emotion
amongst any of us, but we all knew that this was the beginning of the most
serious part of the expedition.'[22]

Mackintosh had decided that he too would lead one of the sledge parties
and now, having seen Joyce and his companions safely over the horizon,
he turned to the final preparations for his own departure, scheduled for the
following day. First he had a haircut and enjoyed what would be his last
bath for many weeks and then he sat down in his cabin to write up his final
orders for the other sledging teams and for Stenhouse, who would remain
in command of the *Aurora*. On a single page of ITAE headed notepaper,
which he addressed to his chief officer, he confirmed that 'This will serve
– in the event of anything happening to myself and not returning – to give
you complete command and authority of this section of the Expedition.
I have verbally told you other particulars relative to the relief of the parties,
and our programme to run thro' until March 1916.'[23] The following day,
25 January, the 'Skipper', Spencer-Smith and Wild followed in the footsteps
of Joyce and his team. Until their return, responsibility for the safety of the
Aurora, her crew and the remaining scientists, lay on Stenhouse's shoulders:
now, at last, de facto master of his own ship.

ADRIFT IN McMURDO SOUND

Before leaving to begin laying the depots for the transcontinental expedition, Mackintosh had discussed with his chief officer his plans for the *Aurora*. 'Owing to the sea ice not having gone out from the vicinity of Glacier Tongue,' Stenhouse later told Shackleton, 'we were unable to take the ship there before his departure but he . . . instructed me to endeavour to find a berth for the ship on the Northern side of the Glacier Tongue, when the sea ice allowed of this. He told me that I should on no account go South of Glacier Tongue.'' As an alternative, Stenhouse proposed that they might find a safe berth further north at Cape Royds, the site of Shackleton's BAE base, but Mackintosh dismissed the idea. He wanted to make the ship the main base for the expedition and to establish a small party at Cape Evans to carry out scientific research; Cape Royds was too far from Cape Evans for this plan to work and too far also from Hut Point, the initial goal of the returning sledging parties. Glacier Tongue, therefore, must be Stenhouse's primary objective. But first, he must land the third and final sledging party which consisted of Hooke and Ninnis in charge of the motor tractor, Stevens, Hayward and Richards, all under the command of Cope.

Landing them proved more easily said than done. The ice around Tent Island broke up continually, forcing Stenhouse to waste precious coal in steaming from place to place in search of a secure anchorage, and only on 31 January were conditions suitably calm and the ice sufficiently stable to complete the operation. And the pleasure felt at the prospect of their departure did not result purely from the thought of their being able, at last, to contribute to the vital work of the expedition. Mackintosh had already found it necessary to admonish Cope for his lack of focus, and Stenhouse and Thomson shared their captain's reservations. 'Sorry to say one or two of the afterguard do not seem to realise what work is ahead of them and the importance of getting down to it,' Stenhouse wrote on the day of their departure. 'Too much talk and armchair discussion etc.,' he added later, 'The transcontinental party are dependent on some of these for their relief; I am sorry for Capt Mac and the ones who count. Query: (Evolution) which is the more advanced, a clean, virile savage or a dirty, anaemic scientist?'[2] Thomson, meanwhile, felt none of the regret that he had experienced when waving off Joyce and his companions: 'I will be very glad to see them landed safely and on their way, as the ship will begin to look like a ship and less like a pleasure yacht out of hand . . . all hands including myself were called to help get the party away, which I found out afterward [meant doing] everything for the party excepting to go away in their stead.'[3]

The officers' pleasure at Cope's departure proved short-lived. By 2 February 1915 the entire party had returned to the ship completely exhausted and reporting that the motor-tractor had so far proved a total failure. On first examining the machine, Hooke had observed that it would be 'Very nice if all goes well with engine. Very rotten if no good.'[4] Now it had proved hardly able to pull its own weight, let alone a train of heavily laden sledges. Three days later the sledgers left for the second time, heading for Hut Point and carrying hastily improvised spares in the hope of resuscitating the broken-down machine. If their attempts failed, they would have no option but to resort to the tried and tested, if backbreaking, method of man-hauling.

The ice, meanwhile, continued to break away with tedious regularity and Stenhouse had little option but to keep the ship constantly on the move, sometimes drifting and sometimes nudging her way back to the pack edge. The officers and engineers worked watch after watch, with a flurry of orders passing from the bridge to the engine-room every hour. 'My word,' an exhausted but admiring Larkman wrote of Stenhouse, 'he gave that telegraph Hell!' By 3 February, in a note addressed to Mackintosh, Stenhouse felt unable to suppress his doubts any longer: 'I have very little hopes of taking the ship to Hut Point or to Glacier Tongue,' he wrote, 'as we have had northerly swells followed by southerly winds and little effect from them . . . I don't think much more ice will leave the Sound; early yet, I suppose, to form opinions.' If he found that his primary objective, Glacier Tongue, remained inaccessible, he stated his intention of attempting to berth instead at Cape Evans and ended his note with the hope that he would see Mackintosh again 'about March 20th, in the best of health and spirits'.[5]

Despite his pessimism regarding the likelihood of being able to winter against Glacier Tongue, Stenhouse remained determined to make another attempt at obeying Mackintosh's orders whenever conditions allowed. Off Tent Island, the ice showed the same tendency to break up, the anchors continually broke free and the blizzards buffeted the ship with unremitting violence. Faced with such trials at Tent Island, could Glacier Tongue be any worse? On 8 February, he made his decision and set a course for the Tongue. With icebergs to dodge and with the land often completely shrouded in mist, no one could afford to slacken their vigilance and everyone came to look forward with intense pleasure to the time when the ice might finally set firm and lock the ship in its grip.

Day after day, Stenhouse and Thomson made the same entries in the log: 'Ice breaking away' would be followed with monotonous regularity by the words 'ship broke adrift' and then they would spend hours drifting in McMurdo Sound until new ice began to form and the process could begin again. On 18 February, Thomson recorded that 'we were experiencing one of our first real blizzards as the land was completely shut in by driving snow and one could not see more than 100yd, which made it very dangerous manoeuvring ship to stop her striking an iceberg or going ashore and to make it more exciting we do not know what water we have under us anywhere . . . I will be very glad when we get into safe winter quarters and frozen in and I think everybody else will echo my opinion on this subject.'[6] In a second report to Mackintosh, written on 8 March and later left at Hut Point, Stenhouse confirmed that 'From the 15th to the 19th we were adrift in the Sound through a heavy blizzard which lasted without any respite for four days. During this time, the land on all sides was totally obscured, a high sea running and heavy growlers and floes over which the seas broke heavily, drifting at a great rate to the NW. . . . Until five days ago we were watch and watch . . . this with the repeated calls in the watch below makes the prospect of a night's rest something to look forward to.'[7]

Between 21 and 24 February, with only moderate breezes, the *Aurora* lay secured to the north side of Glacier Tongue, the position chosen for her by Mackintosh. But at 2 a.m. on the 24th the wind grew in force and then shifted to the north-west, driving the ship broadside on to the wall of ice. Stenhouse immediately called for steam to take her out of the danger zone but with the pack setting in hard all around, he found his vessel being jammed on to the low side of the glacier with her rudder post pressed tightly against the ice wall. At this critical moment, with the ship and her captain absolutely powerless to prevent her being seriously damaged or even destroyed, by sheer fluke, the gale turned to the south-east, blowing the stricken vessel to a safer position. The respite proved short-lived: within half an hour the variable wind changed direction again, reverting to the north-west and once more crushing the *Aurora* against the glacier. Stenhouse ordered fenders to be rigged and tried to manoeuvre his ship out of danger but to no avail. For 6½ hours the wind ground the wooden hull against the ice, before finally shifting to the east-south-east and allowing her to swing away from the glacier, bruised but, by a miracle, still seaworthy. Stenhouse would later claim that this experience had been one of the worst of his entire life: 'frustrated in every move, breaking away from the fast ice in blizzards and then as the ice broke up dodging about the Sound . . . avoiding and clearing floes and growlers in heavy drift when we could see nothing, our compass unreliable and the ship short-handed. In that "homeless" time, I, keeping watch and watch with the second officer, hard-pressed to know what to do in the circumstances, had a glimpse of Hell.'[8]

After this nightmare, Stenhouse decided to return to the comparative safety of Cape Evans and, by 6 p.m. on 24 February, the *Aurora* was riding easy with her anchors lying in 23 fathoms of clear water. Over the next few days the ship yawed heavily in strong to gale force winds but, with the exception of the frequent passage of bergs towards the north-west, conditions seemed more stable and the *Aurora*'s position more secure. Stenhouse sent Thomson out in the ship's whaleboat to take soundings along the coast and he ordered the crew to start building a raft to carry the stern anchors to shore. Once landed, the anchors could be buried in the ice, allowing the ship then to be heaved inwards to her winter resting-place. Keen to complete the job as quickly as possible and to start the process of landing stores for the sledging parties, Stenhouse worked the crew, and himself, hard. 'I wonder,' an exhausted Larkman asked his diary, 'if the absent parties realise that we too are having our troubles – it's rather hard Stenhouse should have to do his 12 hours as a minimum plus whole responsibility.'[9] They finally completed the process of securing the anchors on 8 March.

Mackintosh and Stenhouse had agreed that, at the earliest opportunity, sufficient stores for the sledging parties should be landed at Hut Point. In writing to Mackintosh on the 8th, however, Stenhouse stated that 'after the last party left, the Bay Ice was breaking away in such large sheets as to render the sledging of stores to Hut Point too dangerous a proceeding to be even considered.'[10] Now an opportunity to complete the task belatedly presented itself – an opportunity created by the violence of the weather. In the early hours of 10 March, the wind freshened to a moderate gale and the *Aurora* began to rock violently at anchor. At 4.30 a.m. the anchors dragged and Stenhouse called all hands, as the ship started to drift north-westwards towards Barne Glacier. With the vessel hove down to her bulwarks by the fierce gusts, he found it impossible to haul in the anchors, and had to leave them swinging precariously from the hawse-holes. At 2 p.m., he scribbled in the log, 'Whole Gale; heavy sea; violent squalls; ship driving to leeward but riding easy' and, for the thousandth time, the *Aurora* proved her worth.

Only at 6.30 p.m., 15½ hours after the storm blew up, did the weather begin to moderate. With the opportunism vital to successful polar exploration, Stenhouse now decided that, having been driven from Cape Evans, he might as well take the *Aurora* round to land the stores directly beneath the hut, thereby negating the need to sledge them across the bay once the ice had set. Mackintosh had suggested 20 March as a probable date for the return of all the sledging parties, so it seemed unlikely that all the men of the land parties would be awaiting the ship at Hut Point – but some of them might have returned early. If, by the time the remaining sledgers regained the hut, the ship had become iced-in at Cape Evans, then Stenhouse would signal with rockets to confirm whether they could safely cross the Bay. He gave the order to proceed at half-steam and, at 11 a.m. on the morning of 11 March, the anchors plunged 13 fathoms into the icy waters of Discovery Bay. Almost immediately the process of landing stores began but the trade was not, as might have been predicted, one way: on its first trip, the whaler returned with six filthy and exhausted men from the sledging parties: Spencer-Smith, Stevens, Hooke, Richards, Ninnis and Gaze. And they brought with them a story of intense, gruelling and dangerous work to rival that of the *Aurora*'s crew.

The bad weather that had kept the ship dodging about the bay for the last six or seven weeks had also dogged the sledging parties. Mackintosh's hopes of reaching Hut Point on the day of his departure, 25 January, had come to nothing and he and his companions had got no further than 5 miles from the ship when heavy snow and poor visibility had forced them to make camp. The thick weather continued the following day and it was not until 4 p.m. on 27 January that they had finally pushed their way into the hut. Disgusted by the squalid condition of the building and believing it likely that the sledgers would have to occupy it for some time on their return from the first depot laying expedition, Mackintosh scribbled a note for Stenhouse advising him of his wish that it should be properly cleaned. 'Instruct other parties to keep hut clean,' he wrote in pencil, 'and clean up when sheltering here; expect Cope's party to have everything in order and sorted out, can easily be done with party of 6 . . . will probably have to live here some time, they have heaps of opportunity to get it in order, clean and habitable – it's anything but that now – like a pigsty. . . . Please land a broom for sweeping out.'[11]

The following day Joyce's party also arrived at the hut, having been driven back by the appalling conditions on the ice. Then, having discussed the best way forward, Joyce set off across the Sound towards Black Island while Mackintosh headed on to the sea ice on 28 January. Over the next few days, warm temperatures and fresh falls of snow combined to create dreadful sledging conditions, with the men sinking to their knees with every step and the dogs floundering pitifully. At last, both parties had no option but to begin the backbreaking process of relaying their loads, their progress sometimes amounting to no more than 1 mile for every 5 hours of sledging, with the men marching 3 miles for every mile achieved in their direction of travel. Every few feet, the sledge would grind to a halt, its runners clogged with the soft, sticky snow, and then men and dogs together would have to exert themselves to the utmost to get the 600lb sledge moving again, until another stop a yard or two further on. On 10 February, insult was added to injury when the weather closed around them, keeping all six men tent-bound for 24 miserable hours.

During this period of enforced inactivity, Mackintosh had an opportunity to reconsider his strategy. Concerned about the increasing weakness of his dogs – a number had fallen in their traces totally exhausted and one had died – he decided to bring the eight strongest animals together into one team and send the four weakest back to the hut. He, Joyce and Wild would press on, while Spencer-Smith, Jack and Gaze would return to base. Following this plan, the parties separated and when Spencer-Smith and his companions had last seen the Skipper, during the afternoon of 11 February, he and his team were making good progress towards the south, the more powerful dogs apparently being able to pull the sledge with only minimal assistance from the men. In contrast, hindered by their own exhausted dogs, two of which died en route, Spencer-Smith's party made slow progress towards Hut Point and, with their supplies of food and fuel running low, they were glad when they met Cope and his five companions on 18 February.

After the early failure of the tractor and their return to the *Aurora*, Cope's party had eventually abandoned the machine altogether and set out from Hut Point on 7 February. Apparently oblivious to the deck officers' views regarding his own person, Cope left a brief note at the hut, advising Stenhouse that 'We are off today. Tractor will not go so we are man-hauling all goods across to the Bluff – all well. . . . Please give my love to Thomson and the whole of the engineering staff.'[12] Stevens, too, left a letter for Stenhouse: 'We are about to clear,' he wrote 'and I am sorry to see your masts still in the offing – you will be chafing at delay . . . I am glad to say Cope still continues to belie the Skipper's distrust. He is doing A1 and I hope and think he will continue to do so.'[13] Unfortunately, these hopes proved ill founded. Under Cope's apathetic leadership, the sledge party made poor progress, clocking up no more than 20 miles in a week and, by the time they met up with the returning Spencer-Smith, Cope's frustrated men were teetering on the brink of mutiny. Finding that the ascetic chief scientist, Stevens, seemed hardly capable of continuing the punishing sledging programme, the selfless Jack volunteered to take his place among the outward-bound party. And so Spencer-Smith, Stevens and Gaze waved farewell to their colleagues and headed northwards to Hut Point, which they reached on 22 February. Ninnis, Hooke and Richards, who after another gruelling week on the blizzard-swept barrier had been sent back to the hut to conserve food, joined them there on 2 March. These, then, were the six smoke-blackened scarecrows brought aboard the *Aurora* on 11 March. None of the returning sledgers had seen or heard of Mackintosh and his two companions for exactly a month.

While at Hut Point, Stenhouse unloaded sufficient provisions to last twelve men, on full rations, for approximately two months. This supply, he believed, should be more than sufficient to support the six sledgers when they returned to the hut and keep them well fed until the sea ice was able to support their weight, enabling them to sledge across the Bay. Now he weighed anchor and steamed back towards Cape Evans with the intention of making another attempt to secure the ship for the winter. Inevitably, the weather wrecked his plans.

The *Aurora* dropped anchor off Cape Evans at 9.10 p.m. on 11 March but, by 6 o'clock the following morning, a moderate breeze had given way to stormy conditions and, once again, the anchors began to drag. Soon the *Aurora* was adrift in McMurdo Sound, passing first Barne Glacier and then Cape Barne and on to Cape Royds. 'We only missed Cape Royds by about two hundred yards,' wrote a relieved Hooke. 'Three times it looked certain that icebergs were going to take us, but providence was with us.'[14] At midday, Stenhouse noted in the log: 'Storm; heavy sea running; thick driving mist, frequent and continuous violent squalls; ship with heavy list to leeward [port] and spraying heavily. . . . Everything obscured by drift beyond a ship's length. . . . Ship rolling and labouring heavily.'[15] To make matters worse, in the bitter cold, the spray froze instantly, festooning the spars and rigging with glistening stalactites and giving the *Aurora* the eerie appearance of a ghost ship. Life on board became perilous as well as unpleasant as men slipped and fell on the violently rolling decks and tackle became clogged with ice.

The following day the weather moderated, allowing Stenhouse to work the vessel back towards Cape Evans. By the early afternoon of 14 March, he felt able to bring the ship close enough to the pack edge to start the process of securing her with a series of wires running to the shore; using these, the anchors and the windlasses, he intended to heave the ship into her winter resting place. Although the continuing gales often put a severe strain on the wires, causing them to hum and whine, the ice gradually began to fill the bay; sometimes the wind and currents broke it up and sent it scudding northwards, but it always reformed. Over the next few days, as the new ice began to coalesce, locking the ship into place, Stenhouse put more anchors ashore and hove the ship in as tightly as possible. Then began the process of tidying the ship, clearing her decks of the accumulated clutter and giving her the ship-shape appearance that he and Thomson so prized – a transformation much aided by the landing of the dogs that had been picked up with the sledge parties.

On 20 March, with McMurdo Sound now frozen over as far as the eye could see, Stenhouse finally felt confident enough to give Larkman the order to draw the fires and blow down the boilers for the long winter ahead. On this very day, he had hoped to be able to pick up Mackintosh at Hut Point, but there was no sign of the Skipper and the ship now seemed secure for the winter. Three days later, preparations began for landing the scientists at the Cape Evans hut. The whaleboat plied the short distance between ship and shore carrying scientific instruments, supplies and some of the personal effects belonging to Stevens, Spencer-Smith, Gaze and Richards, and by 5 p.m. the four men were endeavouring to make themselves comfortable in their new home. That same day, Hooke observed ominously that 'Towards midnight the pack ice started to come in at a rate estimated to be two miles per hour. All the weight of the ship was thrown on one or two wires and a tremendous strain was set up and there was an immediate danger of the ship pulling the "bits" or breaking the wires. Should this happen, as we have no more wires, we should have to drift with pack, an unpleasant prospect.' Unpleasant, too, for the men who would thereby be marooned ashore.

Over the next few weeks, the ice spread and then contracted, advanced and retreated, like breath on the face of a mirror. Stenhouse kept a constant watch on its fluctuations around the ship and across the Sound; indeed, the ship's log became more akin to a diary of ice movements, with only the briefest accompanying descriptions of the weather and of the crew's activities. Of course, the safety of the vessel and, ultimately, of the crew and land parties, was largely dependent upon the ice conditions but, also, by making a detailed record, Stenhouse knew that he might also be lending aid to future expeditions into the Ross Sea.

In leaving the *Aurora*, Mackintosh had made it absolutely clear that Stenhouse's primary duty must be to ensure the safety of the ship and the well-being of the crew – other considerations must be secondary. The work that Stenhouse detailed in his log, therefore, revolved largely around making the ship ready for the winter ahead but also around making her fit for her eventual return to sea. Besides the constant tending of the wires and anchors, often still being placed under enormous strain by the frequent blizzards and the shifting of the ice, he focused the crew's attention on the repair and re-rigging of the damaged jib-boom, work which they completed during the first days of April. Thereafter, they concentrated on the rigging of the wireless aerials.

Captain Scott had refused to take wireless on the *Terra Nova* because of its bulk, but Mawson's expedition had carried a full set of Telefunken equipment on the *Aurora* in 1911. Unfortunately, the Australian expedition's unintentional landing at the windiest place on the face of the globe had made the establishment of the wireless station extraordinarily difficult and severely limited the range and clarity of the signal. Nonetheless, in the AAE's second year, some messages had been successfully sent and received via Macquarie Island and important experiments had been conducted in the transmission of time signals to determine longitude. The Ross Sea Party's possession of wireless would enable messages to be sent between the Antarctic and Australia as well as facilitating easy communication between the ship and the scientific party in the hut.

Hoping that work on the aerials would be completed during his absence on the depot-laying expedition, Hooke had left detailed instructions with Stenhouse. 'Having fully appreciated your offer to have aerial erected (if possible) during my absence,' he had written on 30 January, 'I have attached necessary particulars. If aerial is erected [it] will save an immense amount of time as, in any case, I would be dependent upon your assistance. Also the increasing cold is a considerable factor.'[16] Despite Hooke's confident assertion that the construction and erection of the aerials would 'not entail extra work on yourself or your staff', the reverse proved to be true and the sailors spent many days labouring on the triangular constructs and then hoisting them up the fore and mizzen masts. Work on securing the aerials continued until the beginning of May and, with so many distractions, it was not until 6 April that Stenhouse could record that additional sledging rations had been sent ashore.

Increasingly concerned at the continued absence of the sledging parties, by 15 April Stenhouse had decided that a reconnaissance party should be sent to Hut Point and then, if necessary, out on to the ice shelf to look for them. 'You will take charge of sledging party,' he instructed Ninnis, ' . . . Proceed, by previously discussed route to Hut Point. . . . Do not attempt a passage to Hut Point over sea ice. . . . If, on your arrival at the hut, you find no traces of the parties, provision your party for 21 days and proceed to Corner Camp. . . . On your return to the hut, signal Cape Evans as follows: 1 Rocket = arrived here and am returning, 2 rockets = arrived all OK all hands returning. . . . Good luck!'[17] Not everyone considered the expedition a good idea: Spencer-Smith, in particular, thought risking additional lives, in order to confirm the fates of those perhaps already lost, to be pointless. Ninnis, meanwhile, in a private note to Stenhouse, confirmed that 'I have not packed away any things as I expect to return so soon but, if otherwise, then A.P. S-Smith and you will please act as I ask you to do in my letter to him. . . . Diaries might be censored by A.P., or rather "scanned" before being referred to at any time.'[18] In the event, Ninnis's anxiety for the privacy of his diary proved unnecessary. Concerned about the condition of the ice, Stenhouse abandoned the expedition and instead he had a sledge of provisions hauled round to the south side of Cape Evans, where it was linked to the sea ice by a 40ft rope ladder. This would offer easy access to Mackintosh, Cope and their parties should they attempt a passage around the bay.

In a letter written on 26 January, and left for Stenhouse at Hut Point, Mackintosh had asked his chief officer to devise some form of signal to indicate whether the ice was safe for the returning sledgers to attempt a passage across the bay. On the evening of 16 April, therefore, the men in the Cape Evans hut sent up a rocket to tell Mackintosh that the ice on the south side of the Cape would support a man's weight. They then waited for some kind of answering signal – but none came. Either the sledgers had not returned or they had not seen the signal or, possibly, they might even now be making their way towards their anxious friends. There was no way of knowing. Despite this disappointment, on 24 April, Hooke and Gaze sledged out to plant a depot flag to indicate the location of the ladder and the sledge loaded with supplies. If the depot-laying parties, weak and starving, were trying to make their way to the Cape Evans hut and the ship, this small fluttering rag at the end of a bamboo pole might actually save their lives.

Over the next few days the weather offered very little opportunity for sledging. At 8 p.m. on 24 April, Stenhouse noted in the log that the sky had the distinct appearance of a blizzard and, by midnight, the wind had picked up to near gale force. By the early hours of the following morning, the blizzard was in full spate, sweeping the bay clear of ice and making the iron-hard, ice-covered rigging whine and whirr. 'This is dreadfully disappointing,' Hooke observed, 'as we hoped we had at last a safe position.' Every now and then, a violent squall would lash the ship, freezing the spray as it whipped it from the surface of the sea and then flinging it into the faces of the few men brave enough to venture on to the slippery decks. The blizzard continued with only the briefest of lulls for four days and only on 30 April could work again begin on rigging the wireless aerials. As the wind died down, the ice once again began to creep into the bay, turning the surface of the sea opalescent and leaving the cables and wires mooring the *Aurora* glittering in the moonlight like spun glass. But with the return of the ice came the ice-pressure, and soon the stern moorings began their endless song.

The formation of the ice also made communication with the shore easier. On 1 May, the crew landed five bags of coke for the scientists inside the hut and the following day a hunting party from the ship killed and brought on board two seals. Earlier in the year Stenhouse had stopped the indiscriminate shooting of birds, at the same time expressing his regret that 'several of the crew and I am sorry to say the after-guard also shoot for shooting's sake and numbers of skuas, petrels etc are wounded and left in pain.' Killing for food, on the other hand, was perfectly acceptable: fresh meat prevented scurvy, the bane of Antarctic exploration, and some variety in the men's diet helped to keep up morale. Stenhouse himself admitted that he found fried seal 'most enjoyable' while Thomson thought that 'penguin meat is absolutely the best substitute that I have tasted for beef steak'.

The next few days brought a strange mix of mysterious omens and a calmness that might lull even the most hardened explorer. The omens began on the evening of the 2nd, when Stenhouse observed the flight of a comet over the northern slopes of Mount Erebus. The comet showed a brilliant red and left a white tail slicing like a scar across ten degrees of the horizon. But any nervousness that the more superstitious members of the crew might have felt were then allayed by days of moderate, even kindly, weather, with light winds and a sea so still and unruffled that it allowed the pack to creep into the Sound unchallenged. On the afternoon of 4 May, Stenhouse even took a break from his shipboard duties to sledge out to within half a mile of Little Razor Back Island, where he discovered that the ice seemed to be holding quite firm. Then, during the evening of 5 May, all on board heard a distinct rumbling from Erebus and the ice began to crack and break as the sea beneath it rolled in a heavy swell. It appeared that the Antarctic landscape was about to awaken.

On Thursday 6 May 1915, a fine clear sky arched overhead, light breezes from the east-south-east gently strummed the rigging, and the usual routine of work continued on ship and shore. Around 4 p.m., however, Stenhouse noticed that the sky had a 'blizzardy appearance' and at 8 p.m. the after-moorings came under an immense strain as the threatened gale struck the ship. Over the next hour, the blizzard grew in intensity until, at 9.45, the *Aurora* lurched and the screeching of the chains and wires reached a crescendo. Listening from his cot, Thomson thought 'the strain was so great that something had to go: either the decks with the bits or the wires. I soon found out which it was as the two wires parted with reports like the report of guns.' On the bridge, meanwhile, Stenhouse found it 'Most hellishly fascinating to listen to wires and chain breaking' until he was distracted by Scotty Paton, the bosun, rushing across the deck, hurricane lamp in hand. 'She's away wi' it,' he yelled, and even as the blizzard tore the words from his lips, the massive slab of ice containing the *Aurora* broke free from the shore with a great rending crack. 'Any ass could see and feel and hear it,' an irritated Stenhouse later scribbled in his diary, 'but the Bosun is frightfully garrulous.'[19]

With the vessel's exposed side acting like a great sail before the wind, the gap between the ice-bound ship and the shore widened with every passing second, the void filled with violently churning granite-grey waves and glistening shards of ice. In this emergency, the first priority must be to haul in the dragging anchors, which were causing the ship to heel over and placing tremendous strain on the windlasses. 'As the ship, in the solid flow, set to the NW,' Stenhouse later wrote in his diary, 'the cables rattled and tore at the hawsepipes; luckily the anchors lying as they were on a steep sloping bottom, came away easily, without damage to the windlass or hawsepipes.' He also ordered Larkman to raise steam in the hope of being able to work the *Aurora* back to shore once she had extricated herself from the floe. But with the boilers totally cold and the machinery partly dismantled for essential repairs, there could be no immediate prospect of firing the engines. In the meantime, whenever they had a moment to raise their heads against the wind's icy blast, Stenhouse and his crew could see the light burning in the window of the hut at Cape Evans: a tiny flickering, yellowish light, gradually dwindling to a speck before it disappeared altogether in the whirling drift snow. In the hut, completely oblivious to the drama being enacted within a few hundred yards of where they sheltered, the members of the land party carried on their usual routine, sleeping or yarning, as the blizzard swept the helpless *Aurora* into the midst of McMurdo Sound. Some of them would never see the ship again.

An hour and forty-five minutes after the wind snapped the moorings and flung the 600-ton vessel out to sea, the slab of ice entrapping the *Aurora* began to break up. For an hour or so, the great splinters of shattered floe played a restless tattoo on the ship's timbers as they scraped past. An admiring Thomson believed that 'the pounding this ship got would have sent almost any steel ship to the bottom but this old ship stood it wonderfully well'. By midnight the most immediate danger had passed as the pack again began to close up, the noisy jostling of the great plates dying away as they froze into a solid mass. At 12.45, when the moon broke through the clouds, Stenhouse could see the ice stretching away into the distance to the north and south, one unbroken mass. The ship had developed a heavy list to port, but he remained optimistic about the chances of getting back to Cape Evans once Larkman and Donnelly had managed to raise steam. They had continued to work on the engines throughout the night and had already managed to free the main blow-down cock of the accumulated ice by pushing a hot iron down its length. With the fires lit in the furnaces and water beginning to flow in the boilers, Stenhouse felt satisfied that they had struck 'the first blow in our defence against the terrific forces of Nature in the Antarctic'.[20]

PRISONERS OF THE PACK

Having spent 7 May 1915 in a flurry of activity, liaising with the engineers, plotting the ship's position and overseeing the laborious process of bringing sea-ice on board for cooking purposes, it was not until the morning of the 8th that Stenhouse found an opportunity properly to survey his surroundings. To the south, the sky glowered black and threatening; the Western Mountains loomed indistinctly through the haze astern; and Cape Bird and Cape Barne could just be seen on the port and starboard bows. Since breaking adrift the *Aurora* had swung round until she now lay with her head pointing east. Her starboard side, therefore, faced south: a prey to every gust of wind that scoured the Antarctic plateau before rolling out over the pack to blow the helpless ship ever northwards. 'So this is the end of our attempt to Winter in McMurdo Sound,' Stenhouse wrote on 9 May, 'hard cheese after four months buffeting, for the last seven weeks of which, we nursed our moorings . . . five weeks to the middle of winter, no sun, little and uncertain light, blizzards; no immediate water supply . . . fast in the pack and drifting to God knows where. . . . Well! We are all in good health . . . good spirits and we will get through . . . we hope!'[1]

During 10 and 11 May, the blizzard reached such terrific force that it became practically impossible for a man to work his way down the deck and Stenhouse admitted that, in all his years at sea, he could 'never remember such wind force'. Added to the intense anxiety felt by all, the enforced confinement below decks brought latent disagreements bubbling to the surface and the mood on board became grim and fractious. 'People are inclined to get a little restless now,' Thomson noted on the 17th, 'and little quarrels are continually arising which I have to patch up. I have a few little rows of my own now and again but I think I am mostly right in telling people off a bit.'[2]

Desperate to alert the outside world to the expedition's plight, Stenhouse ordered that every effort should be made to raise Macquarie Island and each evening, despite the fact that the wireless masts bent before the wind like fishing rods, Hooke tapped out his plaintive messages. The evenings were known to offer the best climatic conditions for such work but, hour after hour, his headphones emitted nothing but static. In ominous contrast to the silence of Macquarie Island, however, the pack was seldom quiet. Throughout May, a continuous grumbling could be heard, interspersed with loud explosions as the ocean swells caused the ice to flex and crack; then the blizzards set in, grinding the rough edges of the broken floes together in a perpetual sawing motion and driving the whole mass gradually to the north-west.

On 25 May, Stenhouse observed 'a scene of chaos all around; one floe about 3ft in thickness had upended and driven under [the] ship on port quarter; as far as can be seen heavy blocks of ice screwed up on end and the scene is like a graveyard.' His description was depressingly apposite: the combination of sea, ice and wind were subjecting the *Aurora* to enormous pressure and, if her timbers splintered and the ship foundered, the lives of all on board would almost certainly be forfeit. The perpetual darkness emphasised the eerie and depressing qualities of the petrified seascape still further, with only a faint grey arc of light being visible to the north either side of midday. 'The dim light and glow in the Northern sky is a most melancholy sight,' Stenhouse commented a few days later, 'giving rise to many different speculations and thoughts; in that light people are living . . . soon it will [be] shining over battlefields. To us it appears, that arc of twilight, a gate to all that is – soon the gate will be closed.'³ With the *Aurora* in imminent peril of being crushed, and with the feelings of powerlessness likely to sap morale still further, he decided that he must prepare to abandon ship. Should this become necessary, the eighteen men on board would have to take to the ice with four sledges and one month's rations. They would then head for the nearest land, six men making a high-speed dash for Cape Evans while the remaining twelve followed as quickly as possible, killing seals and penguins en route and building depots in case of an emergency retreat. With the uncertain condition of the ice and the risk of a strong blizzard scattering the floe, it was a risky proposition – but there seemed to be no viable alternative.

Of course, despite the enormous pressures being exerted upon her, the ship might not be destroyed. If she remained ice-bound but static, then Stenhouse would land a party of three towards the end of August when the sea ice might be judged safe. These men would then proceed to Cape Evans to make contact with the sledging parties. If, on the other hand, the ship remained trapped and the pack continued to trend northwards, once the ice broke up he would sail to New Zealand. Reinforced with additional officers and men, he would then head south once more to relieve Mackintosh and complete the depot-laying for Shackleton's transcontinental party.

Despite the extreme danger of his own position, it was the fate of the men at Cape Evans that gnawed most relentlessly at Stenhouse's peace of mind. They had limited stockpiles of food, clothing and supplies; they were also completely ignorant of the ship's fate, not knowing whether she had simply been blown out into the Sound or overwhelmed and sent to the bottom. That doubt meant that they could have no idea whether news of their own situation and need of rescue would ever reach the warring and preoccupied outside world. Although Stenhouse would later vigorously defend himself for not having landed more equipment when the ship lay anchored against the ice shelf, he did feel acutely responsible for the land parties. In a position already fraught with risk, what chance would be left to them if the *Aurora* sank?

Whatever the eventual fate of his ship, Stenhouse had more immediate problems to address, not least the shortage of drinking water and the need to gather food. When blown out to sea, the *Aurora*'s freshwater tanks had been nearly empty, the plentiful supply of snow and freshwater ice on shore making their replenishment seem relatively unimportant. But, by 31 May, the supply previously relied upon lay some 90 miles to the south-east and the crew now found themselves in the middle of a vast field of undrinkable salt-laden sea ice. Their only sources of fresh water, therefore, were a large iceberg, broken from the barrier and lying trapped, like themselves, in the pack, and any snow that they might be able to harvest after a storm. For the time being, however, the treacherousness of the sea ice meant that the berg lay too far distant to be approached safely. In such circumstances, any snow flurry, no matter how brief, was quickly followed by a snow-gathering excursion. 'The cracks and lanes have frozen over hard, and the ice seems absolutely safe,' Stenhouse observed, 'but with all the noises of pressure and movement about, I don't like to send anyone too far away from the ship. Suppose we will get plenty of snow "by and by"; up to the present time the snowfall has been extraordinarily small.'

Hunger constituted less of a problem. The *Aurora*'s holds contained reasonable quantities of tinned food but, with no way of knowing how long she might be held in the pack and with the life-span of the tinned supplies uncertain, every contingency must be considered. Every day, lookouts scoured the surface of the ice watching for penguins and seals that might wander close enough to be killed and added to the ship's larder. 'When approached,' Stenhouse noted, 'the Emperor usually comes to meet the hunter, then gets suspicious, turns away, and again, curiosity overcoming him, comes back . . . he gets a "crack" on the neck, then, which bowls him over. If it were not such a cold-blooded affair it would be ludicrous, for if he does not go down at the first blow, he ducks his weird old head and seems horribly surprised.'[4]

As well as ensuring that the crew remained well fed, hunting provided an important recreation for the men and offered ample opportunities to add to the *Aurora*'s collection of biological specimens. Of course, the men specifically tasked with prosecuting the Ross Sea Party's scientific programme were all ashore at Cape Evans, but the ship's crew, too, could make an important contribution. Stenhouse also buoyed up his spirits with the thought that 'With our records of winds etc and drift and set of pack our enforced trip in the pack ice will prove valuable to science',[5] and he encouraged Hooke and Ninnis to send regular weather updates to New Zealand and Australia, via Macquarie Island. Although they could not be certain that anyone received these reports, he hoped that, eventually, they would be collated by professional meteorologists to form a comprehensive record of climatic conditions in Antarctica. With this goal in mind, each evening, with their earphones clamped to their heads like earmuffs and their breath condensing in clouds and coating the timbers with icy rime, the wireless operators crouched over their instruments patiently tapping out their signals. Having transmitted their messages, they would then pause and listen, desperate to hear the metallic clicks of an acknowledgement. All in vain: the proximity of the magnetic pole, interference from the aurora australis and the accumulation of drift snow around the insulators all prevented the wireless from functioning properly and their messages disappeared unanswered into the ether.

'From 2 a.m. until breakfast time,' Stenhouse recorded on 2 June, 'a most peculiar noise arose from under the ice along the starboard side. . . . A most eerie, ghostlike noise, intermittent like a sleeping man breathing thro' his mouth . . . suhh . . . suhh . . . suhhuh . . . suh. I think the noise was caused by underridging ice from the southward. . . . Crew weighing out rations . . . should soon be ready with sledges.' Fortunately, for the time being at least, the sledges proved surplus to requirements. For all the ghostly moaning of the ice beneath her keel, the old ship showed no inclination to sink. The Dundee shipwrights had built enormous strength into her design and she had withstood nearly forty years of punishment as a whaler in northern waters before Mawson purchased her for the AAE. During that expedition she had come close to being wrecked on more than one occasion and she had lost anchor after anchor as the terrific winds tossed her about like a toy in Commonwealth Bay. But she had survived those conditions and, gradually, the crew began to think it just possible that she might now endure all that the Ross Sea could throw at her.

As their initial anxiety slowly wore off, familiarity with the sounds of the pack began to breed contempt, and the crew gradually became more resigned to their new life. Fortunately, most of the men seemed inclined to make the best of their circumstances, despite the harshness of their living conditions. On 14 June, Stenhouse observed that the 'Cook and Steward's room, which is below decks and with Carpenter's and Bosun's rooms, adjacent to the forecastle, has become like a grotto from the frozen breath of its occupants; there is no stove in any of these rooms and what little heat comes from the forecastle stove is inadequate in making any appreciable difference to their temperatures.' In reality, those men whose cabins did have the benefit of a proper stove were often no better off, since the stoves frequently emitted clouds of sulphur fumes which often came close to suffocating their owners. Stenhouse regularly awoke retching and dizzy and, on more than one occasion, the noxious gases actually knocked him out altogether, so that his companions had to drag him into the open air to resuscitate him. But, with being frozen to death the only option to keeping the stoves lit, the risk of asphyxiation was one that had to be borne.

Every member of an expedition that had ever wintered in Antarctica viewed the arrival of mid-winter as a red-letter day. The members of the Ross Sea Party were no exception and when, on 21 June, the sun reached the limit of its northern declination, they could look forward with relief to its return to southern skies. Stenhouse and his companions still faced months of darkness and bitter cold, and there was very little chance of the ship being released until the spring, but at least they could take some pleasure from the thought that the darkness would now begin its long, slow retreat. 'Observed this day as holiday,' Stenhouse wrote that night, 'and in evening had "hands" aft to drink to health of King and Expedition. All hands happy but miss the others at Cape Evans; pray to God we may soon be clear of this prison and in a position to help them. We can live now for sunlight and activity.'

Despite the passing of this important milestone, Stenhouse grew increasingly depressed and anxious. While many of the men seemed to have reconciled themselves to their imprisonment, he found it almost intolerable. In the period preceding the ITAE, he had suffered from acute and debilitating depression, and he had seen the expedition as the perfect antidote, offering distraction in the form of unremitting labour and activity, with the added bonus that he would be exploring new lands, seldom trodden by man. Now he found this dream replaced by a nightmare of enforced inactivity, his ship moribund and useless. To make matters even worse, over everything there lay a pall of doubt and fear regarding the fate, not only of the men at Cape Evans, but also of Shackleton's party. In the cramped confines of the *Aurora*, Stenhouse could not entirely hide his anguish and Larkman certainly recognised that he endured 'mental torments thinking of the Captain's party'. What the engineer probably didn't realise, however, was that Stenhouse's anguish could also twist into bitter resentment which, in the extremity of his depression, he directed at the men whose situation, at other times, he so deplored. 'Through all my waking hours one long thought of the people at Cape Evans,' he wrote on 1 July, ' . . . this is Hell and one must appear to be happy and take interest in the small happenings of shipboard. The people who have to remain on board ship during the sledging etc are like coachmen and grooms – [they] drive to Olympia, and wait outside while the others have the fun. My sincere opinion is that the people who winter ashore have no hardships or frights in comparison with the people on shipboard . . . in the hut one is safe from pressure. . . . This outpouring is from a bad attack of the blues.'

Fortunately for Stenhouse's state of mind, life on board did offer him some diversions – though of a nature which, perhaps, few would have relished. In particular, with Cope trapped at Cape Evans, he took on the additional role of ship's surgeon. During his years with the Weir Line, he had seen men similarly unqualified treat many ailments and perform a variety of operations, from the setting of fractures to a circumcision carried out on the wardroom table, and he probably knew more of makeshift medicine than anyone aboard. Inevitably, frostbites, bruises and strains constituted the most common complaints on the *Aurora*, but some patients brought more challenging ailments to the sick bay. One such was the fireman William Mugridge who suffered from an intermittent rash, with red inflamed skin and occasional blisters. 'I don't know what the deuce it is,' admitted the perplexed medico, 'but the nearest description to it in *Materia Medica*, etc. is pemphigus . . . so pemphigus it is and he has been tonic'd and massaged.'[6] When circumstances demanded, Stenhouse also turned his hand to amateur dentistry. 'Have just returned from an unsuccessful attempt to draw one of Larkman's teeth,' he noted on one occasion. 'He has been suffering much lately and asked me to have a shot at pulling it out. Had two heaves and after nearly heaving his head off desisted as he was on the point of swooning. It is cruel work and Old L. must be a brick to stand it.'[7]

By the middle of July, any distraction, no matter how bloodthirsty, was to be welcomed. Throughout the month, the ship vibrated and shivered as the pressure exerted upon her increased. Occasionally, too, she leapt with a motion that Stenhouse compared to the sensation of a 'kick on the underside of a mattress to a person lying on top'. 'The gigantic force behind the ice sheet can only be fully realised in a position like ours, where one's future seems too uncertain to bear thinking of,' he observed after watching the ice around the ship bend and buckle. 'I am inclined to think that we have set into a cul-de-sac and that we will now experience the full force of the pressure from the South. Here one sees the impotence of man and feels like a pawn in a great game. We have prepared for the worst and can only hope for the best . . . a release from the ice with a seaworthy vessel under us.'[8]

A few days later these hopes received a devastating blow. After lunch on 18 July, a violent concussion shook the ship, followed shortly afterwards by a rumbling sound like chains being dragged overhead. Bounding up the companionway, Stenhouse immediately saw that the great slab of ice holding the *Aurora* had split along the line of the keel and then diagonally from her port quarter. The ice to port had retreated some 15ft and, for the first time since 23 May, he ordered that the gangway be hauled in, in case the cracking indicated an imminent break-up of the floe. Four hours later, however, the ice closed again like the jaws of some colossal sea monster, nipping the ship unevenly and causing her timbers to groan and strain more than ever.

Over the next few days new lanes continually opened and closed around the ship. And gradually, as the pool in which the *Aurora* lay widened and contracted, she slowly turned so that by the 21st her rudder-post pressed against one wall of ice while her bow pressed against another. It was an acutely dangerous position, but not one that could be rectified by any action on the part of the crew; instead, they could only watch, horrified, as the ice began inexorably to squeeze the stricken vessel at both ends. At 5.15 p.m., the colossal weight of the ice against her stern twisted the ship's rudder round to starboard, smashing it beyond repair. The 'solid oak and iron went like matchwood', Stenhouse scribbled in his diary, while Hooke observed that 'In a very few minutes all hands were on deck ready to jump overboard onto the ice. It looked certain that the ship must go.'[9] After two and a half months of constant strain and uncertainty, it seemed that the *Aurora*'s fate was finally sealed. 'An anxious time of open leads, buffetings and squeezings,' Larkman wrote later that day, 'Sleep "All Standing" and emergency sleighs and gear ready for taking to the ice – though God knows there's practically no hope of survival if that comes to pass. . . . 'Tis of interest to see how some are behaving in this crisis – blue funk, calmness, cheeriness, etc are all shown . . . wonderful to note how quiet and retiring our armchair critics are when there's some real hard cold graft to be done!'[10]

The following morning, with the *Aurora* still in the same precarious position, Stenhouse told his men to be ready to abandon ship. She still swam, but there appeared to be no chance of a release and he thought it impossible that she could stand much more. Hooke observed that 'The whole crew are like a pack of schoolgirls, our nerves absolutely shattered. The dropping of a book or the slamming of a door brings us all up with a start.' And yet, to everyone's astonishment, the veteran whaler refused to submit to the inevitable: her timbers groaned and squealed and her sides visibly bulged, but still she resisted. At 2 p.m., desperate to find some way of easing her position, Stenhouse ordered his men to pour sulphuric acid on to the ice around her stern-post.

He hoped the acid might soften or melt the ice and thereby relieve the pressure, but the plan produced no visible effects. Instead, the ship began to buck as the floes forced their way under her stern, causing her to list badly. Then, just as it seemed that the *Aurora*'s destruction was entering its final phase, the situation began to turn in her favour with the very violence of her movement working to her advantage. As she jerked and lurched sideways, the relatively new ice on her starboard side began to crumble, turning the ship so that her vulnerable stern-post no longer pressed against the hard edge of the floe but buried itself instead in the softer ice of one of the recently frozen lanes. By midnight on 22 July, an exhausted Stenhouse could at last note in his diary that the ship rested in a safer position and the next day he felt able to 'thank God that we have been spared through this fearful nightmare!! Shall never forget the concertina motions of the old ship during yesterday's and Wednesday's fore and aft nip.' He and the carpenter continued to check the wells but, amazingly, they showed no evidence of any serious leaks.

All around, the northward-trending floes could be seen splitting into broad lanes from which dense clouds of vapour rose, producing a weird and beautiful effect in the moonlight. Sometimes the leads opened to widths of 300yd, but they then froze again, before once more splitting and repeating the process times without number. Stenhouse thought these newly frozen leads aided the ship's position because they acted as 'springs' or buffers, relieving the pressure that still threatened her timbers, and certainly the continuing violence of the floes' movements made any protection afforded by the springs very welcome. On 25 July, for instance, Stenhouse observed how 'a large field on the port quarter came charging up and on meeting "our" floe tossed up a ridge from 10 to 15ft high. The blocks of ice as they broke off crumbled and piled over each other to the accompaniment of a thunderous roar; one's thoughts cannot be even remembered after witnessing this awesome sight in the hazy darkness and from the deck of a small vessel so close to and at the mercy of a hidden, tremendous force.'[11] He thanked Providence and God for the ship's survival – but he also remembered Alexander Stephen, the *Aurora*'s builder, whom he hoped was 'wearing a "Halo of Happiness" in the place where there are no pressure ridges'.

With the ship apparently out of the most immediate danger, work began on making her seaworthy again. It seemed too much to hope that the leads might broaden to such a degree that they would release her – but the crew's confidence in miracles had been reinforced over recent weeks and Stenhouse wanted to be ready for any eventuality. On 30 July, he and his officers began making plans for cutting away the smashed rudder and rigging steering gear for a jury rudder. Through the early days of August, however, a severe blizzard severely hampered progress, reducing visibility to near zero, covering the decks in drift snow and driving the *Aurora* ever northwards. 'Am sick of the sound of the blasted infernal wind,' a frustrated Stenhouse cried on 4 August, ' . . . din! din! din! and darkness – a beautiful glorious world!!' It was not until the 6th that the blizzard finally died down and, with the long-anticipated return of the sun, the mood on board changed instantly. 'Rose 9.50 a.m. local time,' Stenhouse enthused, 'a glorious joyful sight. We drank to something and with very light hearts gave cheers for the Sun . . . saw one gentleman salaaming the Sun à la Mohammedan . . . we can appreciate what we have passed thro' now.'

Despite frequent interruptions caused by the poor weather, work continued on vital repairs throughout the rest of the month. The conscientious Donnelly, whose lack of sea experience had never proved a hindrance to his effectiveness, spent hours sawing through the iron sheathing and dense oak of the smashed rudder, often risking both frostbite and plunges through the treacherous sea ice. Stenhouse, Mauger and others, meanwhile, worked on the jury rudder, which they manufactured using timber, salvaged ironwork and even concrete, which they had to mix with boiling water. 'Things are running very smoothly aboard the old ship,' a satisfied Stenhouse remarked on 13 August, 'and as each day brings us more light and brighter prospects we are thankful to the Almighty for our safe passage through the dark days.'

The removal of the old rudder began on 23 August, but in temperatures of −20° and with the rudder weighing around 4½ tons, the job proved long and hard. Having cut through a mass of wood and iron, the crew cleared the snow and ice around the ship's stern. Next they attempted to lever the rudder away from the rudder-post, so that they could let it sink. But the rudder had been built on the same massy scale as the rest of the *Aurora* and, instead of falling away from the ship as they intended, they could only make it rock in a see-saw motion, as though it were pivoted below the waterline. The next day, Stenhouse had a complex network of blocks and tackle rigged and eventually, after hours of backbreaking labour, the dismembered rudder lay on the ice a short distance from the stern. 'All the pintles are gone at the fore part of the rudder,' Stenhouse noted, surveying the damage, 'it is a clean break and witness to the terrific force exerted on the ship during the nip.' Two days later, Mauger reported that he had finished working on the new rudder and that it could be installed whenever the *Aurora* reached open water.

Throughout the rest of August and September, the sight of numerous open leads, the occasional feeling of a sea-swell beneath the *Aurora*'s keel and the continuing work on board, kept Stenhouse's mood buoyant. Looking down from the crow's nest on to the ridged and hummocky pack, he thought the extreme cold and the frequent blizzards made an early release unlikely, but still there was a chance; if that chance came, the ship would now be in a much better condition to meet it.

When not working on the sails, rigging or rudder, officers and men alike amused themselves playing cricket and football, sports which Stenhouse considered a 'splendid tonic'. Earlier in the year, he had been concerned to observe that the sedate, indoor lifestyle forced upon them by temperatures of −50° had left the hands 'in poor condition and frightfully soft' but now, benefiting from hard work and regular exercise, he could report that 'We are all in splendid fettle.' Content that the ship continued to drift northwards and that open water lay in quite close proximity, he occupied his own time tending the sick and injured, observing the habits of the penguins and, in the evenings, playing whist and chess. 'Things are running very smoothly on board,' he noted with satisfaction on 8 October, 'and for'ard the ship's company could scarcely be happier.'

He continued to believe that, even when trapped in the wastes of the pack, life could be made tolerable if filled with activity. When the weather made work impossible, however, he fretted and chafed at the uselessness of his existence and at his inability to help his comrades at Cape Evans. In the last days of October, such thoughts became uppermost in his mind and he sank once again into a deep depression. 'These leaden skies get on one's nerves,' he complained on the 24th, 'day after day the same old thing; a ghastly white gloom is all one can see. Have been suffering from severe dose of Blues due, not to the surroundings, but the opportunity to think; I think happiness is a myth; whenever I have leisure the old, old curse comes back to me . . . I think and brood over the use of anything and am worked into thinking that all is chaos.' His companions, too, instead of a comfort became an irritation. 'There are one or two faces on board here,' he growled two days later, 'which give me the "pip" to look at and the trouble is there is no means of getting away from them. One notices small faults in a position like ours, and becomes hyper-critical. . . . It is hard to have to eat at the same board as one who has the vices and manners of a "larrikin". . . . This inactivity is telling on us more than we realise, I think!'

On 21 November, after six and a half months of northward drift, the *Aurora* slid across the Antarctic Circle. For months, there had been little or no appreciable change in her circumstances: lanes continued to open in the ice and sometimes a sea bird normally associated with open water, like a sooty albatross, would glide overhead. But the lanes always closed and the albatrosses invariably found their way back to the ocean without having to sit and wait for it to come to them. The crew frequently heard noises from the pressure and the ship occasionally received a smart blow as the floes moved around her but otherwise things remained much the same. As the Antarctic spring slowly turned to summer, however, there was a perceptible rise in temperature and Stenhouse felt delighted one morning to see melted snow coursing down the ship's scuppers. Of small note in itself, he knew that this tiny torrent indicated that the great slab of ice imprisoning the *Aurora* must also be melting, however slowly. 'This cannot last very long,' he sighed at the end of the month, 'and I think one good hefty blizzard would cause a general break up!'

Despite such hopes, the ice held with sickening tenacity throughout the days leading up to Christmas, a celebration that Stenhouse dreaded. 'This is Christmas week,' he noted on 19 December, 'and likely to be the most miserable one that I have ever spent and they are plenty; there is little fun in spending Xmas in a sailing ship, off the Horn, or in other high latitudes, but it is preferable to being locked in the ice, knowing the dire straits of those at Cape Evans and our inability to assist them and thereby the transcontinental party . . . it seems a mockery to have any jollifications, at all, considering what a useless part we are playing.' But, whatever his own feelings, he tried to hide them from his crew and, on Christmas Eve, he stopped work early and gave the cook permission to use some of the carefully hoarded fuel to make bread – a luxury they had not enjoyed for months. In reality, the thought of such dainties turned his stomach. 'A most elaborate menu has been made for tomorrow', he wrote that night, ' . . . I wish to God the blasted "festivities" were over – it is all forced. To think that we are hogging in to the best, whilst the poor beggars at Cape Evans have little or nothing!' On Christmas Day itself, Hooke noted that 'on the whole, the day passed away well'. Ninnis had manufactured decorative menus, the cook had excelled himself and, after the usual toasts, Larkman rounded off proceedings with his rendition of 'Life on the Ocean Wave' – but all knew only too well that the plenty of Christmas would be followed by scarcity of rations and the longed-for date of their eventual release remained as unpredictable as ever. 'What hypocrites we are!' Stenhouse snarled at the end of the day, 'Thank God that this ordeal is over!!'

Fortunately, New Year's celebrations proved rather more hearty. At odd times during the previous week and throughout the afternoon of the 31st, Stenhouse and the other officers had heard a variety of bizarre noises issuing from the forecastle: clattering and banging and the sounds of disagreements reaching various levels of intensity. Then, just before midnight, the decks echoed with the sound of hobnailed boots and, after a sharp knock, the wardroom door opened to reveal the foremast hands in the guise of a 'fou-fou' band, equipped with a broken-winded melodeon, marline-spikes doubling as triangles, a kerosene tin for a drum and a mouth organ. '[A] more motley crowd than the bandsmen would be difficult to imagine,' an amused Stenhouse wrote later that night. ' . . . It was a comical sight to see

Grady with a kerosene tin slung around his neck, Mugridge with the marline spikes (standing at attention as befits an ex-RN man), Kavanagh with the big drum – an empty venesta case with which he drowned all the other noise – and the other bandsmen with their earnest, serious expressions.' The bosun cried 'Guid New Year' to all and then the band launched into lusty, if rather dissonant, renditions of 'Britannia' and 'God Save the King'. With much slapping of backs and shaking of hands, every man wished his neighbours a better year to come, cheers were given and toasts drunk and then the crowd dispersed. All in all, it had been a hugely successful night, with any disagreements forgotten and, for once, the plight of the ship and of the land parties put to one side. 'So ends an eventful year!' Stenhouse wrote in the early hours of 1 January 1916, 'Although misfortune has dogged our movements, we in the ship can look back with something akin to Awe and with Reverence to the Power which, through all the vicissitudes of fortune has brought us safely in good health and with buoyant spirits to face the next move.'

The nature of the next move, however, remained as uncertain as ever. All around the ship, large chunks of the floe continued to rot and then capsize in the warmth of the sun and Stenhouse still hoped that the break-up might enable him to reach New Zealand, coal, repair and re-supply in time to give succour to the land parties. On 7 January, he mused that 'if we could leave Lyttleton at the end of February, with luck and a quick passage south we might make Hut Point before the general freezing in of the Sound . . . at the worst we could leave stores and clothing and relieve the anxiety of the parties there'.[12] But time was critical and this plan could only work if the pack released the ship in the very near future; the only possible alternative remained a return south as soon as the ship broke free. After another week of strong and variable gales, however, any hopes of either of these plans coming to fruition had dwindled significantly. 'It will be too late now to go North and return in time to relieve the parties South,' Stenhouse decided on the 13th, 'If we break out soon and have luck we might get South but I am not quite so hopeful now as the Blizzard season will soon be along. . . . We seem to be at a dead end.'

'I don't know what to hope for,' he wrote a week later, 'but still one must. To be cooped up in a small ship with chums, and in pleasant surroundings would get stale I suppose; to be in the small ship, with people with whom one has nothing in common (except the present), and in a frozen sea, with the ever-haunting knowledge that the others of the Expedition are in dire need, is worse.'[13] Eleven days later he remained as glum as ever: 'Another month gone and still we are imprisoned. The Transcontinental Party should be at the Beardmore now, if they have made good time; it will be a miserable "home coming" for them, after the hardships of travel, to find not only no relief ship but little stores and a prospect of another Winter in the South.'[14] Over the previous few days, however, some encouraging signs had been observed. The wind had freshened after a lull of many days' duration and some of the bergs in the distance, which had lain trapped like the *Aurora*, could be seen moving with apparent freedom: either wide lanes had opened around them or they had actually been freed altogether. With the ice breaking all around the ship, it seemed just possible that she, too, might soon escape.

In fact, after so much longing and anticipation, the break-up of the floe took everyone by surprise. Saturday, 12 February, started much like any other day, with strong to light east-south-easterly winds and a fall of snow that continued intermittently throughout the course of the day. A close watch had been kept on the ship's wells throughout the drift, even though for much of the time she had been so securely frozen in that there had been little opportunity for water to work its way through her seams. Now, with the prospect of a release much more real, and with the thought of the seams straining and opening in a heavy sea, they had to be observed even more closely. With over 3½ft of water in the wells at 9.00 a.m., Stenhouse ordered that the main pumps be started. Then, when Larkman reported that the pumps were frozen, he had the crew prepare for bucket-baling, forming relays between the main well and the fore hatch, while the engineers worked on thawing out the pump pipes using red-hot irons. It took all day to reduce the water level to 1ft, with everyone far too busy to look over the rails at the changes in the ice around the ship. They could feel a swell beneath their feet – but they had felt many such swells over the previous months and none had proved the precursor of release. But today turned out to be different: new lanes had been opening up and widening all around the ship and, just as work on baling and pumping came to an end, another swell caused the thinning ice crust to flex and then buckle, splitting it into hundreds of jagged pieces.

Within a few minutes, the entire floe had splintered into chunks varying from 5ft to 100ft-square and these fragments were soon jostling against each other and against the ship's sides as the swell rippled among them. The following morning, Stenhouse ordered the setting of the foresail and the fore-top-mast staysail and immediately the *Aurora* began to forge ahead. After nine months of frigid entombment, at last she possessed life of her own, the stained and patched canvas of her sails billowing as they caught the breeze: a sight to lift the spirits of every man on board. Occasionally the ship's reinforced bows crashed into a substantial block of ice, causing the vessel to shiver, and sometimes it became necessary to warp her around a really large piece of floe but her progress remained relatively constant.

'Have hopes of getting to McMurdo Sound if luck holds,' a jubilant Stenhouse wrote on the evening of 13 February, and the following day his hopes seemed well on the way to being fulfilled:

The old ship has been doing great work today, nosing her way thro' heavy pack with no rudder. . . . At breakfast time topsails were set and by 10 a.m. we had worked thro' to a broad lead with few scattered floes in it; thro' this comparatively open water we bowled along for about 100yd when we were brought up suddenly against a floe. It is most interesting to watch the ship working along with an easy but steady motion; occasionally the yards are backed to throw her head off some corner of a floe which has stopped her way and occasionally an ice anchor is put into a floe to warp her but for the greater part of the time she is steering herself.

But, on the 15th, progress ground to a halt. Large pieces of the dismembered floe seemed to have converged on the *Aurora* overnight, hemming her in and making it impossible to manoeuvre. 'This is exasperating!' Stenhouse growled. ' . . . With plenty of coal and a good rudder I do not think that the ship could make progress thro' this ice; I cannot experiment and try the jury rudder with steam on the engines as once we light the fires our chances of relieving the Southern Party go. We must show results for every pound of coal consumed now.'

This same frustrating state of affairs continued for the next week, with the crew trimming sails and warping the ship with ice anchors in a desperate attempt to reach open water. Leads continued to open and close all around, but the rudderless ship's lack of manoeuvrability made it impossible to take advantage of the short-lived opportunities presented to her. 'This is hard luck!' a disgruntled Stenhouse complained on 17 February, 'I feel that we are taking things too easy and not trying hard enough and yet it is no good battling against this with steam power for we would use all our meagre supply in reaching the limit of the ice in sight and then be in a hole with neither ballast nor fuel.' The situation worsened during the night of the 21st, when the north-westerly swell increased and a cross sea began to beat the *Aurora* backwards and forwards between the great shards of ice, first smashing her into the floe ahead before allowing her to rebound on to the one lying just astern. 'The old ship vibrates throughout,' Larkman wrote, 'her timbers groaning and creaking with every shock . . . this pounding must be doing considerable harm. . . . Really things look more hopeless than ever.'[15] And, to add to the anxieties of the crew, they could clearly see that the powdered ice between the floes had begun to freeze, binding the great chunks together again and threatening to halt the ship's movement permanently.

The violence of the elements continued intermittently throughout the rest of February. Sometimes Stenhouse felt convinced that all the signs indicated open water in the near vicinity but at others it seemed that they were as deeply embedded as they had been in the depths of winter. He hoped desperately that the onset of a gale might scatter the pack before it once again coalesced but any increase in the wind inevitably meant that the ship began her destructive dance among the floes. On the last day of the month the force of the impacts became so strong that he felt sure that the hull must be punctured and, sure enough, at 9 a.m. Larkman reported that the *Aurora* had sprung a leak close to the propeller shaft, just beside the stern-post. Mauger managed to stop the worst of the leak by stuffing the seams with a mixture of cement, oakum and Stockholm tar but the repair could be only temporary and, besides, the propeller also seemed in imminent peril of catastrophic damage. 'This pack is a dangerous place for a ship now,' an exhausted Stenhouse scribbled in his diary that evening, 'it seems miraculous that the old Barky still floats.'

On 1 March, after spending most of the morning scanning the ice field from the freezing heights of the crow's nest, he reached a momentous decision: 'In view of the fact that progress, for many days now, has been impossible with light and chiefly unfavourable winds and also taking into consideration the imperatives of getting clear of this dangerous pack, I ordered steam on the main engines at noon. The pack is still very close but we must waste our coal before the ship is smashed up. With the lighting of fires, while yet in the pack, goes our last chance of relieving the people south.' Despite having been trapped for nine months, he had resisted every temptation to start the engines, pinning his hopes on the thought of being able to relieve Mackintosh and Shackleton before the close of the Antarctic sledging season. Now those hopes lay in tatters and he could only attempt to save his ship and then return in the spring. It was a bitter realisation.

At 5.15 the following afternoon, Larkman reported that working pressure had been achieved. Still unable to ship the jury rudder because of the risk of it being damaged by the floes, Stenhouse had ordered that a spare spar be rigged to act as a temporary rudder until they reached open water. Now, with this make-do contrivance suspended from her stern and with the light northerly breezes plucking the smoke from her funnel, the *Aurora* began to push her way through the ice. But 3 hours later a heavy floe fouled the propeller and, with the gathering darkness making it impossible to clear the screw, Stenhouse had no option but to order 'all stop'.

The pack only opened sufficiently to allow real momentum on 6 March and even then it continued to be a very stop-and-start kind of affair. Furthermore, as Stenhouse explained, even this relative freedom of movement brought its own challenges: 'Without a rudder (neither of the jury rudders can yet be used amongst these swirling, rolling floes), the ship requires a lot of attention. Her head must be pointed, between floes, by means of anchors (ice) and warps or by mooring to a floe and steaming around it. . . . We made a fairly good course towards two bergs, to our Nor'ard and about 5ft Northing when, darkness coming on, the men could no longer venture onto the floes (with safety) to fix the anchors.'

Progress remained agonisingly slow throughout the next few days. Sometimes leads opened, allowing the ship to move forward under steam; at others, the floes became close-packed, making it impossible to warp ship; and, of course, once she stopped, the swell and the jagged lumps of ice began to beat their interminable tattoo along her bruised sides. 'During evening,' Stenhouse recorded on a typical day, 'the NW swell increased and ship started a "cannon off the floe" game. When this is on nothing else matters much. The old ship has stood some tremendous buffeting up to the present time and one wonders exactly how much more she will take – and swim.'[16] To make matters worse, the bergs which had given early warning of the looseness of the pack had now worked their way back among the floes; if they continued on their present course, they would threaten a catastrophic collision with the ship.

Fortunately, by 9.30 a.m. on the 10th, the worst of the danger was past. The pack had begun to open into wider and wider lanes allowing the *Aurora* to take a zigzag course to the north-north-east and, more importantly, beyond the bergs large stretches of open water could be seen. The ship's steel-clad bows sliced through the loose brash and smaller floes and it seemed, at last, as though she might actually be able to cut and ram her way to freedom. Speeds remained variable over the next few days, with occasional heavy knocks and a constant risk of the ship settling back into the pack, but, at 2.00 p.m. on Tuesday 14 March, after ten months, or 312 days, in the pack, the *Aurora* broke through the last belt of brash ice and out into open water. 'Spliced the Main Brace,' Stenhouse wrote that evening, 'and blew three blasts of farewell (to the pack) with the whistle.'

Now all that remained to him was to nurse his battered, rudderless vessel across one of the stormiest stretches of sea on the face of the globe; repair, refit and coal her; and then make the return journey to McMurdo Sound. Perhaps, after all, the Main Brace had been spliced a little too early.

AURORA REDUX

On 14 March 1916, the *Aurora* broke free into a world of high, tumbling seas and contrary winds. In these conditions, chronically short of coal and with only a cobbled-together jury rudder with which to shape her course, sometimes the old ship drifted helplessly, quite unable to make steerage way. At times, indeed, as she span among the giant waves, it seemed that she had escaped the floe and reached the open sea only to be overwhelmed and sent to the bottom, her vital message regarding the plight of Shackleton's Ross Sea Party undelivered. No shipping hove into view through these desperate days but at last, on 23 March, the long-dormant wireless crackled into life and Hooke began a series of exchanges with Bluff Station, New Zealand, and then with Wellington and Hobart. After so many months of uncertainty, Stenhouse could finally report his ship's position and request help for the Ross Sea Party. He could also send a message to his anxious family, who had received no word from him since he sailed from Australia. 'Ship driven by blizzard from winter moorings May,' he telegraphed, in what must have been one of the most welcome and yet most worrying messages ever received by a father, 'set northwards twelve hundred miles locked in ice; nipped; heavy pressure July; lost rudder; ship severely strained . . . jury rudder, no anchors, short fuel; expect to arrive early April.'[1]

Despite establishing wireless communication with the harbourmaster at Port Chalmers, Stenhouse strongly resisted offers of assistance for his ship. He knew that, by accepting such an offer, no matter how well-intentioned, he might invite a salvage claim from any captain involved in the *Aurora*'s rescue: an embarrassment and liability that the ITAE could well do without. By 31 March, however, any hope of making New Zealand without help had all but disappeared. In the rising sea the jury rudder had become useless and the *Aurora* began griping to windward and pitching heavily; to make matters even worse, by 7.40 a.m. the wave-whipped cliffs of the Snares, one of New Zealand's sub-Antarctic island groups, could be seen to starboard. With his vessel no longer under control and being driven on to a rocky shore, Stenhouse had no choice: he must accept outside aid. Hooke tapped out another message and, at half-past midnight on 2 April, the searchlight of the tug *Dunedin* swept the *Aurora*'s battered hull. Then, at 3.30 a.m., a cheerful hail greeted the ears of the expeditionaries: the first voice they had heard from the outside world since departing from Macquarie Island over fifteen months earlier. As he supervised the securing of the *Dunedin*'s towline, Stenhouse must have believed that, at last, he could look forward to completing his mission. Having once reached New Zealand, he would be able to refit the *Aurora* and then take her south once more to relieve Mackintosh and his fellow-sledgers. In reality, he would soon find himself caught up in a storm as violent in its fashion as any that he had experienced in the frozen south.

The *Aurora* finally tied up against the Port Chalmers wharf at 10.45 on the morning of 3 April, having, at Stenhouse's request, been allowed to enter the harbour under her own steam and without a tow. Through a display of what Shackleton would later call 'fine seamanship and dogged determination,' Stenhouse had 'accomplished successfully one of the most difficult voyages on record in an ocean area notoriously stormy and treacherous'[2] and he had done so without the loss of a single man. Now, as he stepped ashore, the *Aurora*'s bewildered master found himself the hero of the moment, with literally thousands of spectators lining the wharves to gape at the ship and its crew, raised so miraculously from the dead. Of course reporters, too, descended en masse but Shackleton's contract with the *Daily Chronicle* in London meant that Stenhouse was allowed to speak to no one but the *Chronicle*'s representative in New Zealand, the editor of the *Otago Daily Times*. 'We had hoped that when we came back it would have been with all our party on board,' he told George Fenwick, in his first interview. 'I am sorry that Sir Ernest Shackleton is not with us. As to the party we left ashore, we know nothing about them at present, but they were all well when we left.'[3]

While the members of his crew accustomed themselves to the sights and sounds of civilisation and absorbed the fact that the war, far from being over, continued to drain the life-blood of Europe and the colonies, Stenhouse immediately busied himself with preparations for a return south. Nothing had been heard of the *Endurance* since she had departed from South Georgia at the beginning of December 1914 and to many observers it seemed that two relief expeditions were now called for: one to the Weddell Sea and one to the Ross Sea. Of course, everyone recognised that even a single expedition would be immensely costly, but no one seemed sure where the money would come from. While the *Aurora* was still at sea, Stenhouse had telegraphed Shackleton's agents in London to request the necessary funds to pay off his crew and to repair his ship, but the reply he received turned out to be anything but reassuring. Frederick White, the expedition's secretary, told him that the ITAE's finances were in complete disarray and that he was 'unable [to] send sum required as no funds available. . . . Cannot find five hundred pounds [with] which [to] credit you'[4] – hardly a surprising revelation perhaps to anyone who had been involved in preparing the *Aurora* for sea in 1914. With the expedition clearly unable to help itself, appeals were made to the Australian, New Zealand and British governments and, for the next two months, the telegraph cables on the ocean floor glowed as the different government offices sought to define and limit their contributions. Eventually, all three set up their own Relief Committees, though all were to work together, and they agreed that Britain should meet 50 per cent of the costs, with New Zealand and Australia splitting the remaining 50 per cent between them.

Just as these negotiations drew to a close at the beginning of June, the receipt of a telegram by the Admiralty in London changed the situation dramatically. In his interview with George Fenwick, Stenhouse had stated that 'Shackleton is the finest leader I know, and the most courageous of men, and I am fully confident he will win through.' The telegram received in London now showed how well-placed that confidence had been: it had been sent from Port Stanley in the Falklands and it announced that, against all the odds, Shackleton was indeed alive. Suddenly, the drift of the *Aurora* became old news and the reporters began a mad scramble to tell Shackleton's remarkable story. Weary of battles, bloodshed and ever-lengthening casualty lists, their readers could now regale themselves with stories of heroism and hardihood in an arena where men fought against blizzards and ice floes rather than machine guns and barbed wire.

The *Endurance* had left England for Buenos Aires on 8 August 1914 and, by the beginning of November, she had reached the whaling station at Grytviken, South Georgia. Here, her crew replenished the ship's coal bunkers in readiness for their assault on the south and Shackleton canvassed returning whalers regarding the prevailing ice conditions. The news had not been good. All the reports confirmed that the pack-ice stretched much further north than might have been expected at that point in the season and Shackleton could only pray that it would not prevent him reaching his destination. He knew only too well that the annals of polar exploration were littered with schemes warped and broken by unexpected movements in the ice. Erich von Drygalski's *Gauss* Expedition had become trapped in 1902. Between 1903 and 1904, the *Discovery* had been hemmed in at McMurdo Sound and, most recently, in 1911, Mawson's plans for the AAE had been seriously compromised by the length of time it had taken to find a viable route through the pack. Although Shackleton had always stated that an inability to start the transcontinental crossing during the Antarctic summer of 1914–15 would not be catastrophic, a failure even to reach his chosen jumping-off point could spell disaster.

The accuracy of the whalers' claims regarding the ice was quickly proven. Within a few days of departing from Grytviken on 5 December, the *Endurance* had reached latitude 57° South and already she resounded to the bumping and grating of ice against her hull. Confronted by such conditions, Shackleton had little option but to pursue a course to the north-east. Three weeks later, just as the *Aurora* prepared to leave Hobart, the *Endurance*'s progress had been reduced almost to a standstill, as strong winds packed the ice ever more tightly around her. On 30 December, she limped across the Antarctic Circle and then, on 8 January 1915, after another week of incessant scraping and grinding, she had broken into open water stretching for 100 miles due south. By the 15th, only another 100 miles had separated Shackleton from Vahsel Bay, the spot he had chosen to make his landing. Then, four days later, at 76° South, the expedition's progress finally ground to a halt as a combination of east-north-easterly winds and a sudden, catastrophic drop in temperature allowed the ice to coalesce into a single, impenetrable mass. The *Endurance* was beset.

At first, Shackleton hoped that the ice might break up and allow him to continue his journey that season. But, as day succeeded day with no discernible change in conditions, he and his crew had been forced to accept that they must wait until the Antarctic spring before continuing their journey. On 22 February, locked in the drifting floe, the *Endurance* reached her furthest point south: crossing the 77th parallel in longitude 35° West. During the succeeding months, as she drifted gradually to the north-west, she ceased to be a working ship and instead took on the role of a winter base. The expeditionaries made themselves as comfortable as possible and occupied their time with a variety of tasks. They replenished their larder by hunting penguins and seals; they undertook occasional sledging expeditions, as much for recreation as for the purposes of exploration; and they collected geological specimens and dredged the sea floor for Antarctic flora and fauna. The real work of the expedition would have to wait.

On 3 April, Shackleton observed the first signs of pressure in the ice. Tell-tale groans and creaks filled the air as the pressure began to break up the great slabs of ice, causing the enormous shards to tumble over each other, forming great heaps and ridges of debris. In the following months, the pressure increased intermittently and by the end of July the *Endurance*'s situation had become precarious. On 1 August, only eleven days after the *Aurora*'s rudder had been smashed in the Ross Sea, the same fate befell her fellow-expedition ship. Leads opened around the *Endurance* and then, as the ship turned in the open water, the floes closed in again, nipping her with all the power of millions of tons of compressed ice and sheering off the blade of her rudder. By 30 September, the ship was being subjected to enormous pressure, her decks shuddered and squealed, her beams began to arch and

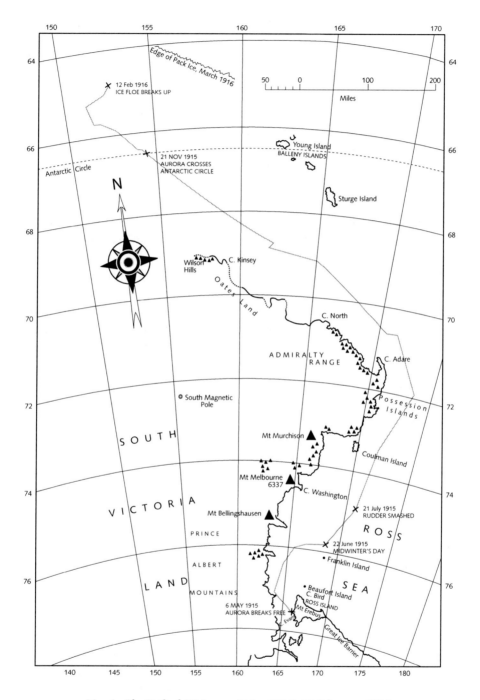

Map 1. The Drift of SY *Aurora*, 6 May 1915–12 February 1916.

her stanchions buckled. Shackleton knew that the *Endurance* could not last much longer and on 23 October she quivered as her starboard quarter was forced against the edge of the floe, fatally twisting her stern-post and starting the heads and ends of her timbers so that water cascaded into the stricken vessel. On the 26th, he gave the order to abandon ship.

Depressing though it might be to see her smashed and broken, a tangle of shattered planks, fallen masts and twisted rigging, the destruction of the *Endurance* came as a surprise to no one and Shackleton had had ample time to transfer all vital equipment and supplies to the floe. Now he must devise and execute a plan to save his men. In the 281 days of her imprisonment, the ship had drifted 570 miles to the north-west and Shackleton calculated that the best chance of salvation lay on Paulet Island, where he could expect to find a hut built by the Swedish explorer, Otto Nordenskjöld, and stores cached by an Argentinean relief vessel. With this goal in mind, he organised his men and dogs into parties intended to haul the ship's boats in the direction of the island. They began their 346-mile trek on 20 December but, with the ice quickly degenerating into soft sticky sludge, too unstable for hauling and yet too tightly packed to launch the boats, they were soon forced to abandon their plan. Instead Shackleton decided to make camp and wait for conditions to improve or for the floe to break up so that they could take to the boats.

Their wait at the aptly named Patience Camp proved much longer than expected. It began on 27 December and lasted until 9 April: the most miserable three months of the entire expedition. The treacherous condition of the ice made movement all but impossible and food stocks dwindled so that the expedition teetered on the brink of starvation. Recognising that the chances of any further sledging were now reduced to zero and with meat in such short supply, Shackleton gave the order for the expedition's dogs to be shot. Now the party must look to the three ship's boats for its salvation. By 17 March 1916, the expeditionaries had drifted to within 60 miles of Paulet Island, but the floe upon which they stood continued to disintegrate. They might still head for the island or, alternatively, they might cling to the crumbling floe in the hope that it would carry them to Deception Island. Alternatively, they could sail for Elephant Island in the South Shetlands, which they sighted on 7 April.

Shackleton decided on the latter course and, on 9 April, as the floe cracked and split beneath his feet, he ordered the launching of the boats. After hours of hard rowing in the brash, which fouled the oars and wearied the weak, cold and hungry men still further, they made a temporary camp on the ice. But they rested only fitfully; the floe continued to crumble throughout the night and one man nearly plunged to an icy grave when a large crack opened beneath him as he slept. After another exhausting day of rowing, they spent the night of the 10th on the ice. From then on they remained in the boats, at the edge of the pack to begin with and then in the open sea, anxiously fending off floating blocks, listening to the blowing of nearby whales, and being tortured by a combination of freezing spray, hunger, thirst and seasickness.

On the morning of 15 April, the twenty-eight ice and salt encrusted scarecrows, some now incapable of speech and others barely able to walk, landed on the barren shores of Elephant Island: it was the first time they had stood on dry land since the beginning of December 1914. Then, while his men feasted on the meat of seals they slaughtered on the beach, Shackleton considered his next move. He knew that the island could offer only a temporary home to his men. It lay 1,000 miles from the point at which the *Endurance* had been beset and well outside the regular shipping lanes: he and his companions might starve to death or die of exposure before anyone so much as thought of looking for them here. Another boat journey was called for.

The voyage Shackleton now determined to make would be perhaps the most perilous undertaking of the expedition so far: 800 miles across some of the stormiest waters on the face of the globe to the whaling station at South Georgia. He would take only one boat, the *James Caird*, which would be improved and reinforced, using materials salvaged from the other boats, and five men, all of them professional sailors, would accompany him: Worsley, Crean, McNeish, Vincent and McCarty. On 24 April, this select band waved farewell to their twenty-two companions and hoisted sail. If all went well, they hoped to return in a matter of weeks to rescue their friends. If they did not reappear, then Shackleton and his fellows might be assumed to have been lost, and another boat would have to be launched in the spring.

For fourteen days the *James Caird* beat her way to the east-north-east, sometimes cutting her way through the crests of giant, granite grey waves, at others wallowing in bottomless troughs, at every moment in danger of being overwhelmed. Shackleton had divided his crew into two watches of three: one man steering, another tending the sail and a third baling or attempting to chip ice from the hull and rigging to prevent the boat becoming top-heavy. Meanwhile, the watch 'below' would try to rest in their sodden, freezing reindeer sleeping bags. On the eleventh day of this gruelling odyssey, a mountainous wave nearly capsized the tiny vessel, lifting her high into the air and then throwing her down into a maelstrom of swirling green water and foam, but somehow she survived, with the crew baling for their lives. By a miracle, at 12.30 p.m. on 8 May, they sighted the rocky coast of South Georgia. But with a storm lashing the ocean into spume and spray, they was no chance of making a landing and for another two days the starving, parched and exhausted men lay hove to waiting for a lull in the weather.

Eventually, they managed to make their landing during a brief calm on the morning of the 10th and they spent a few days recouping their strength, slaking their thirst at a freshwater stream and eating chicks snatched from a nearby albatross colony. Shackleton, meanwhile, planned the last stage of his epic journey: the crossing of South Georgia's Allardyce Mountain Range to reach the whaling station at Stromness. Two of the party, McNeish and Vincent, were too ill to attempt the hitherto unclimbed range, much of which exceeds 6,500ft in height, so they were left to shelter beneath the upturned *James Caird* in the care of McCarty, while Shackleton, Crean and Worsley prepared for the ascent. They started at 1 a.m. on 19 May and had climbed to 3,000ft by dawn. With no map to guide them, they spent many precious hours scaling slope after slope, only to find their way blocked by sheer precipices, so that they had to retrace their steps and try again in a different direction. Then, with darkness descending and with no tent or sleeping bags to protect them from the plummeting temperatures of a sub-Antarctic night, the three men made a desperate resolution: to toboggan down the valley side into the thickening mist – whether to safety or certain destruction they had no way of knowing. They linked themselves together, and sitting upon coils of their climbing rope, launched themselves into the unknown. Two or three minutes later, they drove into a thick drift of snow, having hurtled up to 2 miles down the mountainside – the only damage they sustained being more tears to their already threadbare clothing.

Jubilant but exhausted, they continued to walk throughout the night of the 19th, crossing crevasses, floundering down snow slopes, cutting steps into blue ice sheets and lowering themselves through the icy torrent of a mountain waterfall. But, at last, during the morning of 20 May, the three filthy, bearded ragamuffins reached their destination. They presented themselves to the disbelieving eyes of the station manager at Stromness and, after a bath, a shave and a meal, Worsley left on board a whaler to recover the rest of the party from the other side of the island. Then, on 23 May, Shackleton started on his first attempt to reach his men at Elephant Island. The attempt was a desperate one and no one felt surprised when the steel-built *Southern Sky* was forced back by the ice. Disappointed but undeterred, Shackleton then made for the nearest wireless station, on the Falklands. From here he sent the telegram that announced to an astonished world both his own survival and his desperate need for help to pluck his men from their barren, wind-swept rock in the South Atlantic.

The extraordinary story of his adventures brought Shackleton enormous public support and acclaim but, as he sought to arrange the rescue, he became increasingly concerned that the government-sponsored Relief Committees did not share the public's enthusiasm. Instead, as time passed, he came to fear that they intended, at best, to force him into a secondary role and, at worst, to deny him any involvement at all in the denouement of the *Endurance* Expedition. His suspicions were well-founded. His maverick approach to fund-raising and organisation and the poor management of the opening phase of the Ross Sea expedition had won him few friends in official circles. Now, news of the loss of the *Endurance*, the near loss of the *Aurora* and the plight of both arms of the expedition seemed to vindicate the scepticism of many officials. Ignoring such emotive factors as individual heroism, they argued that, when considered objectively, the ITAE had been an unmitigated disaster. This being the case, was it right that the rescue of the survivors, a rescue moreover funded from the public purse, should be entrusted to the man responsible for the fiasco?

Dauntless as ever, Shackleton carried on regardless and, while the British government formulated plans to send Scott's old ship, the *Discovery*, south, he continued with his own schemes for the rescue of the *Endurance* survivors. He made two more attempts to reach them, but on each occasion the pack-ice drove him back; then, at the end of August, he made his fourth and final attempt, on board the Chilean steamer, *Yelcho*. On 30 August, the *Yelcho* broke through the pack and, with hope and fear vying for dominance in his heart, Shackleton approached Elephant Island in one of the ship's launches. As he anxiously scanned the beach for signs of life, one by one, twenty-two blackened scarecrows appeared from inside the upturned boats beneath which they had been sheltering for four months. 'Thank God!' he cried as the keel of his boat struck the shingle: in a miracle that would come to epitomise man's determination to conquer seemingly insurmountable odds, he had managed to save all the men of the *Endurance*. Unfortunately, this success would do nothing to stifle the determination of Shackleton's enemies to sideline him and, balked in their efforts to exclude him from the climax of the Weddell Sea element of his expedition, they now turned their attention to the Ross Sea. And Stenhouse, too, would discover that his loyalty to his leader would leave him tarred with the same brush.

In the period preceding Shackleton's reappearance, in his dealings with the various governments, Stenhouse had received much valuable help from Leonard Tripp, an old school friend of Shackleton's. As well as being sympathetic to the ITAE, Tripp brought a legal training and considerable diplomatic skills to his dealings with all parties and it was at least partly due to his ministrations that the three governments eventually accepted responsibility for the fate of the Ross Sea Party. Ever since that acceptance, money had been rolling in and, at last, work on refitting the *Aurora* could begin. The ship surveyors at Port Chalmers had started work on 29 June and it quickly became apparent that it was little short of a miracle that the veteran whaler had survived at all. Her months in the ice had left her very badly strained; bow and stern had both sagged by nearly 8in; many of her planks had started; her iron knees needed replacing; and large portions of masts and rigging were no longer serviceable. A sum in the region of £6,000 would be required to complete the necessary work and it was abundantly clear that only the exacting standards of the Dundee shipwrights had prevented the *Aurora* from sharing the fate of the less fortunate *Endurance*.

Although work progressed swiftly, to his intense irritation Stenhouse found that his role in supervising the refit was to be a distinctly subservient one, with real authority lying with an appointee of the New Zealand Relief Committee, Joseph Kinsey. Kinsey had considerable experience in such matters, having acted as an agent for Scott, Mawson and Shackleton, but he also stood high in the ranks of those who doubted Shackleton's competence as an organiser. 'From my first meeting with Mr Kinsey,' Stenhouse later told his leader, 'I knew that he was extremely bitter against you and during one conversation he made disparaging remarks about you – naturally I could not listen to these and from that time forward I noticed a marked difference in his attitude towards me.'[5] Worse was to come.

On 4 October, while visiting the Otago Club in Dunedin, Stenhouse picked up the *Otago Daily Times*; in its pages he read that 'It has been decided that Captain Davis, who accompanied Captain Scott on his last voyage, shall command the relief expedition. . . . Captain Davis is expected to reach New Zealand next week.' The Captain Davis mentioned in the article was no less a person than John King Davis, the very man to whom Shackleton had first offered the command of the *Aurora* in 1914. Upon the reappearance of the ship in March and the resulting flurry of speculation regarding the fate of both arms of the expedition, Davis had been asked to take command of the *Discovery* and to undertake a relief expedition to the Weddell Sea. Initially reluctant, he had eventually accepted the appointment on the condition that his command should be absolute and undivided. Although news of Shackleton's success made it appear that Davis's services would no longer be required, at the beginning of September he was surprised to be asked to take command of his old ship, the *Aurora*, and to go in search of Mackintosh and the other men stranded on the shores of the Ross Sea. After due consideration, he agreed.

Stenhouse was furious and he entertained no doubt that the Committee's decision to replace him resulted from his refusal to listen to Kinsey's insinuations. 'There have been many influences at work of which I know nothing,' he wrote to Shackleton, 'but I am convinced that as I was under your orders and intended to abide by them Mr Kinsey determined that someone appointed through him should take command who would be entirely independent of you. Mr Kinsey told me that the Imperial Trans-Antarctic Expedition had finished as far as the Relief Committee were concerned and that you had nothing whatever to do with the matter. . . .

It seems extraordinary that people who have been entrusted with the affairs of this relief expedition should behave in such an underhand and un-British manner. . . . Had I been prepared to humiliate myself and renounce my contract with you, there would, in my opinion, have been no change of the command of the *Aurora*.'[6]

Others shared Stenhouse's outrage. Leonard Tripp admitted that 'it made my blood boil to think that Stenhouse had been so badly treated in New Zealand,'[7] while all of the *Aurora*'s officers, with the exception of Ninnis, vocally expressed their complete confidence in and support for the man who had brought them safely home. Whatever his personal feelings, however, Stenhouse's primary concern remained the relief of his friends and colleagues in the Antarctic. He told Tripp that 'Naturally, having been treated in a most un-British way, I feel that justice has not been done, but I want to do all in my power to assist in the rescue of my comrades in the South.'[8]

In a placatory gesture, Davis offered him the post of chief officer and, had he been able to act independently, Stenhouse would almost certainly have accepted but, as Shackleton's representative in New Zealand, he felt his hands were tied. Without Shackleton's direct sanction, he could not acknowledge any other body's power over his ship or its personnel. 'I note that you state that with the approval of the Secretary of State and the Governments of the Commonwealth and New Zealand you have assumed command of the Relief Expedition,' he told Davis, 'but I have no official intimation of this, and therefore am in duty bound to retain command of the *Aurora* until notified of the wishes of the owner of the ship. . . . I must therefore decline to acknowledge the right of anyone save my owner to give me directions. My plain duty is to remain in command of the ship until officially notified of my owner's desire to have me superseded.'[9] Davis's reply was curt: 'I gather that you do not recognise the right of the representatives of the Governments who are paying you to give you directions. I am regretfully obliged to recommend to the Committee that your services be dispensed with immediately.'[10]

Throughout the preceding weeks, Shackleton had impressed on Stenhouse, by a series of telegrams and letters, the importance of not giving an inch and, on the explorer's arrival on the scene on 2 December, everything seemed set for a show-down. Instead, after some initial bluster, Shackleton agreed to subordinate his own feelings to the welfare of the men in the Antarctic. He told the Committee that he would accept its appointment of Davis so long as he, Worsley and Stenhouse were allowed to accompany the expedition. Neither Davis nor the Committee could, with any semblance of good grace, refuse to allow Shackleton a part in the rescue of his own men. So far as Stenhouse and Worsley were concerned, however, Davis remained adamant: he would not sail with Shackleton's lieutenants. According to

Tripp, 'Captain Davis had said that under no circumstances would he have Stenhouse on board, his reason being that Stenhouse would always be a disappointed man.'[11] No attempt at reasoning would sway Davis and, though Shackleton expressed his wish to remain true to a man who had always stayed loyal to him, an approach was eventually made to Stenhouse and Worsley. In the interests of the men in the Antarctic and in order to avoid further friction, would they voluntarily step aside? If they agreed, the New Zealand government would pay their wages and those of their fellow officers, thereby relieving a burden on Shackleton, and they would be given a first-class passage home to England. In reply to this suggestion, Stenhouse stated that 'if Shackleton told him to serve under Davis he would be perfectly loyal to Davis, and if necessary would black the boots on the ship.'[12] Despite this moment of melodrama, when the request was repeated, both Stenhouse and Worsley agreed that they would abandon their intention of accompanying Shackleton. It was a bitter pill to swallow.

The *Aurora* sailed, with Shackleton as a supernumerary, on 20 December 1916, and Stenhouse and Worsley waved her off. Over nine months had passed since she had broken out from the pack-ice and nineteen since she had been driven from her moorings at Cape Evans. Now the two sailors could only wait and, while they speculated about the fate of Mackintosh and his companions, get to know one another better. The New Zealander was Stenhouse's senior by fifteen years, but both men had been apprentices in sail and both loved sailing-ships more than anything else in the world; they also loved adventure, but there the obvious similarities ended. For all his passion and enthusiasm, Stenhouse could sometimes appear dour and remote to the men under his command, particularly when he suffered one of his periodic bouts of depression; Worsley, on the other hand, was jovial, ebullient and daring even to the point of recklessness. Indeed, while Shackleton quickly learned to place absolute confidence in his seamanship, he doubted Worsley's suitability for command and had even opined that 'Captain Worsley . . . is not the type of man to hold men well together; he is a bit excitable and is of a rather curious tactless nature.'[13] In spite of their dissimilarity, however, or perhaps because of it, the friendship between Stenhouse and Worsley developed quickly and it would endure for a quarter of a century. Now, while they waited for news, the two explorers travelled to Christchurch, where Worsley's family lived, and then on to Otira Gorge in New Zealand's Southern Alps for a three-day camping excursion. They were back in Wellington for the *Aurora*'s return on 9 February, and no one was more eager than Stenhouse to welcome the ten castaways back to civilisation. When the *Aurora* berthed, however, he discovered that only seven of the men he had involuntarily left in Antarctica had lived to tell their tale. Aeneas Mackintosh, the Revd Spencer-Smith and Victor Hayward were all dead.

After separating from Spencer-Smith, Jack and Gaze on 11 February 1915, Mackintosh, Joyce and Wild had continued on their depot-laying expedition covering between 5 and 12 miles a day, building cairns at regular intervals, and reaching latitude 80° South on the 20th. There, they built an 8ft cairn over a substantial cache of supplies intended for the transcontinental party before commencing their long trek back towards Hut Point on 24 February. The return journey had rapidly degenerated into a living hell. Two dogs had died of exposure even before they began, leaving them with only seven to help them on their way; they had only enough rations for ten days, leaving men and animals desperately hungry; and, to add to their woes, the weather closed in, often forcing them to waste precious days confined to their tent, sleeping in bags that were either frozen solid or, when the temperature rose, reduced to a sodden mass of stinking and moulting reindeer skin.

By the 26th, the party had 160 miles left to travel with only one week's rations, while the dogs, in the last stages of starvation, had been reduced to eating their harnesses, leather, rope, rivets and all. By the night of 3 March, all but one of the dogs were dead and, with the temperature plummeting to −28°F, the outlook for the party was grim indeed. Fortunately, progress became more rapid when the onset of a southerly wind allowed them to hoist a sail made from the tent's floor-cloth, though trimming the sail led to a number of frostbites. The one meal a day they allowed themselves and their frequent inability to sleep, reduced their vitality still further and made them even more prone to frostbite, so that the bodies of all three men soon became a mass of agonising sores. But they struggled on, sometimes managing little more than 2 miles, despite a day's hauling, at others covering up to 9 miles and eventually, on 25 March, nearly two months after their departure, they reached Hut Point. It had been an incredibly gruelling marathon and one that had reduced the men to shambling, blackened skeletons, covered in suppurating ulcers – and yet this proved to be only the beginning of their trials.

Cope, Hayward and Jack were already resident at the hut, having reached it shortly after Stenhouse had picked up the other sledgers. Despite his anxiety to make contact with Stenhouse, the open water of McMurdo Sound prevented Mackintosh from reaching the *Aurora*. As a result, he and his companions spent more than two months living a strange troglodyte existence, dependent for heat upon a blubber stove which gradually turned their skin, hair and clothing black and greasy. It wasn't until 2 June that they managed to cross the Sound to join Spencer-Smith, Stevens, Gaze and Richards and by that time the *Aurora* and her crew had been missing for nearly a month, their fate remaining a complete mystery. The situation of the men at the hut was serious but not immediately threatening. Coal, meat and clothing were all in short supply, partly because only small quantities had been landed from the ship, which everyone had expected to winter at Cape Evans, and partly because some of the stores that had been landed had been swept out to sea with the ship. The limited supplies that had been landed could, however, be supplemented by the stores left by Scott's men and by hunting seals and penguins.

Over the next three months, the men prepared for the next sledging season, which began on 1 September. Mackintosh's plan was that three sledging parties would be formed, each containing three men; the tenth man would remain at Cape Evans to undertake meteorological observations. In total, the sledging parties would carry 4,000lb of supplies for their own consumption and for the depots they intended to lay for the transcontinental party. They would lay the first depot at Minna Bluff, 70 miles from Hut Point, and then a further depot at each degree of latitude. The last depot to be laid would be located at the foot of the Beardmore Glacier. Moreover, since only four serviceable dogs remained, the men would do the vast majority of the hauling themselves. The task before them was immensely daunting but Mackintosh had no choice. Completely unaware that the *Endurance* had never even reached Vahsel Bay, he believed that Shackleton and his fellows remained entirely reliant upon the depots to be laid by the Ross Sea Party; failure to lay the depots would be tantamount to manslaughter.

After a series of journeys to ferry the supplies to Hut Point, the real depot-laying expedition began on 9 October, with the three sledging parties being made up of Mackintosh, Spencer-Smith and Wild; Joyce, Cope and Richards; and, finally, Jack, Hayward and Stevens. Gaze remained at Cape Evans nursing a frost-bitten heel. Over the next two months, during a series of journeys between Hut Point and the depot at Minna Bluff, the three teams stockpiled nearly 3,000lb of provisions. Often the going proved extraordinarily tough, with the men's rate of progress sometimes being reduced to a handful of miles each day, and suffering from painful attacks of snow-blindness and frostbite but, by the end of December, the Bluff depot had been laid. Now they could begin the process of ferrying stores to the string of depots they intended to lay between the Bluff and the Beardmore Glacier.

Despite a faulty primus stove forcing Cope, Jack and Gaze (who had now replaced Stevens) to return to Cape Evans, the remaining six men continued to push south throughout January 1916 and, by the 18th, they had laid depots at 80°, 81°, and 82° South. Only one more depot, to be laid at 83°, at the foot of the Beardmore Glacier, remained, and they decided that they would proceed together. But tragedy was about to strike. In the last stages of the expedition, Spencer-Smith had begun to suffer from painful and swollen legs and, by noon on 22 January, he felt unable to proceed any further. Keen to complete the depot-laying, Mackintosh agreed to the invalid's suggestion that the rest of the party should continue, leaving him with a tent and sufficient provisions to last until their return which would be about a week later. After crossing a field of heavily pressured ice, caused by the collision of the Beardmore Glacier with the Barrier ice, they laid the final depot on the 26th and, relieved and jubilant to have completed the work of the expedition, they started back in the middle of the afternoon of the 27th. Two days later, they found the patient churchman still lying prone within his sleeping bag, quite unable to move. Even more worryingly, Mackintosh, too, was in the last stages of exhaustion.

Against the odds, over the next fortnight the party made rapid progress, often covering over 15 miles in a day, and on 12 February, they were able to replenish their stores from one of the depots they had laid earlier in the season. But, from that point, the weather and the quality of the surfaces over which they travelled rapidly deteriorated and their pace slowed. On the 18th, a severe blizzard set in, confining the entire party to their tents for five miserable days. Rations for both men and dogs became severely depleted and, even worse, oil for the stove also ran perilously low. On 23 February, a break in the weather allowed the party to continue, but by mid-afternoon Mackintosh had to admit that he could proceed no further. Fully aware that any further delay would probably cost the lives of the entire party, Joyce, Hayward and Richards determined that they would continue with the four dogs in a desperate attempt to reach Minna Bluff, 12 miles away; Wild would remain behind to look after the two invalids.

After floundering through thick drift snow and howling blizzards, with their limbs frost-bitten and swollen, the party under Joyce finally reached the Bluff depot at 3.25 a.m. on 26 February. It had been a close-run thing, and Joyce believed that another day's delay would have killed the entire party; now they must recoup their strength and the dogs', as quickly as possible, and return to collect the three men still lying on the barrier. Weakness and poor weather delayed their start until midday on the 27th and the men's chronic debility reduced their progress to a crawl but, at last, at 12.45 p.m. on the 29th, they reached their companions. They found the indomitable Wild remarkably hale and hearty – fitter, indeed, than the ailing Hayward – but Mackintosh could barely stand and Spencer-Smith lay in a deep hole melted by his body heat. The entire party, with Mackintosh and Spencer-Smith lying on top of the sledges, staggered into the Minna Bluff depot at 5.45 p.m. on 1 March. With a fortnight's rations taken from the depot, the party continued the following day.

Blizzards, the bitter cold and freezing drift snow made the next few days an appalling ordeal, with the men made weaker every day by the onset of scurvy. By 4 March, Hayward, too, had been reduced to lying on one of the sledges and all the work of hauling fell on Wild, Joyce, Richards and the four dogs. And yet, with the wind behind them, the party still managed between 8 and 11 miles on those days when the weather permitted them to travel. On the 7th, hoping to increase the party's speed, Mackintosh volunteered to stay behind with three weeks' provisions while the rest pushed on, which they did the following day. But the decision made no difference to Spencer-Smith, whom his companions had now dragged 300 miles across the barrier. During the bitterly cold night of 9 March the man whom Stenhouse had described as 'the finest parson I have ever met' died in his bag as his friends slept around him. They buried him a mere 30 miles from Hut Point, which the rest of the party reached on 3 p.m. on 11 March. By the evening of the 18th, Mackintosh, too, had been picked up, severely lame and weakened but still alive. The entire party had been on the ice for over five months; it had covered 1,561 miles; and it had laid all of the planned depots for the transcontinental party.

Tragically, after enduring so much, the lives of Mackintosh and Hayward were thrown away. After a lengthy period of recuperation, Mackintosh's anxiety to ascertain the fates of the rest of his party and of the *Aurora* overcame his caution. On 8 May, he determined, in the face of opposition from Joyce and others, to attempt to cross from Hut Point to Cape Evans on the still young sea-ice stretching across the Sound; the only man to accompany him was Hayward. The two men set out at 1 p.m. and had last been seen about a mile from Hut Point. At 3 p.m. a blizzard had descended and within a short time it had been raging with considerable violence. The young ice upon which the two men travelled had broken away and both had been carried out to sea. Despite numerous searches, their bodies would never be recovered.

Joyce, Richards and Wild did not manage to cross the bay until 15 July, where they found Stevens, Cope, Gaze and Jack safe, but completely unaware of the fate of Mackintosh and Hayward. For six more months, the seven survivors of the Ross Sea Party waited in the Cape Evans hut for a rescue which they were unsure would ever come. They assumed that the *Aurora* had been lost with all hands in May of the previous year, and so the outside world must be in ignorance of the expedition's plight. By the time the *Aurora* finally reached them on 10 January 1917, the rigours which they had endured for so many long months had reduced some of the castaways to unrecognisable, shambling and inarticulate wretches. And only then did they learn the fate of the *Endurance* and discover that all the privations of their two years in the Antarctic had been for nothing since the transcontinental party had never even set foot on the Antarctic continent. The depots which they had struggled so hard to lay would be left to disappear into the drift snow.

THE MYSTERY SHIPS

With Shackleton and all but three of his men safe, Stenhouse could at last think of returning to Europe to join the war effort. When the *Aurora* had left Hobart on 24 December 1914, few on board had still believed that the war with Germany would be a short one. Long before they sailed, the battles of Mons, the Marne and Ypres had all been fought, effectively dispelling any hopes of a swift and easy victory for either side. It's unlikely, however, that any expected the conflict still to be in full and bloody spate by the time they returned to civilisation. Initially, for most of the expeditionaries, ignorance regarding the conduct of the war and, more immediately, the fates of friends and family had been their greatest anxiety, and Stenhouse had been no exception. As time passed, however, and the thrill of exploration had given way to frustration and boredom, concern for his loved ones in Europe had been replaced by a more selfish desire: that the struggle between the great powers should be as protracted as possible. 'I shall be glad to get out of this mess,' he had written longingly on 19 November 1915, 'and if all turns out well get to the front after this ghastly inactivity.' Compared with the feelings of impotence that he endured during the *Aurora*'s drift, the intense, remorseless action of war seemed a panacea.

After his arrival in New Zealand in April, Stenhouse had been desperate to play his part in relieving the men of the Ross Sea Party, but the months of bitter wrangling had only exacerbated his desire to get to the front. Now he could at last join the fight and, in fighting, perhaps quell the violence of the emotions currently vying for dominance in his heart: relief for the men saved, sadness for those who had been lost, and disgust at the treatment he had received at the hands of the Relief Committees. With this goal in mind, on 20 February he and Worsley, in company with John Cope, boarded the RMS *Makura* bound for England. Like Stenhouse, Worsley already held a commission in the Royal Naval Reserve and, believing themselves ready for immediate action, both men reported to the Admiralty shortly after disembarking at Liverpool on 9 April. To their intense disappointment, however, the Royal Navy appeared to think that they required additional training before setting them loose on the enemy and, instead of being appointed to ships, they were ordered to HMS *Pembroke*, a naval shore station at Chatham, to undergo training in anti-submarine warfare.

Without question, in sea warfare, the submarine constituted the greatest and most destructive innovation of the modern age. Although Germany had lagged behind Britain in commissioning its first submarine, the *U-1* not being launched until 1905, four years after the Royal Navy's *Holland 1*, it was German naval tacticians who first realised the true value of this new weapon. That submarines could successfully engage large and well-armed surface warships had been amply demonstrated on 22 September 1914, when *U-9* attacked and sank three British light cruisers, *Aboukir*, *Hogue* and *Cressy*, in the English Channel. But such victories only tended to reinforce the view of submarines as auxiliaries to surface fleets, useful as scouts and capable of sinking enemy warships certainly, but not offering any major strategic or tactical advantages. This perception changed fundamentally at the beginning of 1915 when German naval planners suggested that, if stationed astride Britain's trade routes, a fleet of 200 U-boats could so interrupt her supply of foodstuffs and raw materials that Britain would be forced to sue for peace. A sustained U-boat campaign, they claimed, could become the 'magic bullet' so desperately needed to end the bloody stalemate on the Western Front.

In the early days of February 1915, this new strategy came into play, with Germany committing its still small U-boat fleet to a campaign which targeted both Allied and neutral ships, particularly in the Western Approaches. Unfortunately for Germany, however, the tactical benefits of sinking nearly 1 million tons of Allied shipping in a mere seven months were more than balanced by the strategic consequences. In particular, U-boat attacks on passenger ships carrying American as well as British citizens constituted a major propaganda disaster. Most notorious of all, on 7 May 1915, without warning, *U-20* torpedoed the Cunard liner *Lusitania* off the coast of Ireland, killing 1,198 passengers and crew, including 124 Americans.[1] Further sinkings, including that of the passenger ship *Arabic* on 19 August, raised American outrage to such a pitch that President Wilson's government issued a furious protest to Berlin, leaving Germany in no doubt that a continuation of the campaign would result in the USA declaring war. Fully aware that such an eventuality would spell almost certain defeat for its own forces, the Kaiser's government immediately backed down, bringing unrestricted U-boat warfare to a close at the beginning of September.

Seven months later, with the slaughter in the trenches showing no signs of abating, the Germans tried again. And this time the submarine commanders were told that, as a matter of policy, they might attack shipping without surfacing, thereby substantially increasing the likely loss of life among those on board the target vessel. To reduce the risk of civilian casualties, the German High Command issued instructions that passenger liners should not be attacked but, in reality, it took little more than a week for the rule to be broken and, on 24 March 1916, the steamship *Sussex* plunged to the ocean floor carrying the bodies of yet more Americans. President Wilson threatened to sever diplomatic relations and once again Germany promised to restrict its submarine activity. Nevertheless, losses to Allied shipping increased throughout the remainder of 1916, rising from 37,000 tons in June to 180,000 in December.

With an American entry into the war seeming ever more likely, by the beginning of 1917 the German government had decided that the chance of defeating Britain through the resumption of unrestricted submarine warfare more than outweighed the risk of accelerating an American declaration. The assumption behind this decision was that, to all intents and purposes, the war would be over before the Americans could mobilise and ship their troops to Europe. Just as Stenhouse and Worsley boarded the *Makura*, therefore, the Battle of the Atlantic entered its most destructive phase, with a quarter of all ships leaving Britain's shores being sunk before they could complete their return journey. The German navy had not been able to bring into play the 200 submarines that it calculated as being necessary to achieve its overall goal but, despite this shortfall, it had brought Britain's civilian population close to starvation. The Royal Navy laboured under no illusions: something must be done, and done quickly, if Britain was to avoid defeat.

The most important element in Britain's response to the looming catastrophe proved to be the introduction of the convoy system. Despite the success of convoys during the Napoleonic Wars, the senior officers at the Admiralty strongly resisted this initiative, fearing that it would strip the Grand Fleet of its cruisers; but Lloyd George overruled them and, from 10 May 1917, all ships crossing the Atlantic travelled in convoy with Royal Navy protection. Convoys, of course, were essentially defensive in nature; but the Navy had also developed other stratagems with which to take the war to the enemy. With his training at HMS *Pembroke* completed towards the end of April, Stenhouse learned to his delight that he would now be given the chance to play a part in these offensive operations: on the bridge of the already legendary Q-ship, HMS *Penshurst*.

In the days when depth charges and the hydrophone were still in their infancy, the Q-ship, or 'mystery ship' constituted one of the Admiralty's only weapons against the submarine scourge. In essence, the Q-ship was a man-of-war disguised as an innocent or, better still, as a particularly vulnerable merchantman: just the kind of prey that the German U-boat commanders continued to snap up in such huge numbers. Acting as decoys, the Q-ships' highly dangerous role would be to loiter in the U-boat hunting grounds, often impersonating a ship in distress, and literally inviting attack. Reluctant to squander their torpedoes on sinking this kind of small tramp steamer, most submarine commanders chose to surface in order to use the long-range, 4.1in guns mounted on their outer casings. In imminent peril of being sunk by this gunfire, the Q-ship captain would perhaps make some show of resistance, usually consisting of a feigned attempt to escape. Next, seemingly intimidated by the German firepower, a 'panic party' would lower the boats and row away from their vessel, leaving enough men hidden on board to work the ship and lay the guns. Once the submarine ceased firing and approached close enough to properly examine its prize, the Q-ship crew would drop their guns' disguises, which often consisted of false deck-house or lifeboats, and return fire. With luck, the German vessel would be taken completely by surprise and sunk before it could do too much damage to the Q-ship; if the Q-ship sank, however, the Admiralty considered such a loss a price worth paying for the destruction of an enemy submarine. All in all, the plan was beautifully simple – and immensely dangerous for the men on the decoy.

The Royal Navy commissioned its first Q-ship, the SS *Vittoria*, as early as 29 November 1914 but neither she nor her immediate successor, the SS *Antwerp*, ever succeeded in sinking an enemy submarine; indeed, the crew of the *Vittoria* never so much as saw a raised periscope. But, with an anti-submarine arsenal practically devoid of weapons, the Admiralty could not yet afford to write off the experiment as a failure. Instead, knowing the suspicious nature of most U-boat captains, they sought to make the Q-ships more convincing. Success, they determined, depended on three critical factors. First, the Q-ship must be perfectly suited to her patrol zone; at the most basic level, a ship disguised as a collier should not mingle with a fishing fleet. Second, her appearance and behaviour must in no way be compromised by her armament or by the fact that her crew consisted of Royal Navy sailors. Lastly, and perhaps most crucially of all, her captain must be hand-picked for the role.

E. Keble Chatterton, a lieutenant-commander of the RNVR and the first historian of the Q-ships, believed that captaining these vessels demanded very specialist skills and character traits:

It was an exploit calling for supreme bravery, combined with great fighting skill, sound seamanship, and a highly developed imagination. . . . The slow-reasoning, hesitating type of being was useless in a Q-ship; equally out of place would have been the wild, hare-brained, dashing individual whose excess of gallantry would simply mean the loss of ship and lives. In the ideal Q-ship captain was found something of the virtues of the cleverest angler, the most patient stalker, the most enterprising big-game hunter, together with the attributes of a cool, unperturbed seaman, the imagination of a sensational novelist, and the plain horse-sense of a hard business man. In two words, the necessary endowment was brains and bravery.[2]

Finally, in order to lull the suspicions of an experienced submariner, the captain and officers of a Q-ship should be intimately familiar with the appearance and behaviour of tramp steamers, oil tankers and colliers. This last requirement resulted in the bulk of Q-ship officers being recruited from the ranks of the Royal Naval Reserve: men who had spent their entire professional lives on just the kind of vessels that the Q-ships now attempted to impersonate; men, moreover, who possessed the individuality and self-reliance so essential to the command of these irregular vessels. When judged against such criteria, Stenhouse, who combined a Merchant Navy training with the resourcefulness and independence essential for Antarctic exploration, must have seemed an ideal choice.

His new ship, the *Penshurst*, had been commandeered from the Power Steamship Company of London in November 1915 and then fitted out for Q-ship service by Admiral Sir Stanley Colville near Scapa Flow. With her three masts and single funnel, 225ft long and 35ft in the beam, Colville had thought the *Penshurst* ideal for decoy duty but her new RNR captain admitted to very different views. Commander F.H. Grenfell, a retired officer who had rejoined the Navy at the outbreak of war, thought his new command 'the last ship they should have used for the purpose, being of a design quite unusual and instantly recognised after once being seen'.[3] Although she drew only 15ft, giving her the distinct advantage of not being 'worth a torpedo', Grenfell also found that she lacked stability in rough weather and, with 'the old bitch rolling like gorblimey', life on the *Penshurst* could be profoundly unpleasant. 'Damnably uncomfortable,' he wrote on 29 December 1915, 'cabin not cleaned out and filthy, heater upset and spilt paraffin all over the floor. Has no bath – and all for 1/6 a day!'[4] Despite these failings, under Grenfell's able command the *Penshurst* would eventually prove one of the most successful of all decoy ships.

But success did not come quickly. After being commissioned, she spent twelve long months cruising off the north coast of Scotland, off Ireland and in the English Channel without luck, her crew growing sick of her leaking decks, her paper-thin partitions and her incurable tendency to roll. Then, on 30 November 1916, while attempting to salvage the wreck of a ditched seaplane from the Channel, the *Penshurst* was attacked by *UB-19*. Delighted to find a steamer in such a vulnerable situation, with her crew engaged in trying to raise the aeroplane and rescue its crew, Ober-Leutnant

Erich Noodt had approached incautiously, only to find himself steaming directly into a hail of shells from the *Penshurst*'s single 12-pounder and two 3-pounder guns. Taken completely by surprise, the Germans had been given no chance to retaliate and, in a matter of minutes, the accurate fire of the Royal Navy gunners had riddled the submarine's conning tower and hull. She foundered almost immediately, taking seven of her crew down with her. Success followed success and, in the next four months, the *Penshurst*, under Grenfell's command, engaged and sank *UB-37* and damaged a further three submarines. Then, in March 1917, after a campaign that had already made her one of the most successful of all Q-ships, the *Penshurst* was attacked by a U-boat captain who either saw through her disguise or was simply more wily than his peers. A sharp engagement ensued and this time, instead of sinking her opponent, the British ship suffered such serious damage that she nearly sank herself and had to be towed into Portsmouth for emergency repairs. With Grenfell invalided ashore after this battle, command of the *Penshurst* passed to his first lieutenant, Lieutenant Cedric Naylor and, joining the ship on 28 April, it was under Naylor that Sub-Lieutenant Stenhouse would learn his trade as a Q-ship officer.

The officers and men who served on Q-ships could expect excellent rewards and recognition for their service: the crew of one ship earned between them eight Distinguished Service Orders, twelve Distinguished Service Crosses, one French Croix de Guerre, twenty-five Distinguished Service Medals and nine were Mentioned in Despatches. At a time when the Admiralty desperately needed to show that the U-boats were not invulnerable, the crews could also expect a share in the £1,000 prize money offered for every submarine destroyed. But, of course, there was a price to pay. As a decoy, every Q-ship must look as inoffensive and vulnerable as possible; she must operate in the shipping lanes most frequented by the U-boats; and she must deliberately eschew the protection of the convoy system: she must, in essence, make herself an easy target for every marauding U-boat and do everything possible to invite an attack. Furthermore, although most U-boat commanders preferred to conserve their limited supply of torpedoes for the biggest steamers, all the Q-ships faced the risk of being torpedoed and sunk without being given the opportunity to engage their enemy. Finally, and rather ironically, submariners tended to view the Q-ship crews as pirates, waging war by unfair means, and their crews risked being shot if captured. Whatever the possible rewards, therefore, Q-ship service demanded discipline, patience and nerves of steel.

Stenhouse's first opportunity to demonstrate these characteristics came on 2 July in the Western Approaches. At 1.30 p.m., as the members of the forenoon watch finished their dinner and the cooks prepared to clean up the mess deck, lookouts spied a submarine crossing the ship's bows at a distance of about 6,000yd. Word quickly passed among the forty-five-strong crew and tension mounted. The *Penshurst*, meanwhile, continued on her course, seemingly oblivious of her enemy's proximity. Satisfied that the ship in his periscope's view-finder was all she seemed, the U-boat captain ordered his vessel to a position four points on the *Penshurst*'s bow at a depth of 60ft and allowed his prey to shorten the distance. Watching the movements of the submarine's periscope from the corner of his eye, Naylor judged that his opposite number intended to launch a torpedo and, without displaying any concern to his watching opponent, told his officers to prepare for evasive action. Sure enough, a few seconds later, he saw the tell-tale disturbance of the water as a single torpedo left the submarine's forward tube and began streaking towards the hull of his own ship. Just as it seemed that the torpedo must strike, with impeccable timing, the *Penshurst* completed a turn and the torpedo sped on, passing within 10ft of her bow.

On Naylor's order, Stenhouse and the rest of the crew now began the well-rehearsed 'panic' intended to deceive their attackers: they swung out a boat and, with all the appearance of a pell-mell attempt at escape, clumsily lowered it to the surface of the sea. Next, men began jumping into the boat and immediately started rowing away from her. At 3.35 p.m., 5,000yd from the Q-ship's port bow, the waters began to froth and churn as the dark grey hull of the U-boat broke the surface. As the foam slipped from her flanks, officers appeared in the conning tower and a gun crew took up their positions. At 3.39 precisely, the bombardment began, the German gun crew working with practised efficiency, loading and firing and then tossing the empty shell casings hissing into the sea.

For more than half an hour, the men hiding on the *Penshurst* endured the thump and crash of shell after shell from the submarine's 4.1in gun, biding their time and waiting for the submarine to come within range of their own smaller calibre weapons. At last, at 4.13, the U-boat closed to 4,500yd, ready to give the battered steamer the *coup de grâce*. The *Penshurst*'s gunners immediately leapt from their hiding-places to reveal their weapons, increased since Grenfell's command to two 6-pounders concealed on the lower bridge; a single 12-pounder hidden inside a false lifeboat on the main hatch in front of the funnel; and two 3-pounders in the after deck-house. The guns immediately began to play on the submarine's exposed hull and conning tower, scoring hit after hit. But many Q-ship gunners had discovered that submarines possessed greater resilience than might at first appear and they could sustain serious damage to their conning tower, a superstructure separated from the main hull by a watertight hatch, and even numerous holes in their outer hulls without foundering. Sixteen times the U-boat echoed with the clank of the *Penshurst*'s shells striking her hull, but still she swam. Then, with his vessel's combustion engines undamaged and offering a surface speed of around 16 knots compared to the *Penshurst*'s 10, the U-boat captain wisely decided that discretion formed the better part of valour. To the fury of Naylor and all of his men, the German managed to limp his vessel out of range of the Q-ship's guns and then, with astonishing luck, he also evaded the three destroyers called up by Naylor during the action. Against all the odds, both the U-boat and the Q-ship had lived to tell the tale of their engagement.

A few weeks before this skirmish, Stenhouse had written to Leonard Tripp to tell him that 'Since my arrival in England I have been in the "Scrap" so have had little or no time for "looking up" the people I had intended to (I have had only three days at home). . . . I am fit and enjoying life immensely although the "fed-up-ness," caused by the mismanaging Relief Committee, has not yet worn off.'[5] Part of this 'fed-up-ness' had resulted from his concern that the Admiralty might see his conflict with the Relief Committees as being his fault. Now he could begin to lay these doubts aside. Had the Admiralty really entertained any doubts about his ability, they would surely have posted him to some far more obscure position than the bridge of one of its most successful Q-ships; the role he played on the afternoon of 2 July also brought immediate recognition and rewards. On 29 August, the *London Gazette* announced that Cedric Naylor would add a DSO to his DSC for 'services in action with enemy submarines'; it also confirmed not only that Stenhouse had been promoted from Sub-Lieutenant to Acting-Lieutenant but that he had also been Mentioned in Despatches. Finally, in his report on his junior officer's conduct and ability, Naylor wrote that Stenhouse had 'Shown much keenness in making himself proficient in all duties and in acquainting himself with all matters pertaining to the Service. He has energy and is an officer of promise.'[6]

Delighted though Stenhouse must have been with this recognition and with the reassurance it gave him that the Relief Committee débâcle would not stand in the way of his promotion, he must have been disappointed and bemused to learn that he would now be transferred from the *Penshurst*. His frustration, however, quickly turned to elation when he discovered that the man commanding his new ship, the *PQ-61*, was no less a person than Frank Worsley. The two friends had met whenever the demands of the service allowed, but now, for the first time, they would actually serve together: Worsley as captain and Stenhouse as his first officer.

Since leaving Chatham, Worsley had been in Belfast, supervising the fit-out of the *PQ-61*, and it was here that Stenhouse joined him ready for the ship's commissioning on 31 July. But, having expected excitement, adventure and glory to a high degree, both men soon became disappointed at the profound lack of interest that the U-boats took in their vessel. Week after week, the *PQ-61* patrolled her designated zone, while everyone on board did their utmost to give their vessel the appearance of an inoffensive coasting steamer. All to no avail: fully alive to the threat posed by the Q-ships, something about the little ship seemed to make the Germans suspicious. 'I am afraid,' Worsley wrote some years later, ' . . . that our shape was rather too orthodox and typical of Admiralty-build, for we could never persuade submarines to attack us, or at all events to do more than fire torpedoes at us, however much we flirted with them.'[7] As with so many aspects of warfare, however, long periods of boredom, albeit boredom with more than a tinge of nervous tension, could give way, in a matter of seconds, to intense and violent action. In the case of the *PQ-61*, that transformation occurred at the end of September, nearly two months after the ship's commissioning and almost three months since Stenhouse's last action.

During the late evening of 25 September, when cruising about 40 miles off the south coast of Ireland, the *PQ-61* received orders to locate and then escort into harbour the oil tanker, *San Zeferino*. The tanker was travelling as part of a convoy but during her Atlantic crossing she had developed problems with her steering gear which rendered her unable to perform the zigzag manoeuvres designed to minimise the risk of being torpedoed. Limping along at the rear of the convoy, she looked so obvious a lame duck that a really cautious U-boat captain might even have suspected her of being a Q-ship. The seas remained moderate but, by the time that Worsley found the *San Zeferino* at 11.15 p.m., a patchy mist had begun to drift in, reducing visibility to about three-quarters of a mile. The *PQ-61* then took up position about two cables ahead of the tanker's starboard bow and, carefully observing her progress, commenced the usual zigzagging avoidance tactics.

At 5.57 on the morning of the 26th, the inevitable happened: a huge concussion shook the *San Zeferino* as a single torpedo exploded beneath her engine room, killing three men and letting in a flood of freezing water. Neither Worsley nor Stenhouse, standing on the bridge of the *PQ-61*, heard the explosion and only when they saw the tanker settling by the stern did they realise what had happened. In answer to their signals, the master of the stricken ship confirmed that his vessel had been hit but, with her boats swung out, she was in no immediate danger of sinking; more importantly, the submarine had been spotted to the north-west. Dropping speed to reduce the risk of detection, the *PQ-61* set off in pursuit: there would be no attempt at disguise now; if seen, the U-boat would be immediately engaged. Unfortunately, the patchy sea mist had now thickened to a dense, clinging fog and the *PQ-61* rapidly lost touch with the tanker and, in order to render her any assistance necessary, Worsley had to order his ship about.

But first, in a last-ditch effort to make contact with the enemy vessel, he decided to attempt 'sound camouflage'. This involved gradually reducing the revolutions of his ship's propeller in an attempt to fool the submariners into thinking that the *PQ-61* had abandoned the sinking *San Zeferino* and was retreating. If the Germans believed that the escort had left the scene, then they might decide to surface in order to finish off their victim with gunfire. The ruse worked like a dream. The *PQ-61* completed her turn and then came back towards the tanker from a different direction, intending to cross the tanker's bows before heading down her port side and under her stern. As she did so, Stenhouse, straining to see through the fog, spotted the conning tower of the submarine, about half a mile away on the starboard beam, heading west at a speed of around 9 knots. 'Hard a-port and full speed ahead!' cried a jubilant Worsley.

The submariners were taken completely by surprise – their first intimation of the *PQ-61*'s proximity coming with the crash of a 12lb shell as it struck their vessel close to the conning tower. Next, the horrified men saw the enormous bow-wave heading towards them as the Q-ship reached her full speed of 24 knots. 'We certainly must have looked like the Angel of Death to those unfortunate Germans,' Worsley noted. Travelling at such a speed, the Q-ship's bow would naturally sit high in the water and an impact with the submarine could have ripped out her keel. To prevent this, at the last moment Worsley gave two orders: 'stop engines' and 'prepare to ram'. With her impetus suddenly checked, the *PQ-61*'s bows dropped down about 2ft into the water and at the same moment officers and crew threw themselves to the deck. 'As the bows fell,' Worsley recorded, 'the ram caught the submarine amidships, tearing her sides open and rolling her beneath us, and immediately afterwards we were shaken by a tremendous explosion.'[8]

For one horrible moment, it seemed as though the *PQ-61*, so intent upon the destruction of one submarine, had been torpedoed by another, just in her moment of victory. Fortunately, it quickly became apparent that the explosion must have resulted either from the rupturing of the submarine's hull or from the detonation of the explosives she carried. Stenhouse leapt to his feet and yelled into the speaking tube to the engine room, had the engines or propeller been damaged from the impact and subsequent explosion? No, came the almost instantaneous reply, the *PQ-61* had survived the encounter unscathed. Amazingly the clock stood at 6.30 a.m. – only 33 minutes had passed since the explosion beneath the *San Zeferino*'s engine room. Now the wreckage of the submarine that had fired that shot, the *UC-33*, had begun her long spiral down to the ocean floor carrying the bodies of all but one of her crew. The only submariner to be plucked from the oil-stained water was Ober-Leutnant Albert Arnold, the U-boat's captain, who had been thrown clear from her conning tower as the Q-ship's reinforced stem cut her in two.

Now it only remained to take the *San Zeferino* in tow: but that proved easier said than done. The tanker dwarfed her rescuer – 7,000 tons against a mere 600 – and the *PQ-61* had not been fitted for towing. 'Here Stenhouse's splendid seamanship came into play,' noted an admiring Worsley. 'He unshackled a length of our chain cable from the anchor, dragged it aft, and connected it to the oiler's heavy steel towing wire. It was a ticklish business in a heavy sea, for we had to make the cable fast in the very confined space between our twenty depth charges.'[9] With each of the depth charges containing 400lb of TNT, and working in uncertain light on a heaving deck, the job demanded great skill and dexterity, but eventually Stenhouse signalled to Worsley that he could take up the slack. Then they began the long, slow and dangerous tow to Milford Haven, which the two ships reached at 9.15 p.m. – a full 12 hours after they had first taken the *San Zeferino* in tow.

For their parts in sinking this U-boat, Worsley received the first of his two DSOs; Stenhouse, as first officer, received the DSC; and two petty officers were awarded the DSM for their excellent steering and gun-laying. Perhaps more importantly for Stenhouse, his continued success as a submarine-hunter resulted, on 3 October, in his being appointed to his own command: the Q-ship *Ianthe*.

In later days, Stenhouse would admit that 'it is hard for a master to go back to mate without regret or bitterness' and, after commanding the *Aurora* for so long, it had not been easy for him to accept a subordinate role in the Royal Navy. But he believed that duty must take precedence over any personal considerations, and he had stuck to his allotted task and done everything possible to learn the skills of a dedicated submarine-hunter. Now, at last, he reaped his reward. Moreover, it seemed that the Admiralty flag-officers had decided that his reward should perfectly accord with his abilities and experience because they appointed him to one of their thirty-four Q-ship sailing sloops. As E. Keble Chatterton observed, 'In the whole of the Royal Navy there were hardly any suitable officers nowadays who possessed practical experience in handling schooners. This was where the officer from the Mercantile Marine, the amateur yachtsman, the coasting skipper, and the fisherman became so invaluable.'[10] This should, therefore, have been Stenhouse's opportunity to excel on his own terms, but time was against him. In the early days of the war, many submariners had been fooled by the Q-ships and many had fallen victim to the British ships' hidden guns. But, just as importantly, some had escaped – and with every submarine that returned to its harbour, more and more tales spread regarding these disguised warships. Submarine commanders became increasingly circumspect about attacking such vessels and Q-ship successes dwindled.

If, however, the increasingly wary U-boat commanders declined to attack the *Ianthe* as she sailed in her designated waters, other opportunities existed for Stenhouse to demonstrate his ability, quick thinking and courage. By the end of the war, Britain's inshore waters teemed with mines: some strung in defensive chains around harbour mouths, others floating free, either because they had broken from their moorings or because they had been released by enemy vessels like the *UC-33*. In the early months of 1918, while operating close inshore, Stenhouse spotted one such mine from the bridge of the *Ianthe*. All Q-ships carried rifles and pistols but the mine seemed immune to small-arms fire, the bullets either bouncing from its rounded iron sides or splashing harmlessly into the water. If left free, the mine contained sufficient explosives to destroy or seriously damage any ship that collided with it and something had to be done to neutralise the threat.

With a heavy sea running and darkness setting in, Stenhouse ordered that a boat be lowered. Accompanied by a couple of able seamen he then pulled over to the mine, which could be seen occasionally on the smooth slope of a wave, the water foaming round the detonating horns studding its sides. At Stenhouse's feet lay a coil of light rope and, once he had approached as close as he dared without risk of striking the mine, he told the rowers to hold position while he stripped off his pea-jacket and sea boots. A moment later he gripped the end of the rope between his teeth and plunged into the churning water. Watching anxiously from the deck of the *Ianthe*, his crew saw him reappear a second later as he swam the few remaining yards to his goal. With his teeth beginning to chatter and his fingers growing numb, he now had to pass the end of the rope through the hinge-bolt on the mine's side. 'That was all,' wrote one journalist, 'seeming almost as easy as cracking an egg. But this has to be remembered – a circular mine afloat in a gale is not an egg in a cup, but tossing and swirling death.'[11] With the cold sapping his strength and his sodden clothes beginning to drag him down, it was only with a supreme effort of will that Stenhouse managed, at last, to pass the end of the line through the bolt and then make it secure with a knot. And all of this had to be achieved without inadvertently knocking against the horns studding the mine's surface both above and below the water.

With the line secure, Stenhouse turned back towards his waiting boat. Those few yards now seemed immeasurably further than they had on his outward journey and sometimes the boat disappeared altogether from his view as it sank into a trough between the waves. Eventually, though, the men in the waiting boat could reach down and grasp their skipper by the scruff of the neck; heaving his dead weight over the gunwale, they then draped his pea-jacket over his shoulders and began to row back towards the *Ianthe*. Once they had regained the ship's side, the mine, at the end of its long rope, could be towed to calmer water, where the marksmen among the crew might take a better aim. A short time later the stillness of the early evening was punctured by a sudden flare and the boom of a violent detonation: one mine less to threaten Allied shipping.

This incident formed the last of Stenhouse's actions with the Q-ships – but he had no reason to fear inactivity or boredom. In the autumn of 1918, a letter from the War Office brought a sudden and unexpected end to his service afloat. The letter, addressed to the senior officer in Falmouth, requested that Stenhouse be released from his naval duties to undertake specialist work in North Russia, 'where it is considered his experience will be of great value to the State'. Whatever value he could bring to this new theatre of war, he would very soon learn that it would subject him to conditions every bit as cold and explosive as mine clearance in the granite grey waters of the English Channel.

WAR IN THE ARCTIC

The war in the east had not been going well for the Allies. Despite a standing army of around 1,200,000 men at the outbreak of war, poor communications, chronic shortages of weapons and munitions and inept leadership had led to defeat after defeat for Tsarist Russia. Destruction of her Second Army at Tannenberg in August 1914 proved to be the first in a string of military disasters resulting not only in huge losses of men and equipment but also in widespread demoralisation. Defeats in Massuria and Galicia completely overshadowed victories such as the capture of the Austrian fortress at Przemyl in March 1915, and the collapse of General Alexei Brusilov's offensive around Vilna in September 1916 led to the near-total disintegration of the Russian army's fighting spirit. Worn down by appalling casualties, divided leadership and terrible living conditions, on 12 March 1917, the military garrison at Petrograd mutinied. This mutiny, in turn, sparked a revolution that precipitated the abdication of Tsar Nicholas II and the establishment of a provisional government under Alexander Kerensky. As War Minister and then Prime Minister, Kerensky felt honour-bound to continue the struggle against Germany but, in September 1917, the last Russian offensive of the war ended in a humiliating defeat at Riga. A second revolution, this time led by the fervently anti-war Bolsheviks under Lenin and Trotsky, overthrew Kerensky's government on 7 November, and was quickly followed by the opening of peace negotiations at Brest-Litovsk in December.

Initially optimistic that the onset of democracy would energise the Russian war effort, the British, French and US governments had watched the rapidly unfolding events in the east with growing consternation. In particular, they realised that Russia's exit from the war might result in a colossal transfer of German fighting units from the Eastern to the Western Front, just when the Allied armies were recovering from the huge losses sustained during the Nivelle Offensive and Passchendaele. Equally troubling to Great Britain was the thought of Germany capturing Russia's northern ports. If the German Navy established U-boat bases at the permanently ice-free port of Murmansk on the Kola Inlet, and at Petchenga on the Russian–Finnish border, these bases would become operational just when the Atlantic would be crowded with troop ships carrying fresh American soldiers to Europe. The fact that the military storehouses in Archangel, on the south-eastern tip of the White Sea, bulged with supplies sent to Russia from the west constituted less of an imminent threat. Nevertheless, the thought of these supplies being captured by the Germans and then being turned against their donors was too bitter to be easily borne.

The signing of a punitive peace treaty between Germany and Russia at Brest-Litovsk on 3 March 1918 brought an end to German advances into Russia and prevented the capture of Murmansk. But it also meant that the German High Command was now free to start the transfer of its troops to the Western Front. Fully aware of the probable consequences of this freedom, Allied hopes now centred on the conviction that many Russians, particularly those of the officer class, might be willing to reopen the Eastern Front if given adequate encouragement – encouragement which must inevitably take the form of military intervention. The Allies reasoned that, with fighting recommencing on its eastern flank, Germany would be reluctant to transfer too many of its eastern divisions to the west. This reluctance would give the British and French armies an opportunity to lick their wounds in comparative peace and allow the so far untried American troops to complete their combat training before being thrown into the front line. But the Allies now had to decide whether a military intervention should be mounted in support of, or in opposition to, Lenin's revolutionary government. The success or failure of their enterprise would be almost wholly dependent on this decision.

One observer on the spot, the British diplomat Robert Bruce Lockhart, believed that March 1918 was the month during which the Bolsheviks were most amenable to an understanding with the Allies. Deeply distrustful of both British capitalism and German militarism, they currently viewed the latter as the more immediate threat and would willingly have broken the terms of the humiliating treaty forced on them by Germany. Fearing that German victory in the west might result in renewed aggression in the east, they also wanted help to train the new Red Army. But the Allies loathed the very idea of revolution and, finding it impossible to accept that Tsardom was gone for good, they preferred to side with Tsarist *émigrés* rather than with a revolutionary government actually in power. Lockhart firmly believed that the 'White' Russians had no real interest in reopening the Eastern Front and that they were concerned solely with fighting the Bolsheviks. But the Allies continued to prevaricate until, with the re-establishment of an active and vigilant German embassy in Moscow, the opportunity for a pro-Bolshevik intervention had been lost.

The alternative was a military intervention without Bolshevik connivance. Such a strategy entailed huge risks since any unauthorised landing on Russian territory would inevitably be viewed as anti-revolutionary. This interpretation would almost certainly result in an expeditionary force having to fight against two enemies: the Germans and the Bolsheviks. Lockhart considered that such a campaign would be a terrible mistake, capable of success only if the Allies committed significant forces to its prosecution. But he correctly predicted that widespread repugnance at the idea of an invasion of Russia would lead to a half-hearted compromise.

After much heated deliberation, the Allies decided to commit what amounted to little more than a token force to the new campaign. The result of this decision was the formation of what one of its senior officers later called 'one of the most motley of forces ever created',[1] consisting largely of British, French, American and Canadian units – the majority of whom had previously been deemed unfit for service on the Western Front. These waifs and strays, many of whom had received no combat training, let alone instruction in the use of skis and snowshoes, would now be committed to a theatre of war subject to climatic conditions never before experienced by British soldiers. The first tiny contingent, 150 Royal Marines, landed at Murmansk in April 1918, followed on 23 June by a larger body of infantry and by a squadron of Allied warships: two British, two White Russian, one American and one French. The Allied troops, numbering some 2,500 in all, faced approximately 50,000 German troops positioned just across the Russian border with Finland.

Despite this numerical imbalance, the British commander in North Russia, Major-General Charles Maynard, considered Murmansk to be defendable. In particular, the land routes from Finland were very poor and, during the summer months, boggy tundra made it impossible for any but small bodies of troops to manoeuvre. The anticipated German advance, therefore, must come either by rail, along single-track lines from Petrograd to Murmansk, and from Petrograd to Archangel, or by water. Several water routes existed, leading by lake and river to the Kola Inlet, but waterborne operations were rendered extremely difficult by a lack of facilities for the embarkation of large numbers of troops and by the fact that the rivers, as well as being tortuous and fast-flowing, passed through large tracts of extremely inhospitable countryside. If they were to be used at all, then the Germans would find it necessary to employ specially adapted boats and these would inevitably be in very short supply. Overall, the railway lines must be the preferred option for any large-scale advance against the Allies; but the railways crossed countless bridges, making it relatively easy for the defenders to hamper an enemy's advance.

The identity of this potential enemy, however, remained uncertain: it could be either German or Russian – or both. Resentful of the Allied decision to land troops on its sovereign territory and fearful that the Germans might accuse it of collaborating with the western powers, Lenin's Bolshevik government finally declared against the Allies at the end of June 1918. Immediately afterwards, troops from the two divisions of Red Guards stationed in the area made a rather faint-hearted move against British positions in Murmansk. Despite being heavily outnumbered, and resorting largely to bluff, Maynard succeeded in foiling this attempt to oust him. Heartened by this initial success on 7 July, the Murmansk Council declared against the Bolshevik government – on condition that the Allies continued to bolster their position with supplies of food, war materials and money. By mid-July, Maynard's forces had systematically disarmed the entire region north of Kandalaksha and firmly established themselves along the whole of the railway line from Murmansk to Soroka on the western shore of the White Sea; the Bolsheviks had offered only token resistance. Next, they occupied Archangel, which had been ice-free since May. They completed this operation, in the face of firmer Bolshevik opposition, on 30 July. Archangel then became an independent command under another British general, Edmund Ironside.

With their position secured, at least for the time being, the Allies now had to decide on their longer-term strategy. Murmansk and Archangel had been denied to the enemy and, while the Germans had been able to transfer significant numbers of troops westwards, Maynard calculated that another 40,000 had been tied down in the east at a critical period. But events on the Western Front quickly overshadowed this minor victory. By the autumn of 1918, it had become clear that Germany's fighting spirit was waning fast. She had wasted the last of her strength, including the units transferred from the East, in General Erich Ludendorff's abortive offensives around Amiens and Armentières. Ludendorff won great tactical victories but, crucially, he achieved no overall strategic breakthrough and, in five months, he lost nearly 500,000 men. After four years of unmitigated bloodshed and brutality, the Allies could at last discern a glimmer of light at the end of the tunnel.

But growing confidence in the west was matched by doubt and hesitation in the east. The Allies' conviction that Lenin and Trotsky were German agents whose influence would be short-lived had so far proved ill-founded and the hope of establishing a cordon sanitaire to prevent the spread of the Bolshevik contagion had been dismissed as impracticable. Despite Germany's growing weakness, Maynard felt absolutely certain that the Allied presence must extend through at least one Arctic winter – even longer if the Allies decided to campaign actively against the Bolsheviks.

This being the case, it became essential that his inexperienced troops should be given the benefit of expert advice on how to survive and operate during an Arctic winter. Candidates for such work were thin on the ground but, not many months previously, the names of a group of men well-versed in the arts of survival in frigid climes had been splashed across English newspaper headlines. Chief among them was that of the most famous of all surviving Antarctic veterans, Sir Ernest Shackleton.

Ever since the conclusion of the *Endurance* Expedition, Shackleton had been seeking a military post. Disappointed in his hopes of a command in the front line, he had recently undertaken a successful diplomatic mission to South America for the Department of Information. Now, at last, he reaped the rewards of his patience: those rewards being the rank of major in the British Army and military duties, albeit of a very specialised nature. Moreover, given the peculiarity of the work it now employed him for, the War Office gave him something approaching *carte blanche* in the recruitment of his men. The first officers to be transferred to Shackleton's command were Leonard Hussey and Alexander Macklin of the *Endurance*. Then, in the middle of September 1918, in London, he met Worsley, en route to Gibraltar to take command of the Q-ship *Pangloss*. Already concerned that the opportunities for U-boat hunting in the Mediterranean had significantly diminished in recent months, it did not take much to persuade the New Zealander to join the new venture. 'Of course,' Worsley wrote to Leonard Tripp, 'nothing would do me until I got my old pal Stennie with us, and Sir Ernest applied for him.'[2] This application produced the War Office letter of 5 October ordering Stenhouse to North Russia and, in response to the summons, towards the end of October he joined Shackleton, Worsley and Hussey on board the steamer *Ella*, bound for Murmansk.

Except for a brush with a U-boat shortly after sailing from Newcastle, the voyage proceeded uneventfully. The *Ella* passed unscathed through the minefields protecting the Scottish coast and plunged north. She sliced through the turbulent waters of the Norwegian Sea, crossed the Arctic Circle, skirted the Nordkapp, or North Cape, and then began her south-easterly course towards Murmansk. Shackleton told his wife that 'Life goes on much in the same way and the weather has grown cold with occasional snow-squalls and then is clear at night with beautiful aurora swinging across the big starred sky; the tang of the North wind brings back the South to us all.'[3] On 31 October, the *Ella* and her escorts entered the narrow estuary that snakes its way inland from the Barents Sea. For the last few miles of the voyage, they slowly wended their way between high, rugged banks, for the most part clad with fir trees, and then, rounding a bluff headland, reached Murmansk itself.

Murmansk harbour was a hive of activity and, as the *Ella* made her way through the jumble of shipping, Stenhouse could cast an appraising eye over the neighbouring vessels. HMS *Glory*, the flagship of Rear Admiral Green, the senior Royal Navy officer in the White Sea, lay berthed on the one hand; on the other the waters lapped against the sides of the veteran Russian battleship, the *Askold*, known to sailors as the 'Woodbine' because of her five smoke-stained funnels. In the shadow of these giants lay the *Josephine*, once the luxuriously equipped pleasure-yacht of William Rockefeller but now, like many a Romanov princess, scraping by in reduced circumstances, a scruffy maid of all work. Other smaller craft rode at anchor in the fairway or alongside the dilapidated-looking quays and between them scurried ugly bull-nosed tugs towing lighters piled high with stores and equipment.

Before the war, Murmansk had been non-existent: the only inhabited spot being the fishing village of Kola, 6 miles away at the head of the inlet. Then, when the Western Allies began to ship large quantities of stores to equip the Tsar's massive but ill-prepared army, it had been found necessary to construct a railway to transport these supplies inland. Murmansk formed the railhead and the town had grown around the hutment erected by the international band of navvies employed in the railway's construction. Not long after Stenhouse's arrival, the Special Correspondent of *The Times* landed in Murmansk. He wrote that the town 'to-day may be likened to the left luggage office of Noah's Ark: every breed is found within its limits'; they included Americans, Russians, Italians, French, Serbians, Karolians, Finns, Letts, Lithuanians, British and 'Chinese whose compatriots on the Bolshevist side act as executioners for Lenin'.[4]

At first glance, the town appeared quite picturesque, even romantic. It lay in a cup formed by the surrounding hills; a higgledy-piggledy collection of log cabins nestled on the eastern shore of the estuary while, to the north, snow-capped mountains showed through the morning mist, their foothills blackened by a dense covering of firs. The railway linking Murmansk to the Archangel–Petrograd line, 500 miles due south, swept round the edge of the water, right up to the quayside, and the movement of trucks upon it added to the impression of industry and purpose. Closer inspection of the town, however, revealed dilapidation, filth and a lack of sanitation which four months of Allied occupation had done little to improve. One British officer passing through the town en route to Archangel told a correspondent that he 'only went ashore once, but once was really quite enough. No words can adequately express the nastiness of Murmansk, the mixed inhabitants and the rare quality of the smells are unique.'[5] Another said of the sanitation: 'Imagine the worst – multiply it by some big figure, and you'll get somewhere near the mark.'[6] The roads, too, were little more

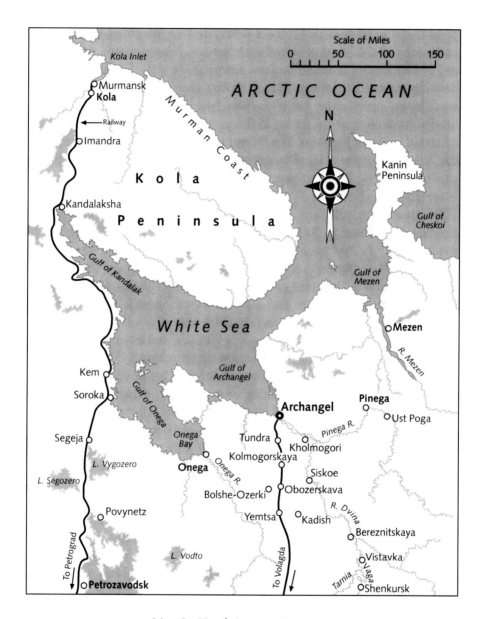

Map 2. North Russia, 1918–19.

than unmade muddy tracks, the hillsides showed hardly any evidence of cultivation and, all around, stretched tracts of dark, monotonous forest dissected by tumbling, rock-strewn rivers. In the late autumn, the scene presented a grim enough prospect. In the fast approaching winter, with its months of semi-darkness and with temperatures sometimes plunging to 75° below zero, it would become more dreary still, the trees weighted down by masses of snow and the bubbling rivers frozen solid. The town was also an armed camp since Maynard had found it essential to provide numerous strong guards, owing to the persistent attempts at looting made by armed gangs of Russians. The Murmansk Council may have declared for the Allies, but many of its citizens remained sympathetic to the Bolshevik cause and the Bolshevik propagandists had already proved extremely adept at spreading disaffection.

Whatever the opinions of the Canadian and British soldiers who accompanied them to Russia – and, in time, they too would reveal a susceptibility to Red propaganda – Stenhouse and his friends rapidly demonstrated a willingness to make the best of their situation. The mood of the group remained buoyant and optimistic, not least because Shackleton, after months of frustration and disappointment, now felt that he could make an active and valid contribution to the war effort, if not quite in the front line then close to it. Stenhouse and Worsley, meanwhile, were 'happy as sandboys' as they investigated their new surroundings.

Worsley joked that 'what I'd like would be for us to finish up each driving a dog-team over the snow into Berlin'[7] but, within a fortnight of his arrival at Murmansk, it became clear to Stenhouse that his original expectation of conducting operations against German troops had been overtaken by events in the west. Having weathered the storm of Ludendorff's offensives, the Allies counter-attacked in force. The exhausted and demoralised German armies buckled and, on 11 November 1918, the war finally ground to its conclusion. In Russia, however, the conflict continued uninterrupted. Not only did the onset of winter make the immediate withdrawal of Allied troops a practical impossibility, many in the west felt a deep abhorrence for Bolshevism and continued to hope that something could be done to prevent its spread. The still-numerous Russian officer class had been expected to reopen the Eastern Front against Germany; might it not also be relied upon to resist Lenin and his upstart Bolshevik government?

While the Allied governments considered their positions, the men under Maynard's command continued their fight: against both the Bolsheviks and the Arctic winter. As soon as it had been confirmed that Lenin's government had become a legitimate target, an avowed enemy, the British press, had begun to publish articles as virulently anti-Bolshevik as their reports, for four long years, had been anti-German. And, in exactly the same vein, the newspapers spared their readers none of the details of Bolshevik atrocities, citing cases of rapine, murder and looting that would not have been out of place in the most febrile reports of 1914. For his own part, nearly a quarter of a century later, Stenhouse would tell his sister that he found it 'splendid to think of the Prussians and Russians, two heathen nations, killing each other off . . . weed strangle weed!'[8], and now he showed no reluctance to engage this new enemy.

In exactly the same way that his career in the merchant marine had made him an ideal Q-ship officer, willing and able to work outside the formalities and conventions of the normal life of the Royal Navy, these same qualities made Stenhouse perfectly suited to the irregular life of Murmansk. The atmosphere was quite informal and, with other Antarctic veterans like Victor Campbell joining them, Shackleton thought it 'more a happy family than a rigid mess'.[9] Officers and men eschewed standard issue uniform and, as another officer reported, 'go about here in any old clothes and no one looks like a soldier. . . . There is no "spit and polish" here, no parades, no reveilles, no lights-out, no padres.'[10] The environment also bore a strong resemblance to that of the Antarctic; the same officer noted that 'I live with a collection of other lost souls in a place colloquially known as the "slum." It is a sort of shed in which Serbs have died of typhus and Russians have lived in squalor, and is now inhabited by mice and bugs. Water freezes 3ft from a red-hot stove. My bed is 18in from the stove, which keeps me just comfortable when it is glowing; I hang my sheepskin coat on the head of the bed, and then button it so that it makes a cone over my head and saves my nose from frostbite.'[11]

These conditions, exacerbated by long hours of darkness, caused many of the Allied troops to loathe Murmansk. But to Stenhouse and Shackleton, to whom such hardships were neither new nor particularly harsh, the place had its own quite potent appeal and they grew to love the snow-clad landscape. They had expected the countryside to be flat and uninteresting; instead, they discovered rolling hills clothed with birch forests and, nestling in innumerable valleys, beautiful lakes covered with black translucent ice. Bilberries and bog myrtle peeped through the snow, the latter filling the air with its sweet scent when crushed underfoot. In his years at sea, Stenhouse met many seamen from these regions and he later stated that 'It was always a mystery to me why these Russian Finns left their own country, with its lovely woods and lakes, to battle round the Horn in foreign ships.'[12]

Maynard described Stenhouse's job as being 'supervising and training mobile columns in which his intimate knowledge of Arctic conditions and requirements were of utmost value'.[13] And, despite the unexpected departure of Worsley, who had received orders to proceed to Archangel, Stenhouse threw himself into the task with all his accustomed enthusiasm and vigour. As the long Arctic winter began to take the country in its icy grip, the work increased and Shackleton found that 'Stenhouse and Hussey are twin towers of strength though not equal in size.'[14]

The building work necessary to house all the men had been delayed until the last minute and one of Stenhouse's most important tasks was the examination of the huts to establish whether any modifications might increase their effectiveness. In a diary entry that might have been written in the Crimea sixty-five years earlier, one civilian contractor commented that 'For every man killed at the Russian front, we shall be losing twenty by exposure at the base. The neglect of proper housing accommodation [is] nothing short of criminal.'[15] At other times, Stenhouse and his fellows delivered lectures to the troops on how to avoid frostbite, linking their talks to their own recent experiences. Worsley, who delivered similar lectures in Archangel, told a correspondent that his audience 'said either I was a liar or it was better to be in North Russia than the Antarctic; which was just what I was trying to drive into them; what a jolly good place we were in after all.'[16]

Most importantly, since Maynard wanted to retain his ability to conduct tactical manoeuvres even in the depths of winter, an intense and focused programme of training was developed and delivered by veterans of both the *Endurance* and *Terra Nova* expeditions. Maynard admitted that the formation of seven mobile columns, each with 200 men in its ranks, 'was a matter of no small difficulty, owing to the unavoidably late arrival of many essential stores, and to the time occupied in unloading, sorting out and despatching to the various organising centres the mass of special equipment required'.[17] At first the troops, who possessed no experience of Arctic conditions, floundered about hopelessly on their skis and in snowshoes, and the 'Shackleton boots', a modified form of Eskimo finnesko, did little to help. E. Davey, the contractor who had so criticised the late building programme, related how he was 'Much amused watching Tommies with their Shackleton boots on – my! how the poor chaps slip and tumble about. The leather soles are smooth as a board. They are alright in snow but on the paths they are really too bad.'[18] Fortunately, the issue of football-boot studs helped to remedy the problem and gradually the troops regained their equilibrium.

By the beginning of 1919, the importance of having the mobile columns ready for action was becoming increasingly obvious. In particular, General Ironside's position in Archangel looked extremely vulnerable and reinforcements needed to be sent from Murmansk as quickly as possible. As a result, in the cold, dark early months of the year, Stenhouse began a series of train journeys southwards, away from the relatively secure enclave of Murmansk and into the Kola Peninsula and Karelia. His orders were to see to the safe transportation of troops to Soroka, via Imandra and Kem, whence they would proceed by sledge and by ski the 150 miles to Onega, before the final leg of their journey to Archangel.

The trains on which Stenhouse travelled offered only basic accommodation, consisting of an ordinary freight wagon called a *chepluska*, 20ft long by 10ft wide, with sliding doors on either side. Luckily, bunks and stoves had been fitted to the wagon and Stenhouse and his travelling companions succeeded in making themselves fairly comfortable. Over the next few weeks, however, Stenhouse came to realise that, if the trains could be made tolerably comfortable, little could be done to make them reliable. Reporting to his superiors in London, General Maynard asserted that:

One of my chief sources of anxiety has been the maintenance of railway communication with my southern garrisons. At the time of the Bolshevik withdrawal, a large number of railway employees joined the Bolshevik forces, and many more fled to the south subsequently, owing to my inability to feed and pay them. Those who remained were for the most part discontented and sullen; strikes were frequent; the repair of locomotives ceased; and, during the whole of last summer, the upkeep of the permanent way was totally neglected – a neglect which is bound to have a most disadvantageous effect on traffic so soon as the thaw commences.[19]

Experiencing these problems first hand, Stenhouse put it rather more succinctly, grumbling to his diary that 'This railway is a joke.'[20]

On his very first journey, scheduled to depart Murmansk at 10 p.m. on 3 January, an asthmatic engine wheezed up to the waiting train on time but then proceeded to shunt his wagon about the sidings all night before finally abandoning it on the wharf. It remained there for the rest of the day and Stenhouse eventually departed 26 hours late, at midnight on the 4th, with Hussey and Macklin waving him off from the platform. These events were a sign of things to come. Over the coming weeks, the trains on which Stenhouse travelled regularly ground to an unexpected and jarring halt. Fretting with impatience, he and his companions would then sit, sometimes for minutes, sometimes for hours on end, among the dark, gloomy woods, silent but for the sudden shot-like cracking of branches overburdened with snow. When the trains were in motion, they rattled and clanked interminably and Stenhouse found that 'Travelling in a truck is a cure for Liver, the "Hump" etc; sudden stops, starts, jerks; a seemingly continuous effort on the part of the truck to jump the lines.'[21] There were some compensations, however, and, as the trains wound their way southwards through the white landscape, the frozen edges of the White

Sea glinting like gunmetal in the distance, Stenhouse could sometimes lean from the wagon's open door and admire the beautiful crimson tints in the southern sky.

It became clear that, if the Bolsheviks did not actively 'stalk' the trains, they were present in sufficient numbers to ensure that the trains seldom passed beyond their surveillance. The unreliability of the engines and wagons used by the Allies also meant that they were presented with frequent opportunities to conduct ambushes. Faced with the destruction of vital railway bridges and other forms of sabotage, General Maynard found it necessary 'to take strict precautions to prevent the frequent and bold attempts at looting made by Russian gangs, whose action is often connived at by the local railway and other authorities'.[22] One such attempt at looting delayed Stenhouse's first journey, though his ignorance that the unscheduled stop had been caused by a raid on the stores wagon led him to remark that 'This is the first "hold up" I have been in and knew nothing about it.'[23]

A few days later, the train's poor state of repair was demonstrated when an axle box on a truck loaded with rum and rations ran hot and burst into flames. With the rest of the passengers, Stenhouse leapt from the train and doused the fire with snow before progressing cautiously to the next station. There he had a 'pow-wow with Russkis and told them that [the] train could not proceed with this truck; eventually got another truck and transferred Rum and Rations to it – much to disgust of Russkis, who were apparently looking forward to Merry Xmas with Rum'.[24] The disappointed Russians enjoyed the last laugh, however, as, within a short distance of the station, the axle box of the new truck, to which the rum and rations had been so painstakingly transferred, also burst into flames. The disabled train limped onwards but, all the time, groups of Bolsheviks could be seen moving among the trees, no doubt hoping that the train's interrupted progress would render it vulnerable to attack.

For all the Allies' attempts to stabilise the situation in the region around Murmansk and to disarm the populace, the atmosphere remained akin to that of any frontier at the edge of civilisation, and the similarities were not restricted to the preponderance of timber houses and ill-made roads. The countryside teemed with armed men: soldiers, deserters, *agents provocateurs*, bandits and terrified citizens. Some were intent on mischief, some were desperate, some merely fearful; but all were equally trigger-happy. Even in the comparative tranquillity of Murmansk itself shots often rang out at night; further south they were a commonplace and travelling by jolting, noisy railway round the southern rim of the White Sea sometimes resembled journeying by stagecoach through America's Indian country fifty years earlier.

The gallant Aurora
pushing through the ice floes.

1. The Steam Yacht *Aurora* of the Imperial Trans-Antarctic Expedition's Ross Sea Party,

2. Members of the Ross Sea Party land stores in early 1915.

3. Climbing from the sea ice to the Great Barrier, summer 1916. The figure in the foreground is Aeneas Mackintosh, leader of the Ross Sea Party.

4. The *Aurora* photographed during her ten-month drift trapped in the ice floes. The footprints of the photographer can be seen leading from the ship's side.

5. Sir Ernest Shackleton setting out to make a last search for Aeneas Mackintosh and Victor Hayward, January 1917.

6. *Left*: The stern-post of *Aurora* showing the colossal damage wrought on 21 July 1915, when the sea ice nipped her and smashed her 4½-ton rudder beyond repair.

7. *Right*: *Aurora* during her emergency refit in New Zealand, April–December 1916.

8. The surviving members of the Ross Sea Party and their saviours on board *Aurora*, mid-January 1917. Left to right: Jack, Stevens, Richards, Wild, Gaze, Joyce, Cope, Shackleton and J.K. Davis.

9. The 'mystery ship', *PQ-61*. On 26 September 1917, the *PQ-61* engaged and sank enemy submarine *UC-33*, earning the DSO for her captain, Frank Worsley, and the DSC for First Lieutenant Stenhouse.

10. Officers and men of the Syren Flotilla patrolling Lake Onega in 1919.

11. RRS *Discovery*, under full sail. Despite Stenhouse's admiration of her sailing qualities, the *Discovery*'s tendency to roll rendered her wholly inadequate for the purposes of the expedition and ultimately led to her being replaced.

12. Officers and scientific staff of the National Oceanographic Expedition of 1925–7, on board the RRS *Discovery*, 1924. Stenhouse (in civilian clothes) is seated between First Officer W.H. O'Connor and the expedition's Chief Scientific Officer, Stanley Kemp. The ship's surgeon, Dr E.H. Marshall, stands behind Stenhouse's right shoulder and Chief Zoologist, Alister Hardy, is on Kemp's left.

13. Stenhouse on the bridge of RRS *Discovery* during the National Oceanographic Expedition, 1925–7.

14. On board the *Discovery*, running the easting down to the Cape, December 1925.

15. Stenhouse and his bride, Gladys, on their wedding day, 2 October 1923. Gladys was the widow of Stenhouse's erstwhile commander and friend, Aeneas Mackintosh.

16. One of the huts inhabited by the members of Treasure Recovery Ltd, during their sojourn on Cocos Island, September–October 1934.

17. Stenhouse, with his back to the camera, and other members of the treasure-hunting expedition on Cocos Island, 1934.

18. *Left*: Frank and Jean Worsley photographed around the time of the Cocos Island expedition.

19. *Right*: Stenhouse on board HMS *Lucia*, standing next to an unexploded charge brought up from one of the wrecks littering Massawa harbour, August 1941.

20. Probably the last studio photograph of Stenhouse, taken in Bedford in 1940.

21. Stenhouse's medals and decorations, including among others: the Distinguished Service Order, the Order of the British Empire, the Distinguished Service Cross, the Great War Victory Medal with oak leaf for a Mention in Despatches, the Polar Medal, the Reserve Decoration and the French Croix de Guerre.

Despite his frustration with the inefficiency of the railway network, Stenhouse thrived on the atmosphere and he made the most of every opportunity to enjoy life to the full, caring little for the dangers which lurked in every wood and behind every corner. Typically, during a stop at Imandra, he welcomed the chance to take a ride across the lake in a two-horse sleigh, in the company of a mysterious Russian lady. 'Good fun driving in dark,' he noted, 'on our return wind sprang up with heavy drift. Cold travelling into wind. Northern Lights came out throwing shafts of green light which lit up the entire country like moonlight. Crossing track revolver shot passed close to us; guard unable [to] detect person who fired.'[25] The combination of the eerie, flickering lights of the aurora borealis, the sleigh-ride and the frisson of danger made a lasting impression on him. In later years, he made much of this incident, describing to the officers of his next naval command the 'beautiful Russian refugee and her doctor husband fleeing from the forces of anarchy, famine and pestilence among the primitive tribes of the outlands'.[26] A few days later, in an episode reminiscent of the harum-scarum bravado of a picaresque novel, Stenhouse dined with Captain Daidoff, the White Russian commander of a local garrison and its outposts. 'Discussing revolvers,' he later scribbled in his diary. 'Daidoff fired his pistol at a chair held at [the] end of table by his Lieutenant!'[27] Fortunately, the chair was the only casualty of this vodka-fuelled antic.

But lawlessness and recklessness were not the only characteristics of a society living on the edge of anarchy and internecine barbarism. On a number of occasions, as he passed through the towns and villages south of Murmansk, Stenhouse saw the local inhabitants attempting to distract themselves from the dangers that surrounded them. Thousands of miles from home, far, even, from the relative comfort and security of Murmansk, he quickly showed himself willing both to divert himself and to help his hosts stem the tide of doubt, depression and uncertainty that threatened to overwhelm them. When observing the life of the British troops in Russia, *The Times*' correspondent remarked that 'any monotony, the concomitant of loneliness, is dispelled by skiing, tobogganing, and other sports'.[28] In Kem, the welcome diversion took the slightly surreal form of a country dance:

Dined at officers' mess; met two Russian ladies, one from Novgorod and one from Petrograd and the Russian Captain of the Port (Polybin). Afterwards went to concert given by party of 'Yorks'; supper then to dance where 'ladies' were masked and dressed in most weird rig-outs. All danced a sort of mixed waltz and [sang?] with great solemnity to accompaniment of melodeon and at times the piano played by British officers which music seemed to throw them out of time. One young girl, who is the leading lady in the local plays, was dressed as a Spanish Senorita and was more Spanish than Russian in her appearance and very nice too![29]

For Stenhouse and for the other soldiers, sailors and airmen of the British Expeditionary Force, such frolics provided a welcome break from the monotony of their everyday existence. And, when not dancing or flirting with the local girls, they could find some solace in the thought that they would soon return home. The people of occupied North Russia, on the other hand, feared that an Allied retreat would leave them to the wrath of the victorious Bolesheviks and, as 'collaborators', they could hope for little mercy. On his return to England early in 1919, Shackleton had done his best to highlight their plight, stating that 'It should be remembered that there are nearly half a million people who threw in their lot with us originally against the Germans, and since against the Bolshevist menace. It is thus not merely a question of saving our own troops, but a moral obligation to civilization.'[30] But, with each passing month, a prolongation of the Allied presence seemed increasingly unlikely, and a mass withdrawal more imminent. Small wonder, then, that the populace should snatch whatever pleasure or entertainment their circumstances afforded and that their laughter and gaiety should sometimes seem strangely brittle.

Whatever his pleasure in his surroundings, Stenhouse's raison d'être in Russia was, of course, his skill in operating in sub-zero temperatures and his most important job the successful transmission of this expertise to the officers and men of the BEF. Having already lectured in Murmansk, he now began the process of disseminating his knowledge further afield, travelling throughout January 1919 to towns such as Kem, Popoff and Soroka to give instruction in sledging and camping. Once his pupils had attained some degree of proficiency, they would then be inspected by General Price, who commanded the southern front.

Stenhouse left Soroka on 17 January and immediately joined a caravan of thirty-four horse-drawn sledges bound for Sumski Posad, 28 miles to the east:

We travelled over beaten trail (good winter road) skirting the shores of the White Sea, at times crossing inlets. Arrived at Sumski Posad 10 p.m., having stopped at one village for tea, where we adjourned to dance in small house filled with people. Unloaded sledges of provisions, at shed attached to partially inhabited monastery. The sledges driven by Russkis, men and girls, then proceeded to their home villages about 12 miles further. The ponies are wonderful little beasts; pulled more than their own weight – some pulling 1,000lb. They had come into Soroka the previous day. The girls too are remarkably fit and strong; they run or walk by their horses over the track when the going is hard.[31]

Since the runners of the sledges in which they travelled were spaced only 2ft apart, with much wider bodies on top, the vehicles proved inherently unstable and prone to overturn. Describing this mode of travel to a friend, Worsley told him, 'when the sledge goes over every ¼ mile or so, it sort of leans on its elbow, looks at you pensively, and then goes on again. Occasionally tho' it goes right over and has to be righted and the occupants in their sleeping bags are rolled back into the sledge by the driver before proceeding.'[32] Fortunately, the thick reindeer sleeping bags and the hay with which the sledges were packed meant that injuries occurred only rarely and, since many of the sledges had been designed to carry two passengers as well as the driver, the occupants could enjoy a relatively comfortable and sociable ride. 'On a fine day with no head wind and temperature not too far below zero,' Worsley recounted, 'you sit up and take notice in your bag, occasionally fingering your revolver to make sure it's ready and pass your time in improving conversation with each other and the driver . . . otherwise you yell Tallyho! . . . and sing ribald or otherwise songs and sailor shanties in more or less unison.'[33]

The move eastwards came not a moment too soon. On 19 January, Ironside's position at Shenkursk, 190 miles south of Archangel, buckled in the face of a sustained Bolshevik attack, forcing him to retreat. As the British forces reeled, Maynard immediately agreed to transfer two infantry battalions and a machine-gun company to Archangel. Now, the training that Stenhouse and his friends had been giving to the British troops came into its own as 2,000 men made their way through the wild and desolate terrain that stretched between Soroka and Archangel.

As part of this critically important troop movement, in early February, Stenhouse took responsibility for the transportation of a shipment of sledges, equipment, horses and 150 huskies brought from North Canada. He discovered, however, that despite their training, the tight-knit mobile columns often broke down. Travelling in parties not exceeding 300, the soldiers would start with their pony or dog-sledges amid much noise and enthusiasm, but many soon became exhausted. The fittest charged ahead while the weaker men lagged further and further behind, forcing Stenhouse to turn back 'with fast horses to pick up the stragglers which had been formed into a cripples' column and were probably having a rough time as the going was hard through the woods and the horses played out. We had cold drive back to Soochaje [sic] . . . where the track meets and crosses the sea ice . . . and the wind was howling with drift from NE.'[34] Despite these problems, the transfer of 2,000 men by land, plus another 300 or so by ice-breaker, had been completed by early March; all arrived safely with only a small number of minor frostbite cases.

With the completion of this operation, Stenhouse's involvement in these often gruelling and occasionally depressing expeditions drew to a close. The successful transfer of a substantial contingent of troops in severe Arctic conditions owed much to his professionalism and to that of his Antarctic companions. This success was further reinforced by the Allied capture of Segeja in mid-February: an operation in which the troops used their winter training for the first time in offensive operations. But, so far, Stenhouse's contribution to the campaign against Bolshevism had been limited to the sidelines; now the plans being laid by General Maynard would present him with an opportunity to step into the centre of the action. And he would no longer be expected to operate on sledges or from railcars; instead, he would be fighting in his natural element: water.

THE SYREN FLOTILLA

On 3 March 1919, for the first time in more than three months, the temperature at Murmansk rose above zero and the daylight hours began rapidly to expand. Snow continued to dominate the landscape and, in the harbour, the *Glory* and the *Askold* still looked like colossal ice-sculptures, their great gun barrels glittering with hoarfrost, but the annual thaw lay just over the horizon. The town's population, both military and civilian, looked forward with keen anticipation to the days when the forests would shed their pall of snow and the innumerable rivers and streams would break their icy bonds once again to boil and seethe along their rock-strewn courses. But General Maynard viewed the coming of the Arctic spring uneasily. He knew that it would bring its own problems; in particular, the retreat of the snows would leave great expanses of thick mud and slush, making troop movements incredibly difficult, while the increased warmth would bring clouds of mosquitoes. If he wanted to push his front-line further south he must do so immediately.

Such an offensive would produce a number of benefits. Firstly, it would extend the hinterland in which the Allied recruiting parties could operate. With the support of the town's Council, for some months the Allies had been enforcing universal conscription in the Murmansk area, but the occupation of additional territory would provide a wider field of operations. The capture of the towns of Povynetz and Medvyejya Gora, on the northern rim of Lake Onega and some 400 miles from Maynard's headquarters, would also help to stabilise his front-line and act as a firmer bulwark against Bolshevik progress northwards. The thought of impending action might also help to stem the growing tide of dissatisfaction and resentment among the troops. The Allied governments' indecision regarding their long-term policy in Russia had resulted in growing unrest in the barracks. Many of the troops considered Russia a backwater in which, despite the end of the wider war, they might be left to rot for months. Few saw the point of their continued presence, and the long winter months of twilight and the determined and highly professional efforts of the Bolshevik propagandists had further sapped their fighting spirit. Lastly, and perhaps most important of all, a campaign might serve to divert the enemy's attention from General Ironside's increasingly precarious position at Archangel.

Of greatest moment to Stenhouse was the fact that the Bolsheviks possessed a flotilla of gunboats currently trapped in the ice of Lake Onega; with the oncoming thaw, these vessels would be released to support land-based troops. Only by capturing the northern shore of Lake Onega and by launching his own armed flotilla could Maynard hope to interfere with such operations; if his forces reached the lake before the thaw they might even succeed in capturing the ice-locked enemy shipping. Initially, however, Lake Onega could only be viewed as a longer-term objective. In the first instance the smaller lakes, Vigozero and Segozero, would have to be captured and then patrolled. Though tactically sound, these plans for waterborne operations presented Maynard's commanders with a number of extremely challenging logistical problems, not least the identification, repair and transportation of suitable vessels, hundreds of miles to the southern front. Such an exercise would have to be managed by a man possessed of considerable logistical skills, knowledge of naval warfare and expertise in the navigation of icebound channels. It did not take Maynard long to identify the ideal candidate.

As commander of what would come to be known as the 'Syren Flotilla', Stenhouse's first job was to establish the size and condition of his squadron. Fortunately, in undertaking this work, he benefited from the services of another seasoned polar explorer, John Mather, who had served as a petty officer on Scott's *Terra Nova*. Mather was a man after Stenhouse's own heart. Nine years earlier, as a junior member of the RNVR, he had helped to load the *Terra Nova* at London's West India Docks. Like Stenhouse, he had been overwhelmed by an urge to join an Antarctic expedition and Captain Scott, who always looked favourably on men from the senior service, had accepted his application. On the expedition Mather had amply demonstrated his organisational capabilities and had often undertaken secretarial and administrative work, at which he excelled. During the war, he had served with distinction in the Royal Navy but, having sailed to Murmansk at the beginning of April 1919, he shed his Navy uniform in favour of army khaki – serving as a major with the Royal Engineers. As the flotilla's Chief Administrative Officer, and Stenhouse's second-in-command, his job would be to help solve the enormous logistical problems attaching to the identification and transfer of suitable boats. He began by conducting a survey of all the available vessels and, having ferreted among the piers and warehouses of Murmansk and the surrounding area, he was soon able to deliver his report. It made distinctly gloomy reading.

The landscape astride the Russian–Finnish border is dominated by rivers and lakes and, anticipating the probability of lake operations, Maynard's force had been provided with a number of motor launches. But these had been expected to operate on the small northern lakes; if operations on the 160-mile-long Lake Onega became practicable, the available boats would be wholly inadequate. Even more worrying than the boats' inherent unsuitability for the role now intended for them was their state of disrepair. Most of them had lain redundant and neglected on the quays at Murmansk for months; they had been boarded over to protect them from the ravages of the Arctic winter but they now mouldered beneath a foot and more of snow. Fortunately, once they had been scraped clean, it became clear that the hulls had not suffered too severely; the engines, on the other hand, 'were very bad. Large numbers of parts were missing and in one or two cases only one cylinder was left out of a four cylinder engine.'[1]

After careful consideration of the available boats, Stenhouse and Mather eventually opted for three American-built submarine chasers. Two measured 72ft long by 13ft 6in across the beam and were powered by three 270hp Duisenberg engines, giving a nominal speed of 28 knots. The third was 60ft long by 12ft with three 200hp Van Blerck engines, capable of 26 knots. In addition to these three boats stored at Murmansk, they chose two 35ft English-built open motorboats. One of these had been found at the Kola base while the other, minus its engine, lay alongside the American boats. As their hulls were cleaned and then caulked and painted, Stenhouse learned that the senior US naval officer in Russia, Admiral McCulley, had also decided to lend two motorboats for lake operations: one from his flagship, the USS *Yankee*, and another from the USS *Galveston*. McCulley's only condition was that these two boats should operate under the independent command of a US Navy lieutenant named Woodward. Finally, a 35ft high-speed motor launch from the yacht *Josephine* brought the total complement of Commodore Stenhouse's flotilla up to eight vessels. The size and weight of the enemy's squadron remained unknown.

On 15 April, Stenhouse and Mather attended a 'Q' Conference at Maynard's headquarters and presented their findings. In particular, they emphasised the pressing need for new boats from England, preferably ones better suited to the kind of work that the Syren Flotilla would be expected to undertake; for properly trained naval personnel; for 3-pounder Hotchkiss guns for each of the boats; and, most optimistic of all, for a fully equipped motor-repair shop to be manned by skilled mechanics under an engineer officer. They left the conference with the understanding that 'all these would be obtained as soon as possible',[2] though, ominously, they received no indication as to when 'as soon as possible' might be. In fairness to Maynard, his hands were effectively tied by his superiors at home, who had proved consistently that they could resist even his most pressing demands for essential supplies and men. The North Russian venture had always been viewed as a sideshow at best, and, at worst, as an expensive folly more likely to generate long-lasting international rifts than to strangle Bolshevism in its cradle. Even with the defeat of Germany, the western governments showed little inclination to commit further resources to the campaign and, as early as January, Shackleton had stated that 'this show will peter out as it is not popular at home'.[3]

In the meantime, the Allied advance to the south of Murmansk was progressing well. By mid-April, an international body of troops under Brigadier-General Price had passed Urosozero on the eastern shore of Lake Undozero, and Stenhouse could expect his flotilla to be called upon at any time. Reassuringly, while he waited, his force continued to grow. On the 19th, an artillery officer, Captain H.F. Littledale, joined the flotilla's staff and, the following day, the new machine-gun officer, Captain R.J. Cholmeley MC, arrived. The promised naval ratings remained conspicuous by their absence, but at least the White Russians had contributed twenty marine cadets under the command of Lieutenant Shulgin and Sub-Lieutenant Annin. Stenhouse wouldn't necessarily have seen these reinforcements as an unmixed blessing. Overall, he had little liking for or sympathy with the Russians – even those who had chosen to fight with the Allies; he preferred the Finns, whom he thought a 'good class of men and higher standard than Russkis'.[4] But it had always been part of the Allies' longer-term strategy to encourage the Russians to take the lead in resisting Bolshevism and this plan held equally true for the Syren Flotilla – whether Stenhouse liked it or not. In fact, the Russian officers chosen to join his command soon proved to be competent and useful and Shulgin, who knew the area, was immediately despatched down the line to reconnoitre and find the best place for launching the boats on to the twin lakes. At first, he hoped that it might be possible to lower them from a railway bridge into the Segeja river, but the water near the bridge tumbled with such violence through a series of rapids that the idea had to be abandoned. Shulgin recommended instead that the light railway between Urosozero and the upper end of the Segeja should be utilised; the boats could then be navigated downriver into Lake Segozero. The boats intended for Lake Vigozero, meanwhile, would have to be detrained at a siding and then placed on skids to be dragged the short distance to the river which drained into that lake.

While Shulgin formulated these plans, work continued on preparing the motorboats for their new role. Despite the promises made at the 'Q' conference, it soon transpired that no Hotchkiss 3-pounders would be made available to the flotilla. Instead eight Russian-made 37mm guns were allocated for its use – but these guns lacked both ammunition and

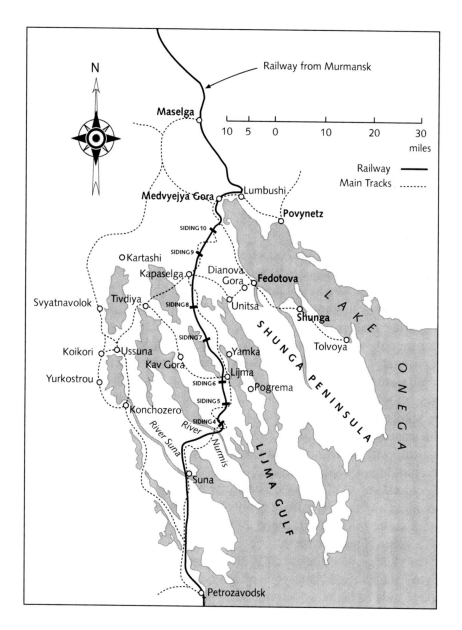

N

Railway from Murmansk

Maselga

10 5 0   10   20   30
miles

Railway ———
Main Tracks - - - - -

Lumbushi

Medvyejya Gora

Povynetz

SIDING 10

SIDING 9

Kartashi

Kapaselga

Dianova
Gora

Fedotova

Svyatnavolok

Tivdiya

SIDING 8

Unitsa

LAKE

Shunga

SIDING 7

Tolvoya

Koikori

Ussuna

Yamka

SHUNGA PENINSULA

ONEGA

Yurkostrou

Kav Gora

Lijma

SIDING 6

Pogrema

Konchozero

SIDING 5

SIDING 4

River Suna

River Nurmis

LIJMA GULF

Suna

Petrozavodsk

Map 3. Lake Onega, 1919.

sights. As ever, necessity proved the mother of invention and engineers at the ordnance workshops in Murmansk started work on designing sights based on those normally used on naval 3-pounders. At the same time, a small supply of ammunition was unearthed at the Russian naval base at Alexandrovsk.

Stenhouse started on the now-familiar railway journey south on 25 April, taking with him the two American submarine chasers with their crews and the *Wahine*, as the yacht from the *Josephine* was now known. The other boats would follow on 5 May, in the charge of Mather. By the time of his departure, Medvyejya Gora lay well within General Price's sights and the original intention of launching the motorboats on to the smaller northern lakes was overtaken by the now practical proposition of launching them straight into Lake Onega. As the Allied advance continued, Stenhouse and his boats followed on the heels of the combat troops, never far from the fighting.

By 11 May, both trains had arrived at Siding 19 on the north-eastern edge of Lake Segozero. While General Price prepared for the attack on Medvyejya Gora by conducting frontal assaults on the intervening trenches and dugouts, Stenhouse and his officers concentrated on preparing their men for their new duties. The American and Russian contingents had been joined on 5 May by the long overdue British personnel – but not the promised naval ratings. Instead, the British boats would be manned by artillerymen from the 420th Field Battery, none of whom had the slightest experience in waterborne operations. At Siding 19 and, a little later, at Maselga a few miles further south, the accustomed stillness of the forests, seldom disturbed by anything but the cawing of crows and the howling of wolves, was shattered by the barking of orders, the dull thud of exploding hand grenades and the crackle of small-arms fire as junior officers instructed their men in bombing and musketry. As a result, by the time they received orders to move closer to the front, the men of the Syren Flotilla were in a much better state of preparedness.

On 19 May, Stenhouse and Mather joined Price in an attempt to find a river which their maps showed to be close to the railway line. If the boats could be launched into this river they might be used to support the planned assault on Medvyejya Gora. To their disappointment, they could find no river that would enable them to put their plans into operation but, for Stenhouse, the reconnaissance was not completely wasted as he found himself on the very fringes of a violent confrontation between Allied and Bolshevik patrols near Lumbushi, to the north-west of Povynetz. Fighting in similar conditions on the Archangel front, Worsley described the nature of such skirmishes:

The forest fighting in the snow was often very exciting. You would slide along on skis in and out thro' the trees as silently as possible, giving orders by signs and all eyes [open] for Bolos. We nearly always managed to spot them as soon or before they spotted us, but it used to make you jump when the first thing you knew was the rattle of their machine guns and bullets singing round your ears like mad wasps. It didn't take over a second to drop in the snow and flatten down then get to work with our Lewis Guns and rifles. . . . Fortunately the Bolo always fired just too high and our people were seldom hurt and more rarely any killed at this game, tho' you could see the trees riddled, gouged and splintered by their bullets about 2 to 3 feet above your head as you lay potting at them.[5]

At the beginning of April, *The Times* correspondent in Murmansk had commented that hand-to-hand fighting with the Bolsheviks added a 'spice of adventure' to the soldiers' lives. For all its glibness, in Stenhouse's case, the comment did come close to the truth and, welcoming any opportunity to close with the enemy, the next day he and Mather again went forward, determined to watch the beginning of the attack on Medvyejya Gora.

Under their observation, the Slavo-British Legion conducted a wide, sweeping movement on the Allied right, clearing the Bolshevik defenders from the village of Ostreche, 7 miles north-west of Lumbushi, before attacking Koldodari. On the left flank, a company of the Middlesex Regiment took Lumbushi after a fierce fire-fight, and in the centre British and Serbian troops surged towards Medvyejya Gora, supported by artillery fire from French field guns mounted on railway trucks. The Bolsheviks fought tenaciously but, by the end of 21 May, the town lay in British hands.

Frustratingly, Stenhouse's squadron had been unable to play an active part in the attack. Unable to find a navigable river, Stenhouse had hoped to bring his boats to the lakeside by railway. But the town's defenders had blown a wide hole in a railway bridge 2 miles from the lake. Now, rather than wait for the bridge to be repaired, he ordered that some of the surrounding fir trees be felled; these were then stripped of their branches and turned into giant rollers on which the boats were dragged the last few miles to the banks of the Lumbushi river. Once launched on to the river, they could be navigated to Lake Onega itself. Here work started on the engine of one of the two larger American-built submarine chasers, which Stenhouse had earmarked as his flagship and which, looking forward to the fear he intended to strike into the hearts of the Bolshevik mariners, he now renamed the *Jolly Roger*.

His plans nearly ended in disaster when, on 28 May, a serious forest fire erupted close to the siding where the boats rested prior to the final stage of their journey. Earlier in the year Stenhouse had criticised the endemic carelessness which, he predicted, would lead to just such an accident, commenting that 'Ground fires have wrought amongst the trees; engines' stacks are insufficiently guarded and wood embers fly in showers into the woods'.[6] Now, the flames danced and leapt among the pine and spruce trees, causing the snow that still clung to their roots to melt and then sizzle with the heat. With every passing minute, the yellow tongues of flame advanced closer to the railway trucks which lay immobile, packed with ammunition and with fuel for the boat motors. The air was filled with the crackling of the fire, strident orders being shouted by the officers and NCOs and by the swish and thwack of clothing and sacks as the troops tried to beat back the flames. A catastrophic explosion seemed imminent but, at last, the railway engineers managed to light the firebox of the engine at the head of the train and the trucks could be moved half a mile, to a safe place down the line. It had been a close-run thing.

To Stenhouse's practised eye it must have been immediately obvious that the newly captured Medvyejya Gora would make an excellent base from which to operate. The Bolshevik withdrawal had been so precipitate that they had destroyed very little. The village offered accommodation for upwards of 2,000 men with good flat ground for more tents, as required. The railway yards and sidings were spacious and there was ample ground nearby to serve as a supply depot. Most important of all, an excellent harbour lay only half a mile east of the village, guarded by a quay along which the railway lines extended. Overall, the protection offered to his small flotilla seemed near perfect. Admittedly, the lack of either a railway or road link to Povynetz would be a disadvantage but, so long as they held the Bolshevik flotilla in check, water transport would suffice. The gradually shelving foreshore and firm beaches even meant that the area would make a perfect spot from which to operate the seaplanes which had been promised from HMS *Nairana*. Given recent experiences with supplies and equipment, however, the provision of the seaplanes seemed highly improbable. As well as its operational suitability, the area around Lake Onega had other attractions. The countryside bore a distinct resemblance to the Highlands of Scotland, with the mirror-like lake reflecting beautiful hills clad in greenery, and mile upon mile of tall firs. The streams which poured into the lake teemed with trout and the richness of the alluvial soil meant that the soldiers could start growing cabbage and cress to supplement their rations.

Over the next few days, as the Allied land forces mounted operations against the local villages still in Bolshevik hands, the Syren Flotilla's boats were brought forward to the shore and launched, one by one. First, the two US Navy vessels, *Atlanta* and *Georgia*, slid into the water, followed soon afterwards by the two Southampton-built open motorboats and the *Wahine*.

Stenhouse with Captain Littledale and Lieutenant Woodward established a patrol on the lake as far as Shunga and Povynetz and, almost immediately, the *Georgia* exchanged shots with a Bolshevik steamer off Fedotova, proving beyond a shadow of a doubt that ice no longer presented any serious bar to navigation. The knowledge that the enemy could now conduct lake operations spurred the Allies to develop better defences at the lake's northern end. In particular, they positioned artillery pieces overlooking the navigable river passage into Lake Onega and laid plans for mine-laying along certain stretches of the lake – plans they abandoned only when it became clear that no mines would be made available to them.

On 4 June the White Russians established an advance HQ at Shunga under Captain Daidoff (the same Daidoff whose impromptu pistol practice had amazed Stenhouse a few months earlier) and the flotilla now became essential for keeping Shunga supplied with rations and ammunition and for supporting its garrison against Bolshevik counter-attacks. In the early hours of the 5th, the Bolsheviks launched a major assault, intended to recapture the town. Fortunately, Stenhouse had foreseen the likelihood of such an attempt and he had ordered Mather to reinforce Daidoff with four of the flotilla's boats. Reporting back a few days later, Mather told him, 'At 0350 we were awakened at the farm by the sound of a heavy bombardment, and at the same time 2/Lt Bunting called us up, having just returned with more ammunition from Medvyejya Gora. I therefore gave orders for all hands to be called and to man the boats for immediate action, and awaited news from Capt Daidoff.'[7] The news, when it came, was not good: the Bolsheviks had landed 300 Red Finns who were now pushing in Daidoff's pickets, supported by shrapnel and high explosive shells fired from four steamers. It appeared that the steamers were attempting to land troops behind Allied lines – a move which must be defeated at all costs, if the Allied position was to be maintained. Mather immediately launched his squadron hoping to engage the enemy steamers and, if possible, force them to withdraw. By 7.20 a.m., the Syren Flotilla was in action. The enemy steamers 'formed into line ahead,' Mather remembered:

> . . . presenting their starboard guns to us [they] opened fire, abandoning the bombardment of the land positions. *Wahine* and No. 9 continued to approach, zigzagging continuously as the range decreased. The first round from the Bolsheviks fell several hundred yards over, and No. 9 opened fire with her 37mm gun, but her shots fell very short, the extreme range of this gun being some 3,500yds. The enemy shortly got the range and shots began to fall all around the two boats, but very few exploded on hitting the water, and none hit the boats though one fell within 30ft of No. 9 and another ricocheted over *Wahine*.[8]

At this critical moment, the *Wahine*'s engines shuddered to a halt and, with shots falling all around her, the motorboat lay wallowing in the swell, helpless.

While his Polish mechanic struggled desperately to restart the engines, Mather signalled to motorboat No. 9 to advise Lieutenant Shulgin that the *Wahine* must disengage. But Shulgin misinterpreted the signal and, instead of going to the crippled vessel's aid, No. 9 turned towards the north and began to retreat, at full speed. At last, the *Wahine*'s engines spluttered reluctantly into life, with two cylinders missing. Smelling blood, one of the Bolshevik steamers now hauled out of line and began to approach. As she gained on the limping *Wahine*, Mather examined his pursuer and decided on his tactics:

> It could be seen that the guns on these ships were mounted aft and that they could not fire ahead, so I intended to wait for her and then rake her with machine guns. However my engines stopped again and resisted all attempts to restart, and the enemy turned and opened fire at approximately 3,000yd, the other ships maintaining their fire from about 5,000yd. A fog bank was seen approaching rapidly from the north east, and I therefore gave the mechanic permission to change the sparking plug; there not having been time to do so previously. . . . Seeing us stopped the enemy began to fire shrapnel, and the first burst immediately overhead. Almost at once however the fog closed down and after a few more rounds of shrapnel the firing ceased. Some five minutes later the repairs were effected and I ordered the boat back to Shunga.[9]

The operation had been successful in that it diverted the enemy steamers from their bombardment of Daidoff's imperilled land forces and eventually persuaded the Bolshevik commanders to abandon their attempted landings. But it had nearly ended in disaster with the narrowly avoided loss of one of the flotilla's boats and, in reading Mather's report, Stenhouse must have entertained grave reservations regarding his squadron's fitness for the purpose assigned to it.

By 6 June, the Allies controlled the entire Shunga Peninsula. Enemy craft continued to be sighted frequently and exchanges of fire remained common but, by now, the rickety flotilla enjoyed the added protection of air cover. Despite gloomy prognostications, the promised Fairey and Short seaplanes had arrived at Medvyejya Gora, transported by rail from Murmansk. Within two days of their arrival, the aeroplanes proved their worth by helping to repel a Bolshevik reconnaissance which threatened Medvyejya Gora. The Bolsheviks had been taken completely by surprise by the appearance of the aircraft and their surprise turned to terror when their pursuers began to drop bombs. None of the missiles hit their targets, but the Bolshevik boats had been forced to retreat in disarray, fleeing in a zigzag course down the lake while their opponents hooted at them and cheered the pilots of the RAF.

Despite her early arrival at Lake Onega, Stenhouse's flagship, the *Jolly Roger*, could not be floated until 6 June, it being found necessary to lay underwater rails to launch her. Triple-engined and triple-screwed, the *Jolly Roger* was the most sophisticated of all the flotilla's vessels, carrying wireless, a naval 3-pounder and several machine guns. But, over the next few weeks, she would come to epitomise the faults of the flotilla as a whole and prove herself the most temperamental of all Stenhouse's charges – no mean feat given that practically all the members of the flotilla broke down with clockwork regularity.

The unreliability of the *Jolly Roger* proved particularly problematic since she was the only boat capable of operating any distance from Medvyejya Gora. On 11 June, during her trials, she bombarded enemy positions at Fedotova and Dianova Gora, scattering a Bolshevik working party attempting to repair damage to Fedotova Bridge, but she immediately developed trouble with the mounting for her 3-pounder and with her reversing gear, and struggled back to base on her midship engine alone: a performance that hardly boded well for the future. On 16 June, further trials took place with a replacement gearbox and she achieved a satisfactory speed of 14 knots on only one engine. But, two days later, during combined operations against Fedotova, she again developed problems with her gun mounting and was forced to return to base for repairs. Despite these teething troubles, on the 20th she achieved a speed of 26 knots on all three engines and, for the next week, Stenhouse employed her in patrolling as far as Rietchnoe. On 3 July, he took her on a long reconnaissance and effected a landing at Pale Ostrov. Not long afterwards, he encountered two enemy vessels off the island of Meg Ostrov and immediately engaged them, spending an hour and a half trading shots with the Bolshevik vessels until the weather began to close in and forced them to disengage.

The *Jolly Roger*'s troubled career came to a close a few days later. On 8 July, she sailed under Captain Littledale's command, intending to visit Shunga prior to making an extended sweep down the lake. Twenty minutes after starting, just as she reached the southern end of Navolok Point, a violent explosion devastated the vessel's fuel room, blowing her half-deck clean over the side and setting her on fire. Initially, Littledale thought that an enemy ship had crept up on him unawares and had succeeded in planting a high explosive shell in his vessel's side. But there were no enemy boats in the vicinity and it appeared that the explosion was just the latest in the

Jolly Roger's ever-lengthening list of mechanical failures. With his small craft spewing forth flames and black smoke, Littledale turned her bows towards the shore. But, taking in water and settling fast, the crippled vessel had little hope of getting so far. With ¾ mile still to go, her engines shuddered to a halt and Littledale ordered his crew to abandon ship. Still smoking, the *Jolly Roger* gradually settled and then sank beneath the surface of the lake, grey now and smooth as a tarnished silver tea tray. She took the bodies of five crewmen with her.

The sinking of the *Jolly Roger* marked the end of Stenhouse's command of the Syren Flotilla. It was a sad note upon which to end his association with a fighting force which he and Mather had managed to form from such unpromising material, but he found that he had little choice in the matter. His oft-ignored requests for a contingent of professional sailors and suitable boats now bore unexpected fruit. On the very day after the loss of the flotilla's flagship, HMS *War Wolf* dropped anchor in Murmansk harbour. She carried on board fourteen RNR lieutenants, twenty-four chief petty officers, twelve leading seamen and eighty-four able seamen, all under the command of a regular Royal Navy officer, Commander Robert Curteis. The new arrivals also brought with them a squadron of twelve motorboats, though, like the vessels they were meant to replace, these boats were better suited to work on the smaller northern lakes than the inland sea upon which they would now be expected to operate. With the exception of the Russians under Shulgin and Annin, the founding members of the Syren Lake Flotilla would now be dispersed.

Over the next few days, Stenhouse completed the transfer of his command to Curteis, discussing with him the situation on Lake Onega and assessing opportunities for further operations. As the two men pored over maps and studied inventories of equipment, Curteis's face fell. 'Before leaving England,' he later reported, 'I made repeated applications to the War Office . . . for a travelling workshop lorry, similar to those supplied to the RAF, to effect the necessary repairs to the motors. I was informed this was unnecessary, as I should find a completely equipped workshop on the Lake. This was not the case, there being no facilities for repair work at Medvyejya Gora whatever.'[10] Listening to such complaints, Stenhouse must have struggled to hide a wry smile from his superior officer. Over the previous three months he and Mather had travelled the length and breadth of the Kola Peninsula and the surrounding country, searching not only for workshop equipment but for boats, armaments, ammunition and men possessing the bare minimum of knowledge for waterborne operations against an increasingly determined and confident opponent. They had also had to invent means by which to transport their precious boats the 400 miles from Murmansk to Lake

Onega through countryside still invested by enemy troops. None knew better that Curteis had good cause for complaint; but in comparison with the situation which they had inherited, his position seemed quite comfortable: he commanded a force of trained men, his supply route was relatively secure and, with the support of RAF seaplanes, the Syren Flotilla had established control of Lake Onega. Overall, Stenhouse could be very well satisfied with what he had achieved. But, like Worsley, who lost command of the gunboat HMS *Cricket* at just the same time, he might also have thought the decision 'a bit hard on us fellows that have been out all the winter, getting done out of it, when there's a good chance of a general advance'.[11]

The situation did have a bright side. Shortly after Curteis's arrival, Stenhouse received orders to proceed to that other bulwark of Allied intervention in Russia: Archangel. Worsley had been stationed there for most of the eight or so months that the friends had been in the Arctic, working with the Army developing transport systems and flying columns and, more recently, patrolling the Dvina river in the *Cricket*. The prospect of a reunion filled both men with the hope that they might be given an opportunity to re-live the glory days of their Q-ship service. But it was not to be. Although Worsley remembered that they enjoyed 'a few more adventures and skirmishes which afforded us plenty of fun with our cheery friends in the Army',[12] in July the Allied command had finally decided to evacuate its troops from Russia and any opportunities for large-scale operations rapidly petered out. By the middle of October the staged withdrawal, conducted under the watchful eye of General Sir Henry Rawlinson, had been completed, and Stenhouse's war was over.

In later years, General Maynard would robustly defend the Allied intervention in Russia: 'To my mind,' he stated in his account of the expedition, 'our action at Murmansk in common with that in other parts of Russia can give rise to no feeling of self-reproach, and to only one regret – namely, that the help we gave fell short of that required to throttle in its infancy the noisome beast of Bolshevism.'[13] By and large, Stenhouse would have agreed with this summary and, unlike the vast majority of his countrymen, he both enjoyed his time in Russia and looked back upon it as something of a highlight in his life. In reality, however, except for the small-scale benefits accrued from the distraction of German forces in the autumn of 1918, the effects of the Allied occupation had been almost wholly detrimental. The Allies had clearly shown that they would have no truck with Lenin's government but they had also revealed that they had no appetite for sustained and active opposition, thereby weakening their own position and sowing the seed for future confrontation. More cruelly, after the evacuation, those who had allied themselves to the western forces, whether voluntarily or by force of circumstance, now became the victims of Communist reprisals. And, finally, by helping, albeit temporarily, to crystallise anti-Bolshevik feeling, the Allies contributed to the terrible civil war that would now ravage post-Tsarist Russia. In the eyes of any objective observer, the Murmansk venture had been a fiasco.

DISCOVERY

Whatever the long-term repercussions of his last campaign, by most people's standards Stenhouse had had a good war. It had been comparatively short; he had come through it unscathed; and, most important of all, it had been packed with the action and adventure he so craved. It had also brought him significant recognition: firstly with the award of a DSC for his part in sinking *UC-33* and, on his return to England, with the additional awards of the Distinguished Service Order and the French Croix de Guerre for his contribution to the Murmansk venture. Nor did his medal tally end with his military service; already a recipient of the prestigious Polar Medal, a month after leaving the Navy he learned that King George V intended to invest him with the Order of the British Empire for his services when commanding the *Aurora*. Added to his other medals, the OBE would make him one of the most highly decorated of all Heroic Age veterans.

But, with his demobilisation in January 1920, Stenhouse faced an uncertain future. Service in Russia had delayed his entry into the cut-throat competition for postwar employment and jobs might prove difficult to find. On paper, he benefited from numerous advantages. In particular, his pre-war career had made him a highly experienced sailor and his part in the Imperial Trans-Antarctic Expedition had brought his name to public notice and allowed him to demonstrate that he possessed both the practical ability and character to command. In the real world, however, it did not take him long to discover that experience and the possession of a medal ribbon more or less would not prevent an unemployed officer from starving. He must find a remunerative occupation, and quickly.

Sitting with his companions around a glowing stove in Murmansk, the irrepressible Shackleton had waxed lyrical about the possible rewards of commercial speculation and he had dabbled in everything from gold mining to the development of 'interrupter gear' for aeroplane-mounted machine guns. It may have been the recollection of these ardently expressed opinions that persuaded Stenhouse and Worsley to try their own hands at business

in the postwar world. Their quickly formed plan was to purchase a small
sailing ship to trade with the new Baltic republics. According to Worsley,
'Stennie reckoned we'd lose over it, and I wasn't too optimistic myself, but
said we'd have to take a gamble as there was nothing else doing for us in
England.'[1] As partners in this venture, they chose four more veterans,
including two other recipients of the DSO: Lieutenant-Colonel Cudbert
Thornhill, erstwhile Assistant Military Attaché to Russia, and Commander
Archibald Cochrane, a great-grandson of Admiral Thomas Cochrane, the
piratical 10th Earl of Dundonald. After a competitive game of billiards
to decide the name of their new company, in April 1920 these officers
registered Stenhouse, Worsley & Co. and then turned their attention to
the purchase of a suitable flagship. They chose the *Annie*, a small sailing
ship without auxiliary engines and with a hold just large enough to carry
150 tons of cargo. And there their plans began to fall apart. The Baltic
freight market collapsed and they immediately faced the need to select
alternative cargo routes.

In November 1920, after being re-rigged and fitted out, the *Annie* embarked
on her first voyage: from Leith to Reykjavik, with Stenhouse, Worsley and
Cochrane on board. The passage proved to be a baptism of fire: storms lashed
the tiny ship as she fought her way across the North Atlantic towards the
Arctic Circle but Worsley, as captain, refused to heave to. Instead, day after
day he drove her on through the hurricane, hoping to make record time. He
remembered that:

Stennie and I never shaved or washed once the whole way – we were too
busy. I had only 14 hours sleep in the 7 days – Stennie a little more – the
last 4 days and nights I had no sleep at all and Stennie and I steered her
ourselves for 48 hours in the worst of the hurricane when a moment
of relaxed vigilance would have shipped a sea that would have swept
everything off our decks and perhaps lost the ship. As it was we smashed
nearly [all] our bulwarks in. However we were both very happy and enjoyed
ourselves royally as Kings of the Sea and Salt of the Ocean![2]

Approaching the craggy Icelandic coast in driving rain and hail, at last
the intrepid pair had no choice but to heave to for 16 hours, while they
waited for the weather and the visibility to improve. Daring to the point of
recklessness, even Worsley had to acknowledge that no sailing ship in the
world could have won a battle against such a terrific inshore gale. When
they finally reached Reykjavik, the two heroes bathed and shaved and then
slept for an uninterrupted 14 hours before sampling the delights of the
town, which included flirtation with the local girls, though Worsley vowed
that he, at least, had seen 'none above the knees!'

Despite the thrill of the voyage and the pleasure of sailing with Worsley, by the time of their arrival in Reykjavik, Stenhouse's doubts regarding the large risks and small rewards attaching to their partnership had crystallised. At the end of December, he and Cochrane left for England on a steamer bound for Leith, leaving a somewhat disgruntled Worsley to load fish for the *Annie*'s homeward voyage. Cochrane's spirit of adventure burned as brightly as Stenhouse's own: during the war, he had served as a submarine commander and, after escaping from a Turkish prisoner-of-war camp, he had walked 450 miles to freedom. Now he proposed a treasure-hunting expedition to Brazil, scene of many of his great-grandfather's adventures. After the bitter cold of Iceland, the lush equatorial forests of South America must have seemed very appealing, as did the rather fantastical prospect of South American gold and diamonds. 'Faith!' noted the rueful and now penurious Worsley, 'we all want some badly enough!' But the planned expedition came to nothing and, for the next two years, Stenhouse followed an uncertain course.

In September 1921, he saw Worsley off on the ill-fated Shackleton–Rowlett Antarctic Expedition and, perhaps somewhat embarrassed by his friend's excess of emotion, carried kisses to and from the New Zealander and his girlfriend. 'Dear old Stennie brought your kiss along and I kissed his old fist where you kissed,' the enraptured Worsley wrote.[3] In his friend's absence, Stenhouse spent much of 1922 in the Mediterranean with Cochrane, working as a partner on board the auxiliary ketch *Annie Reid*, and in the Dardanelles with the Ocean Salvage Company. In 1921, the company had raised the wreck of Britain's first ever aircraft carrier, HMS *Ben-my-Chree*, sunk by Turkish artillery-fire at Kestellórizo in January 1917; now it intended to continue with similar work, salvaging the many vessels sunk around the Turkish coast during the Gallipoli campaign. Based at Chanak and operating from the 311-ton trawler and one-time Q-ship, the *King Lear*, Stenhouse worked with a crew composed of Turks, Greeks, Russians and a handful of Englishmen. He found the job interesting and it gave him a grounding in salvage work that would be useful in later life – but his appointment proved short-lived. By May 1923, he was back in England and as uncertain about his future as ever. Fortunately, his doubts were about to be resolved in an altogether unexpected manner.

In the middle of May, the periodical *Nature* carried an advertisement stating that 'A master is required for service on the Colonial Government ship *Discovery*, whose duties will be mainly research in whaling in the Antarctic.'[4] During his time on the *Aurora*, Stenhouse had opined that 'a man who would cry for another Antarctic Winter Drift like this must surely be mad or imbecile' but, once removed from the stresses and profound uncertainty of that long imprisonment, he had quickly changed his tune. As early as

1917, he had told Leonard Tripp that he and his fellow veterans were 'all looking forward to the time when the war will cease and we shall go into the wilds again', and now the thought of a return to the South Atlantic thrilled rather than horrified him. Delighted to learn that only applicants with special experience of ice navigation would be considered for this new job, he immediately submitted his curriculum vitae. Shortly afterwards, on 27 May, he received a letter inviting him to meet with the members of the *Discovery* Committee, a body formed for the furtherance of specialist scientific research in the Falkland Islands Dependencies. The prize for success at the interview would be command of one of the world's most renowned exploration vessels, the *Discovery*, made famous by Captain Scott's National Antarctic Expedition of 1901–4.

The forerunner of the *Discovery* Committee had been formed in 1917 with the specific purpose of advising the Secretary of State for the Colonies on the means by which the economic viability of the Falkland Islands might be sustained, with particular regard to the preservation of the whaling industry. At the beginning of the twentieth century, Britain controlled the most bountiful whaling fisheries on the face of the globe, incorporating the seas around the Falklands and stretching southwards past South Georgia, the South Shetlands and the South Orkneys to the coast of Antarctica itself. In these cold and turbulent waters the great leviathan, in particular the humpback, fin and blue whales could be found in large numbers. But the whaling industry had become notorious for its prodigality: ruthlessly hunting not only mature whales, but also adolescents, calves and pregnant females. By the end of the nineteenth century, 300 years of intense hunting, made even more destructive by the recent introduction of the small but swift steam-driven whale-catcher, the floating factory and the explosive harpoon, had come to within a hairsbreadth of exterminating whale stocks in the northern hemisphere. And yet, tragically, the unmistakable signs of depletion had done nothing to curb the seemingly insatiable demand for whale products. Changes in female fashions and the growing use of electricity meant that, in the early years of the new century, the use of whalebone for stays and whale oil for lighting had largely been superseded; but the oil was still needed in huge quantities: for tanning, lubrication and the manufacture of soap and margarine.

Nor had the destruction of whale stocks in the north engendered a more rational, conservationist approach among the whalers themselves. Instead, recognising that their northern hunting grounds were becoming exhausted, to meet the never-ending demand they had begun to look further afield. The existence of large populations of whales in the southern seas had been known about for well over a century, having been remarked upon by Captain Cook, but it was not until the northern fisheries had been swept clean that any concerted effort was made to establish the potential of this new pasturage. The Norwegians led the way and other nations soon followed in their wake. In 1904, Captain Carl Anton Larsen built the first whaling station at Grytviken on South Georgia and in no time at all the industry had swung into full and bloody life. Within a year of the founding of the station at Grytviken, the first floating factory sailed into the waters around the South Shetlands and, in less than a decade, a dozen such factories were operating in the region: acting as bases for far-ranging fleets of whalers.

The industry attained its bloody zenith with the onset of the First World War. In addition to the continuing demand for many of the traditional whale products, the war generated an unprecedented demand for glycerine, a vital component in the manufacture of munitions, and in the whaling season of 1915–16, no fewer than 11,792 whales were slaughtered, generating huge fortunes for the industry's leaders.

Peace and the resulting decline in the demand for glycerine did not produce a concomitant reduction in whaling. Instead, the wholesale slaughter continued and it became increasingly clear that, if the world's whale populations and, therefore, the whaling industry were not to be driven to extinction, controls must be imposed. In fact, Britain had already introduced restrictions, but the foreign factory ships operated just beyond her territorial waters, making it all but impossible effectively to enforce the regulations. The situation demanded new laws but it was felt that, if their effectiveness were to be maximised, they should be based upon an exact understanding of the whale's life cycle: of its patterns of migration, feeding and breeding. Such knowledge could only be obtained by a properly instituted oceanographic research expedition, manned by scientists and provided with the latest equipment, and with a ship suited to a voyage into some of the most tempestuous waters on the face of the globe. And, finally, since the expedition would be operating for much of the time among the pack-ice and ice floes on the edge of the Antarctic Circle, the expedition's scientists would have to be supported by a captain and crew experienced in ice navigation.

Despite his qualifications, Stenhouse's appointment to the command of the *Discovery* was very far from being a foregone conclusion. Before advertising the post, the Committee had asked the Admiralty to provide the names of some suitable candidates. These had included Victor Campbell, who had served with Scott on the *Terra Nova* Expedition and with Stenhouse in Russia; Douglas Jeffrey, the navigating officer on Shackleton's *Quest* Expedition; and, finally, Frank Worsley. All had distinguished war records and Campbell, like Worsley, had been awarded the DSO. However, as Worsley was now in Canada, busy running raw spirits to the prohibitionist United States, the Committee met only Campbell and Jeffrey. And, almost immediately, its members struck a problem which would become a perennial one for the expedition: the hierarchy of command. Campbell stated categorically that he would accept the position of captain only if he became at the same time the acknowledged leader of the expedition. Jeffrey expressed similar reservations about the duality of command if the leadership of the expedition was divided between the ship's master and the chief scientific officer, but his objections were not insurmountable. Uncertain how best to proceed, the Committee had decided to broaden its options by advertising the post. Many applied, but the insistence upon expertise in ice navigation succeeded in 'choking off a fair number of cases'.[5]

When the wheat had been separated from the chaff, the Committee decided to interview three of the new applicants: Stenhouse, J.H. Blair, who had been first officer on the *Aurora* during Mawson's AAE, and Commander C.B. Shaw. All attended for interview on 8 June with the result that Stenhouse joined Worsley and Jeffrey on the final shortlist.

About this time, a newspaper reporter described Stenhouse as 'a tall, broad-shouldered Scot, clean-shaven in appearance, and clean-cut in his speech. He strikes one as being like his ship, essentially sea-worthy. Except for his height, which is above the average for a seafaring man, he is a typical sailor. One can understand that those who were under his command on the Shackleton Expedition of 1914 felt safe, even when they found themselves on the *Aurora* drifting 1,500 miles through the long Antarctic night.'[6] The members of the Committee, too, were impressed but they also admitted to entertaining 'some doubt as to the temperament of this candidate'[7] – perhaps rumours regarding Stenhouse's mercurial personality and periodic depressions had reached their ears. To resolve these issues, the Committee asked James Wordie, one of its members, to make further enquiries. He in turn sought the views of another *Endurance* veteran, Dr Macklin, who knew all three candidates. Dr Macklin's opinion would prove decisive: 'I do not think there is much to pick between Jeffrey and Worsley,' he told Wordie, '. . . both are out for themselves.' For Stenhouse, however, he had nothing but praise, stating that he 'is dead loyal to any cause he takes up. I served with him in Russia and liked him. He is a better man than either of the other two . . . Stenhouse is a good man, and an honest one and loyal.'[8] Having received so glowing a reference from such a reputable source, the Committee offered the post to Stenhouse on a salary of £500 per annum during the period of the *Discovery*'s refit, increasing to £700 once she put to sea. Of course, he accepted.

Starting work on 1 August 1923, Stenhouse soon discovered that the task of preparing the ship for a new cruise would be an onerous one. With a price tag of £5,000, the *Discovery* had been purchased as the cheapest vessel suitable for sub-Antarctic research and her condition was poor. A detailed survey showed that her previous adventures had left her badly strained and a lack of air courses had caused many of her inner timbers to rot; her boilers were corroded; and she required new masts, spars, sails and rigging: all of which would prove costly and time-consuming to replace or repair. And, even had she been in much better condition, there were a number of improvements to be made to the configuration of her sailing gear and accommodation. During the National Antarctic Expedition, the *Discovery* had become notorious for her tendency to roll; now, in order to address these problems, her main and foremasts were moved forward and her sail area increased by some 20 per cent. Her engines were totally reconditioned and shipwrights replaced a substantial portion of her oak keel. In addition, carpenters constructed a new wardroom and a laboratory in which specimens of the South Atlantic's flora and fauna might be dissected, labelled and preserved by the *Discovery*'s five-strong scientific staff. Once this veritable rebuild had been completed, the *Discovery* would be, Stenhouse told Leonard Tripp, 'one of the best equipped vessels that has ever left this country,' though he also rather nostalgically opined that 'I don't think any ship could be better than the dear old *Aurora* all the same.'[9]

The refit was undertaken at the shipbuilding yard of Messrs Vosper in Portsmouth. Although the naval architect Sir Fortescue Flannery directed the work, Stenhouse was in constant attendance, offering his expert opinion on matters ranging from the auxiliary compass and the ship's stores to the best length for the bridge and the inadvisability of combining the chartroom and the expedition's library. He also expressed the belief 'that it was essential for the safety of the Expedition that sledging equipment sufficient for the whole party be provided with sledging rations for, say, two months'[10] – the lessons of the Imperial Trans-Antarctic Expedition had not been forgotten. Such weighty matters aside, he also found time to potter among the growing piles of half-rotten ship's timbers, choosing those sound enough for further use. His selection complete, he paid one of the carpenters to make a small occasional table which, embellished with a silver plaque, he despatched to his sister, Nell, as a souvenir.

The security of long-term employment also enabled Stenhouse to make a major alteration in his personal circumstances – by getting married. Tall, powerfully built and ruggedly handsome, many women had found him attractive, even before he added the attributes of renowned explorer and war hero to his résumé. Nor was he averse to flirtation, certainly with the prettier girls of the Kola Peninsula and Reykjavik and, no doubt, with others too. But, so far, he had avoided long-term commitments, and he manfully resisted the matchmaking ploys of matrons such as his Aunt Lizzie who had once artlessly suggested that he might 'make life pleasant' by corresponding with his cousin Sadie: 'a dear girl, with eyes and hair as black as coal.'[11] Now, choosing for himself, he found a woman possessed of the ideal qualifications for the wife of such an adventurous and restless husband: Gladys Mackintosh, the widow of Aeneas.

After his return to England in April 1917, Stenhouse had sought out Gladys to deliver Mackintosh's letters to his family and to tell the widow of his Antarctic experiences with her late husband. Thereafter, he had stayed in touch, visiting Gladys first in Bedford, where she had lived with Mackintosh, and then on the Isle of Wight, where she had bought a house with her sisters in 1919. Of course, Mackintosh's tragic and unnecessary death had been a cruel blow, particularly to a mother with two young daughters to provide for, and Stenhouse had been impressed by the widow's stoicism and courage in the face of adversity. Perhaps, too, Gladys's Scottish birth and her understanding of, and connection with, both the sea and the Antarctic made her especially appealing to a man of his strongly developed proclivities. In Gladys's company he could also meet and talk with other expeditionaries: *Endurance* veterans certainly, but also men like Frank Bickerton, mechanical engineer on the AAE, and a long-time friend of both Gladys and Mackintosh. Romance was in the air in Stenhouse's small circle, as Worsley's courting, too, had turned serious. His eye had alighted on 'a cheery Aberdonian' half his age, named Jean Cumming, and the two explorers and their partners became 'four sweethearts together'.[12]

Stenhouse took the plunge first and, in what *The Gentlewoman* called 'An interesting marriage,'[13] he wedded Gladys on 2 October 1923. For all his dislike of ceremony, he stood by his bride in the strangely anachronistic dress uniform of the Royal Navy, including the sword, cocked hat and tail-coated tunic of Nelson's day. But no one feigned formality when the photographer's shutter snapped shut on the lawns of Kinloch Tay, Gladys's home near Totland Bay, and, instead, the bride and groom beamed at the camera, Stenhouse's chest expanded with pride and pleasure. Of course, he had hoped that Worsley would stand as his best man, but 'Wuz', as hard up as ever, was away on a lecture tour that he could ill afford to interrupt. Instead, Stenhouse turned to Colonel Thornhill, while Gladys's brother, Walter Campbell, gave the bride away.

Having rented a small farm at Horley in Surrey and then a flat on Edith Road in London, the Stenhouses flourished in their new domesticity: their happiness founded on what quickly grew to become a passionate mutual attachment. On 22 June 1924, Gladys gave birth to their only child: a girl whom they named Patricia, with Colonel Thornhill again stepping forward, to act as godfather. Despite this happiness, Gladys can have been in little doubt regarding the probability of long and frequent separation from her new husband and, for all its wearisome delays, work on the *Discovery*'s refit could not go on forever. Soon the old ship would depart on her first

Antarctic cruise in over twenty years and the couple might be parted for two years or more. But they had little choice in the matter: with no private income to support a growing family, they needed the money. Besides, to be truly happy, Stenhouse must be suitably employed. In the Antarctic he had opined that 'Unremitting toil seems to be the panacea for most troubles and I think mortals were intended for it, for only the hard working people seem to have happiness or tranquillity of mind.'[14] Married to a man of Stenhouse's mould, Gladys would soon discover that she too must live by the tenets of this philosophy – whether she liked it or not.

Any gloom at the prospect of his imminent departure might have been balanced not only by hopes for the success of the voyage but also by a substantial pay increase. In August 1924, H.T. Allen of the Colonial Office wrote to Rowland Darnley, chairman of the *Discovery* Committee, stating 'I have always been strongly of the opinion that a salary of £700 is quite insufficient for a man of Captain Stenhouse's attainments, experience and responsibilities. As time goes on one realises more and more that we have been fortunate enough to get an exceptional man for the post.' He also pointed out that 'Shackleton paid Commander Worsley £1,000 a year as Navigating Officer of the *Quest*, and Commander Worsley was an unsuccessful applicant for the command of the *Discovery*!'[15] Darnley sympathised and thought that 'in Captain Stenhouse we have a man with experience almost unique, and much ability and force of character. I may add that he has made himself very useful in matters outside his particular domain.'[16] As a result of these discussions Stenhouse's salary increased to £1,000, on the understanding that he would continue to give the Committee the benefit of his expertise on 'all matters relating to polar exploration, ice conditions, and the like'.[17] Coinciding with a notification that he had been promoted to the rank of lieutenant-commander on the Royal Navy's reserve list, news of the increment must have been welcome. But it's unlikely that it removed some of Stenhouse's nagging concerns regarding his new role.

To many of those involved, the National Oceanographic Expedition constituted a great adventure: an opportunity to study nature at her most harsh, among towering seas and on the edges of a mysterious and beautiful land of ice. But the expedition was to be undertaken on rigidly scientific lines, with little or no place for the kind of muscular exploration which Stenhouse loved and which his old leader, Shackleton, had come to epitomise. Moreover, the science was underpinned by the *Discovery* Committee's primary purpose: to understand the best means by which to preserve the economy of the Falklands Dependencies. The accumulation of knowledge for knowledge's own sake and for the broader benefit of mankind would only be countenanced where such activities complemented the hard-nosed economic demands of the expedition; and of exploration for exploration's sake there would be none. Although twenty years of life on board ship had taught Stenhouse the importance of strict discipline, of adhering to orders without question, this expedition might have appeared to lack soul. And the expedition's newly appointed Director of Research, Dr Stanley Kemp, was hardly the man to allay such doubts.

Previously employed as superintendent of the Zoological Survey of India, the 42-year-old Kemp epitomised the ideal of the ascetic, dedicated and self-effacing man of science. Although one of his team later wrote that 'No finer leader and no better companion for a long and lonely voyage in Sub-Antarctic waters could be imagined,'[18] he possessed little or no ability to inspire any but those who were already members of the scientific fraternity. Stenhouse believed that there would be 'a peculiar and poetic interest in the *Discovery* going into the very latitude where her first commander perished,'[19] but Kemp seemed immune to this poetic interest. 'Our work will be in connection with whaling,' he told the polar historian, Hugh Mill. 'In all probability we shall not cross the Antarctic Circle and I fear we may have little opportunity for coastal surveys.'[20]

Nonetheless, Kemp sketched out a hugely ambitious scientific programme, incorporating a detailed survey of the whole ecosystem of the South Atlantic, from the microscopic animal and plant life known as plankton, to the tiny shrimp-like crustaceans called collectively krill, up to the great whales themselves. So far as the whales were concerned, there was a need to understand their rates of growth, the periods of their sexual maturity, the lengths of gestation and infancy, the rates of reproduction and the nature of their food. The *Discovery* Committee had reached the conclusion that many of these secrets could be plumbed by studying the giant carcasses on the flensing platforms of the whaling station at South Georgia. This decision resulted in the expedition being divided into three parts. The first would consist of a team of scientists operating from a scientific base established among the whalers at Grytviken. But shore-based investigations could only be expected to answer some of the questions regarding the life of the whales. A proper understanding of their living environment could only be gained by detailed oceanographic research, undertaken on board ship. The core of this research would be a methodical survey of the sub-Antarctic waters around South Georgia, supplemented by a less detailed analysis of the oceans spread over a much wider area: from the Cape of Good Hope to the Antarctic Circle. This work would fall to the *Discovery*. Finally, a programme of whale-marking would be undertaken by a subsidiary vessel, possessing the attributes of a modern whale-catcher, and named after the father of Arctic science, William Scoresby. This last element of the expedition would furnish science with a much greater understanding of the whales' habits of migration.

After her lengthy period in dry dock, the Royal Research Ship *Discovery* sailed from Portsmouth on 23 July 1925. All on board were eager to begin their cruise and to head south, but first the ship must pass her sea trials and the effectiveness of some new equipment must be tested. Chief among the latter was the deep-water echo-sounding gear developed by the Admiralty. Fiendishly complicated in appearance, the echo-sounder was actually based on a simple premise: that a sound made in the water will travel to, and bounce back from, the seabed. If the speed at which sound travels through water is understood, then it becomes possible to calculate the distance travelled and, thus, the depth of water beneath the ship, enabling a hydrographer to chart the ocean floor. Despite these plans, however, conditions in the Bay of Biscay made it impossible to conduct the necessary experiments.

As the *Discovery* nosed into the Bay, the glass fell rapidly, much faster than the seasonal norm, and in no time at all the ship was in the grip of a violent gale. Despite the best efforts of the naval architect, the shipwrights and Stenhouse himself, it soon became apparent that the *Discovery*'s notorious tendency to roll had not been cured. Stenhouse reported that 'the wind freshened from NW and heavy swell set in from the WNW causing the ship to roll heavily. Much damage was done to crockery, library, and personal effects. . . . Vessel shipped moderately heavy water which forced its way through ventilators and skylights into the wardroom, cabins and mess-decks.'[21] In fact, the *Discovery* wallowed outrageously, sometimes rolling 43° to starboard and then back again to port, shipping what, to anyone but a seasoned hand like Stenhouse, would be called anything but 'moderately heavy water'.

Much worse than the rolling was the discovery that the quality of the work completed at Portsmouth left much to be desired. During the last months of the extensive refit, the gulls perched on the ship's crosstrees had looked down on a mad flurry of activity. With the workmen under pressure to complete their tasks in time for the ship to reach South Georgia for the beginning of the 1925–6 whaling season, corners had been cut. Now, as the seas swept the decks, foaming at the scuppers and pouring down the companionways, the crew discovered that nearly every hatchway leaked. Rolfe Gunther, one of the expedition's zoologists, recorded his impressions of the ensuing chaos:

The order of our mishaps is not easy to remember. In the violence of a roll two wardroom chairs gave way, while everything that was not lashed down was skating over the decks. One or two of the worst rolls cleared the pantry of crockery, and at the same time the library came adrift, books and battens falling helter-skelter down the companion way, already flooded by cascades of water from the upper deck. The sea on the deck was a foot deep, sloshing first this way, then that. One or two waves forced their way through the wardroom sky-light, pouring in torrents on to the luncheon table.[22]

And H.F.P. Herdman, the hydrologist, told a friend that 'I never saw such a mess as she was in 'tween decks – water everywhere, broken china, food, and "gubbins" of all kinds floating around in the dye from the carpets!'[23]

Faced with such conditions Stenhouse had no option but to put his ship about and fly before the storm while his crew fought with the sails and the green-gilled scientists staggered about picking up and drying out as best they could their precious equipment and books. But, in wearing ship, things got much worse before they got better. The *Discovery* rolled and laboured so violently in the high steep sea that Stenhouse admitted 'I do not think that the masts and rigging could stand if such violent rolling continued for long periods.'[24] In fact, as the chief zoologist, Alister Hardy, later admitted, being struck by this unseasonably violent storm could be counted as 'good fortune', since sufficient time remained to fix the ship's defects before she had to contend with the even more turbulent waters of the South Atlantic. 'The ship has had a severe test,' Stenhouse told the Committee; but he continued to 'think she will be seaworthy when certain obvious defects, disclosed during the gale, have been remedied'.

For the time being, with the ship and the crew looking rather sorry for themselves, the *Discovery* slunk back to England and berthed at the Devon port of Dartmouth for further repairs and improvements. To her surprise, Gladys found that she would be able to enjoy her husband's company for another two months, with the whole family making regular visits to the ship in the balmy late summer's weather. Her pleasure in these visits, however, may have been very slightly alloyed by anxiety as a preoccupied Stenhouse let his two stepdaughters clamber about the rigging in imminent peril of life and limb.

Not until the evening of 24 September could the *Discovery* finally begin her voyage south. Slipping from her mooring in the shipyard of Phillips & Co., she edged her way into the tidal channel of the River Dart and pointed her bowsprit seawards. Flags waved, whistles hooted and, in a lane on the hillside above the town, Stenhouse could see three small figures, the tallest of whom clutched a bundle: Gladys, her two daughters and the baby, Patricia, each fluttering a handkerchief in farewell. And then the ship rounded a bend in the river and town and family disappeared from view. A new voyage into Antarctic waters, Stenhouse's first in nearly eight years, had begun.

OCEANS DEEP

In rough weather, the *Discovery* sailed south-westwards, skirting the coast of Devon and Cornwall, in order to finally complete the testing of the echo-sounding gear and to drop the Admiralty experts at Falmouth. Then, as she headed south at last, the weather cleared, giving way to brilliant sunshine, and the old ship turned into a thing of beauty. Sail after sail was set, and the deck became alive with the music of the sea: the hum of the cordage, the crack of the canvas as it caught the wind and, of course, the hoarse melody of the men themselves. Stenhouse loved the traditional sea-shanties sung by the seamen as they made sail, the rhythm of the songs giving time to the physical labour, and now once again he was in his element. He could not expect to see Gladys and the children for two or even more years and responsibility for the well-being of his crew and of the scientists would at times weigh heavily upon his shoulders, but such thoughts were as nothing to the joy of again being in command of a sailing ship. And not just any ship: but the *Discovery* herself – Captain Scott's ship, famous in the annals of Antarctic exploration; a vessel whose adventures had kept him spellbound when a youth. Soon she was making nearly 9 knots and, with the sun glancing from her polished brass, with the sky and the sea a perfect blue, and with dolphins dancing in the bow-wave, all the omens for the voyage looked favourable.

Believing that 'lubbers have no place on board ship'[1] and remembering the problems encountered on the *Aurora*, Stenhouse may have been doubtful at the beginning of the voyage about the scientists' capacity to accommodate themselves to shipboard life. But his reservations soon turned out to be ill-founded. Kemp's four young assistants quickly proved willing to lend a hand whenever untrained muscle could play a part in hauling on a sheet, and their enthusiasm for the job in hand was quite disarming. If Stenhouse, the adventurer, had remained unexcited by the nature of the work to be undertaken, it soon became clear that the scientists did not share his lack of enthusiasm. Alister Hardy, who had been described to the Committee as 'a very pleasant fellow

. . . Neither a prig nor a pedant'[2] thought the voyage 'a schoolboy's dream come true'[3] and he and his companions displayed equal delight in their move from the laboratory to the field. And the difference in environments could hardly have been more extreme. Admittedly, they spent many long hours cooped up in the laboratory placed amidships, gazing intently through microscopes and into Petri dishes populated with minuscule sea life. But they also passed happy hours squeezed into a bosun's chair slung beneath the bowsprit, rising and falling with the motion of the ship, and wielding a hand-net in the hope of scooping new specimens from the very crest of the waves. When relaxing, too, the officers and scientists demonstrated a willingness to make the most of their situation, particularly on Saturdays when, after a meal of dolphin steaks washed down with wine and port, the labours of the week gave way to entertainments in the wardroom. Mostly, these consisted of songs around the ship's piano ably and energetically played by the Chief Engineer, Lieutenant W.A. Horton.

Despite the growing camaraderie and the beautiful, balmy weather, there was some feeling of dissatisfaction on board caused by the *Discovery*'s relatively slow progress. Anxious to make the best of every light breath of wind, Stenhouse ordered that all the sails be set and the ship became a towering pyramid of white canvas. But fitful winds and the need to conserve fuel meant that she seldom exceeded 6 or 7 knots and often slowed to barely 3 knots per hour. At these speeds, the whaling grounds of South Georgia seemed a very distant prospect, but at least Stenhouse could report that the *Discovery* had become more manageable and that 'in heavy swells and occasional short cross seas which we have encountered, she appeared to behave better than before'.[4]

Frustration at the slowness of their passage aside, the scientists kept themselves occupied in these calm and increasingly warm waters by testing the array of new equipment which cluttered the *Discovery*'s decks. Much of their work would revolve around the analysis of the plant and animal life populating the oceans and, in order to facilitate sampling from considerable depths, the ship had been fitted with an assortment of steam-winches of varying size and power. These winches were designed for lowering and raising a series of nets and bottles for capturing zoological specimens from depths of a few feet to many fathoms, and the wealth of the material brought into the laboratory meant that the five scientists found there were too few hours in the day for its examination, preservation and cataloguing.

Gran Canaria, a massive purple mountain rising abruptly from a sun-flecked emerald sea, became their first landfall in the early hours of 17 October. But Stenhouse paused only long enough to replenish the stores with fresh fruit and vegetables before seeking to intercept the North-East Trades to help speed the *Discovery* on her way towards the equator. Even with the fairest conditions imaginable, the old ship remained sluggish, hardly achieving even 7 knots – largely because of the condition of her hull, made foul by the growth of weed during her long stay at Dartmouth. On 10 November, she crossed the line amidst all the traditional high-spirited horseplay of ritual shaving and dunking, from which no one could claim immunity – not even the stately Dr Kemp.

A failure in the wind beyond Ascension Island, where the *Discovery* partly replenished her coal bunkers, meant that progress remained agonisingly slow. The ship spent whole days becalmed, with not enough wind to give her steerage way; the crew sweltered under a tropical sun and the surface of the sea glistened like a burnished tray, rippled only by the movements of the scientists' sample nets. Herdman told a friend that 'You'll have to excuse this scrawl, but this ship so closely resembles an oven in the Tropics, that the pen falls out of your fingers every few moments from an excess of sweat! The heat is terrible on board, she wasn't built for heat, and everywhere below decks is over 90°F at least!! Besides being airless, she doesn't go fast enough to make her own breeze.'[5]

At last, towards the middle of December, the *Discovery* struck the long-sought westerly winds that would carry her the last 1,000 miles to the Cape, and from being a dead thing she became again a creature with life and motion of her own. In fact, far too much motion of her own. Stenhouse had to report that 'Notwithstanding my remarks contained in my letter dated at Las Palmas 17th October, regarding the rolling of the ship, I am now of the opinion that the ship rolls excessively.'[6] Herdman put it rather more bluntly, claiming that 'She's an absolute cure for sea-sickness – she's never still for a moment – always rolling or pitching even in the calmest weather. . . . I verily believe she'd roll in the lake at Wembley!!'[7] Once again, the scientific work, which had already been interrupted by the need to take full advantage of the light winds, had to be put to one side. Nonetheless, the weight that had been oppressing the crew and scientists in the doldrums lifted and, a week later, as they sailed into Table Bay, they could look forward to a Christmas ashore, and to a bulging mailbag. But letters, no matter how welcome, would fill only a small portion of their time. During their two-month stay in Dartmouth, the crew of the *Discovery* had gained a reputation for hard drinking – Herdman had claimed that 'there's damn all else to do there!' – and now they reinforced that reputation and regularly partied with the local residents from dusk until dawn.

Stenhouse and Kemp had hoped that their stop at Cape Town would last only long enough to fill the ship's coal bunkers and to commission adjustments to some of the winches and other equipment. Christmas and New Year celebrations, however, resulted in a four-week stay. And when, at last, they were able to drag themselves away, the decks of the *Discovery* were made almost impassable by the assortment of presents carried across the gangway. Stenhouse commented distractedly that 'the presents appeared only to be limited by the space available on board. The approximate measurement of all packages was 15 tons.'[8] But only a small proportion of the gifts was for the crew; the vast majority was destined for the residents of the *Discovery*'s next port-of-call: Tristan da Cunha, 'the loneliest island in the world', which they reached on 30 January.

Lying approximately 1,500 miles from Cape Town and slightly more from the coast of South America, Tristan da Cunha sits almost at the centre of the South Atlantic. Rolfe Gunther wrote:

> How different in appearance is Tristan from Ascension. The latter a plateau studded with dwarf craters: the former, though of equal area, consisting of one colossal volcano with only one small subsidiary cone. There does not at first appear to be any ground suitable for a settlement, and the whole island seems cut off from the sea by inaccessible cliffs 2,000 feet in height. Not until we were quite close did the glasses reveal a raised beach on the north-western flank, an area of about two square miles on which are the cottages, the church, the pastures and cattle of the islanders.[9]

This settlement, known as Edinburgh of the Seven Seas after a visit in 1867 from Queen Victoria's second son, the Duke of Edinburgh, was home to a population of 141 in 1926. 'On approaching the anchorage, off the settlement,' Stenhouse reported, 'two boats were seen lying inside the kelp awaiting our arrival' and, as soon as the *Discovery* hove into view, the boats pushed out to meet her.

The ship's arrival counted as a red-letter day to the island's inhabitants, particularly as she brought forty bags of mail: the first postal delivery to the island in over two years. The crew found the islanders, many of whom were descended from a garrison stationed to prevent the escape of Napoleon from nearby St Helena, to be a likeable but somewhat whimsical collection of ragamuffins. All were dressed in a bizarre collection of patched cast-offs of indeterminate age, in one case surmounted by an engine driver's cap. They also spoke in a queer, high-pitched manner with many eccentricities of vocabulary. Dr E.H. Marshall, the ship's surgeon and a brother of the Dr Marshall who had accompanied Shackleton's BAE, noted: 'It has been stated that the islanders appear stupid. This has arisen through not realising that the islanders have a dialect, with a very limited vocabulary, of their own. They are extremely sensitive about their lack of education and little knowledge of English, and this sensitiveness constitutes an obstacle to any scheme of emigration [or] even temporary employment outside the island.'[10] His largely favourable impression was reinforced by the demeanour of the women who 'appeared superior to the men and have a deportment reminiscent of a bygone age, and this in spite of having, apart from their ordinary domestic work, to labour in the fields. The tidiness of their clothes and cleanliness of their person would do credit to any English village.'

During their brief stay at Tristan, the scientists on board the *Discovery* embraced every opportunity to collect specimens of the millipedes, spiders, woodlice and other bugs that made their home on the volcanic island. But it was only with their departure on 1 February that they could at last begin serious scientific operations. Within minutes of their sailing, a 100-fathom dredge brought to the surface a collection of multi-coloured soft coral polyps that made the scientists gasp with pleasure and astonishment. In the 1870s, the *Challenger* Oceanographic Expedition had reported the presence of these life-forms in the area, but Hardy and his fellows could hardly believe their eyes as they sifted through their haul. At last, after such slow progress and the myriad interruptions to their work, they felt as though their expedition was beginning to reap extraordinary rewards. These feelings were reinforced two days later when they completed their first complete set of water samples down to depths of 3,000m. And then, as if in mockery of their excitement and raised expectations, the weather changed abruptly and all scientific work ground to a halt.

The barometer fell rapidly throughout the night of 3 February and, by the evening of the next day, a full gale was whipping the ocean into spume and spindrift. Once again, the *Discovery* laboured in towering seas, with the crew fighting to keep at their stations and Stenhouse, wrapped in oilskins and hanging on to the rail of the open bridge, screwing up his eyes against the flying spray. But now, increasingly familiar with her eccentricities, he felt much greater confidence in the old ship. Compared with his first vessel, the *Springbank*, which he loved dearly, the *Discovery* shipped remarkably little water and he felt able to report favourably on her performance:

As daylight made the wind increased in force with more frequent and violent squalls. At 8 a.m. the wind was blowing with almost hurricane force and the sea was lashed high in a steep and confused jumble. I 'hove to' under storm spanker and with the engines turning at 70 revolutions in order to keep the ship's head to the sea which was breaking heavily. The ship rolled so violently that the stokers carried on their work with extreme difficulty and at great personal risk.

It was found difficult to keep the steam and as it fell, so the ship fell off, and rolling heavily in the trough of the sea, she scooped up green water over the lee rail . . .

The ship behaved wonderfully well and although at times not under command and rolling like a log in the trough of the sea, she shipped little water except that which came over the lee rail. Few ships would have weathered this gale without damage.[11]

Of course, she rolled '45° each way with great regularity', Herdman recorded, but the tough little veteran had held her own in seas that would have overwhelmed smarter and newer vessels.

And yet, despite these qualities, it had become clear that, as an oceanographic research ship, the *Discovery* was fatally flawed. She rolled like a log even in relatively calm conditions and the waters in which she would soon be operating were anything but placid: Shackleton had called them 'the most tempestuous storm-swept area of water in the world'.[12] Trawling and dredging would be difficult at the best of times and, all too often, totally impossible. Stenhouse noted, 'Strong and variable winds with confused seas and swells were experienced during the whole of the passage from Tristan to South Georgia';[13] nevertheless, scientists and crew struggled on and worked their 'stations' – the core of the *Discovery*'s work – as often as possible.

Each station consisted of a detailed observation on a vertical line into the ocean's depths. Having reached the spot chosen for the station, Stenhouse would turn the ship's head into the wind and then, having taken in all sail, attempt to keep her both steady and still. Gathering round their various winches and sounding machines the scientists would wait for his nod and then begin to pay out the long lengths of wire with their sampling bottles and thermometers attached. Of course, at the colossal depths in which they operated it was impossible to drop anchor and Stenhouse had to rely on the occasional use of the engine to keep his vessel static, his job made even more difficult by the fact that the ship's heavy rigging tended to catch the wind like a sail, causing her to move. And too much movement would inevitably result in the sounding line being dragged from the vertical, making the critical assessment of the depth from which the samples were taken quite impossible. Samples would, of course, still be brought to the surface but, in order to chart the life of the ocean, the zoologists must be able to determine the exact depth from which they had been trawled.

Day by day, the weather had been growing colder and, on 16 February 1926, the crew saw their first iceberg: a great chunk of barrier ice some 300ft high and a quarter of a mile long. The scientists, to whom an iceberg constituted an altogether new phenomenon, stood at the rails, entranced. 'The grey of the shadowed portions matched the canopy of cloud above it,' Gunther recorded in his diary, 'and the purity of the lit-up faces was lighter than gold and more radiantly white than snow. . . . The upper portions were rough, and had so cracked about that they had a close resemblance to a castle with turrets built upon an impregnable rock.'[14] After breakfast, they steamed up close and Stenhouse took the opportunity to deliver an impromptu lecture on the formation of such bergs, telling his audience that the floating island before them was but a minute crumb from the vast sheet of ice that covers the entire Antarctic continent and how, over many thousands of years, it had gradually worked its way from the interior to the very edge of the continent, before breaking off and plunging into the waiting ocean.

Over the next few days they saw more and more bergs and in these dangerous waters Stenhouse seldom left the bridge: no one knew better than he the treacherousness of an ice-strewn sea. And he soon witnessed a sight which revealed just how deceptive this arena could be – even to one of his experience:

At midnight on 19th February in a position 56 miles NE of Cumberland Bay large bergs were sighted ahead and on both bows, with many growlers close to the ship. The ship was steamed slowly off and on the ice, until daylight when we found that our course was blocked with large bergs and very heavily pressured close-pack ice. Amongst this was a long ridge ending in steep bluffs about 40ft high which were deeply discoloured where the ice had broken off and had the appearance, even within 2 cables distance, of dark brown rocks. The colours were brown, grey and blue and were distinctly marked in oblique belts like stratified rock. Had I been navigating strange waters I would have reported these as islands, so deceptive was the appearance of this ice.[15]

Over the preceding century, charts of the southern ocean had been peppered with the names of phantom islands: D'Urville's Côte Clarie, Balleny's Sabrina Land and Wilkes's Termination Land, to name but a few. Had it not been for his intimate familiarity with the region, Stenhouse might have added yet another.

Having navigated through the pack without incident, the *Discovery* reached Grytviken, South Georgia, in the middle of the afternoon of 20 February and, at 3.16 p.m. precisely, her anchors splashed into the waters of King Edward Cove. Almost immediately, a small boat put out from the shore and, in no time at all, Stenhouse and his companions welcomed some well-known and friendly faces on board. In accordance with the

Discovery Committee's determination to establish a Marine Biological Station on the island, four scientists under Dr Neil Mackintosh had sailed from England for South Georgia in the autumn of 1924. For more than a year they had been studying the carcasses on the flensing platform of the whaling station at Grytviken, measuring the dead whales, and examining their skeletons and stomach contents: a profoundly disagreeable and malodorous job.

On their approach to South Georgia, Hardy had opined that its rugged and barren scenery 'on a crystal clear day . . . must hold its own with any in the world'.[16] With Mount Paget, its highest peak, thrusting 9,550ft into the sky, the whole of the island's 100-mile length rises from the granite grey waters of the South Atlantic as jagged as a broken bottle; its coastline, too, is serrated by innumerable fjords, which perhaps served to remind the Norwegian whalers of their home, so many thousands of miles to the north. In 1926, South Georgia formed the hub of the southern whaling industry with every member of its small population, with the exception of a small kernel of British administrators, engaged in the hunting and exploitation of the leviathan. Indeed, until the opportunities for whaling were recognised, the island had been home only to thousands of sea birds and seals: mankind preferring to shun its windswept and inhospitable grandeur.

When the *Discovery* made fast alongside the quay of the whaling station, a bizarre and grisly vista opened before her crew's eyes. On shore, the large, barn-like red-brick factories belched out steam into the clear icy-blue sky while the sea lapping against the ship's hull was actually red: dyed by the blood from the half-stripped carcasses on the flensing platform. And in this crimson sea floated innumerable bloated whale corpses, puffed up by the air injected to keep them from sinking and by the noxious gases of decomposition. Most horrible of all, the clean, crisp air of the South Atlantic was laden with the stench from the vats in which the whalers boiled their victims' blubber down to oil. Hardy described it as 'being like a mixture of the smell of a tanning factory and that of fish meal and manure works together with a sickly and almost overpowering odour of meat extract'.[17] To a man like Stenhouse, who regretted the killing of even a single animal to provide essential food, this slaughter on an industrial scale must have been truly repellent.

Soon after his arrival at South Georgia, he undertook an important personal pilgrimage: to the grave of his old commander, Sir Ernest Shackleton. On 9 May 1916, after a 750-mile open-boat journey across the South Atlantic, Shackleton and his five companions, including Worsley, had landed at King Haakon Bay, 30 miles overland from Stromness whaling station. Shackleton, Worsley and Tom Crean had then become the first men to cross the mountainous interior of the island to announce the peril of their fellows marooned on Elephant Island. Six years later, Shackleton's friends had buried their 'Boss' on the island after his death during the early stages of the *Quest* Expedition. It upset Stenhouse when the 'cairn erected on Hope Point to the memory of Sir Ernest Shackleton was found to be badly weathered and almost in ruins'.[18] He also discovered that the grave itself displayed a 'sad state of neglect'. He arranged to have the cairn repaired and re-erected on a concrete platform and the grave weeded and its woodwork repainted: a small enough tribute to the leader whose Antarctic expedition had formed the hub of his own career.

Over the next two months, whenever weather conditions permitted, the *Discovery* engaged in research work in the waters around South Georgia. Work which, Kemp stated, 'Judged from an economic standpoint . . . is the most important that we have to undertake.'[19] The main purpose of the current investigations was to gain an understanding of why the whales congregated in such large numbers around South Georgia. Primarily, this meant a study of the plankton and krill and of the conditions that so favoured their development. The scientists began, on 3 March, by making a line of five stations heading north-east from Cumberland Bay, taking at each a full set of physical observations and vertical hauls. And yet, despite the fact that the line of stations crossed the most productive whaling grounds on the face of the globe, the sampling nets came in empty. The scientists were bemused. It seemed bizarre that the whales should be attracted in such huge numbers to feast on a foodstuff that, to Kemp and his team, appeared conspicuous by its absence. Perhaps the krill gathered in 'patches' or perhaps the giant nets and the vibrating cables from which they hung scared them away. With the wind rising and the *Discovery* tossing with increasing violence, Stenhouse decided to make for the harbour, though he allowed two nets to be dragged behind the ship at depths of 2m and 60m. When the scientists hauled in the nets an hour later, they discovered that their last-ditch effort had paid unexpected dividends. 'It was just on dark when they came in,' Hardy remembered. 'Imagine our excitement and joy as we saw both nets rising to the surface as if aglow with fire – the blue green fire of phosphorescence; each tow-net bucket was full and the sides of each net were plastered thick with krill all glowing brilliantly.'[20]

Unfortunately, the richness of this haul also served to make the paucity of the subsequent investigations rankle deeply. 'These two lines of stations gave us valuable indications of the proper methods of investigating "krill"' Kemp reported; but he added bitterly ' . . . as events turned out, [they] have proved to be our only source of knowledge of hydrographic conditions in the whaling area. Except with horizontal nets we were never afterwards able to make a line of stations.'[21] The delays encountered during her refit, her subsequent battering in the Bay of Biscay, and the agonisingly slow voyage south, had all conspired to ensure that the *Discovery* arrived much later in the whaling season than had been expected. January and February, the height of the summer, had seen much fine weather but, as Gunther phrased it, 'our every cruise in March and April terminated in bad weather'.[22] Often, when the incessant gales eased in their violence, banks of fog would roll silently in from the sea, rendering the rock-bound coast quite invisible. In such conditions, and with icebergs all around, Stenhouse refused to risk his ship.

Since all matters relating to the ship and to navigation lay within Stenhouse's exclusive preserve, Kemp could hardly argue regarding the risks that were or were not worth taking. But the scientist's disappointment and frustration grew with each wasted day and he felt no aversion to sharing his feelings with the Committee. 'It is . . . to the unsuitability of the ship,' he told them, 'that our lack of success is mainly to be attributed.'[23] In making his own report, Stenhouse could not deny that the ship had proved inadequate to the task, though he also paid tribute to the vessel's fine qualities, which he had come to admire strongly:

> There is little doubt that the *Discovery* is the finest ship afloat where ice alone is the test of superiority. I feel that this ship could with safety penetrate into heavy ice where few ships could follow and while appreciating these special qualities I feel that in endeavouring to work lines of stations in the stormy seas between the Trades and the ice we are expecting too much from the ship. Were all research ships built like the *Discovery* our relative standing of efficiency would, I hope, be high, but in comparison with ships of modern build I am afraid that our results make a poor show.[24]

To Stenhouse, whatever her faults, the *Discovery* was a thing of legend and, to a man of his essentially romantic type, the feelings of nostalgia when treading her decks, particularly in an ice-strewn seascape, were strong. Kemp, on the other hand, dedicated and single-minded, had little time for such feelings. To him the *Discovery* had failed and should be replaced as quickly as possible with a vessel better suited to the task in hand. And, in his eyes, Stenhouse's determined refusal to risk the ship, no matter how great the possible benefits to science, made matters even worse – not that he made any concerted effort to explain the possible rewards. So far, relations between the expedition's two leaders remained cordial, but the seeds for future discord had been sown.

The punishment that the *Discovery* suffered while at South Georgia would do little to improve her sailing qualities. On 5 April, a strong gale struck the island and, instead of protecting the bay in which the *Discovery* lay anchored, the surrounding mountains seemed to funnel the wind down upon it. Clouds raced across the sky before being torn into rags and the surface of the bay churned with ever-increasing violence, becoming a maelstrom of whirling green water. The wind gained such force that, high up the mountainside, the waters of a glacial lake could be seen spilling like tea from a saucer and at last the scientists realised what it meant to be on the same line of latitude as Cape Horn.

Moored to a buoy in the cove, as the wind struck her, the *Discovery* began to swing into the steep and rocky north-eastern shore. Fearful of striking, Stenhouse ordered that the ship slip from the buoy and steam over to the weather-side of the cove where he dropped anchor. But the slippery deposits from the flensing platform meant that the anchors couldn't gain a secure hold and they began to drag. Now the ship faced the gravest peril, unable to anchor securely and a prey to the hurricane-force gusts that began to drive her backwards against the power of her engines. 'We again weighed,' Stenhouse remembered, 'and endeavoured to steam to windward but owing to the force of the wind, the light condition of the ship and her top hamper we could not make steerage way. Both anchors were now dropped but with the engines turning at full speed ahead the ship drove to leeward and on to the eastern end of the government wharf.'[25]

On the bridge, Stenhouse and O'Connor, the first officer, shouted orders, raising their voices against the roar of the wind, while sailors and scientists careered about the deck, freezing spray striking them like hail. Gunther and others leapt the short distance between the ship and the shore and ran to grasp and then secure the ropes that were being thrown from the ship to prevent her from sliding backwards. Then the scientists grabbed desperately at an anchor thrown overboard, and carried it up the beach as an additional brake. 'The anchor in,' recalled Gunther, 'we secured the rope to it, but the *Discovery* laughed. She had drifted so far astern that her after-half, caught by the wind, was blown inshore and levered against the crumpled stage, the bows were forced outwards, and our anchor just ploughed up the soil. . . . Hamilton and I must have looked immensely foolish when we stood upon it in the hope of anchoring it the more – and were treated to a ride.'[26] Finally, confident of a soft, sandy shore, Stenhouse ordered Horton, the Chief Engineer, to start the engines again and then he beached the ship, driving her far enough up to protect both her and the jetty from further catastrophe. Cold, soaked to the skin and exhausted, he and the crew could at least be grateful that no one had been harmed or thrown into the freezing wave-lashed sea.

Twelve days later the crew of the *Discovery* ended their frustrating sojourn on South Georgia. Whenever the wind had eased and the fog had rolled away from the coast they had taken up their positions; but the rolling of the ship in the swell had usually prevented the scientists from maintaining their stations on the platforms suspended above the surface of the sea. All too often, when Herdman and Gunther did manage to mount the platforms, they found themselves periodically immersed up to their waists in the icy water as the ship wallowed from side to side. 'Insufficient power and much top hamper make the ship very unhandy,' Kemp complained; 'when she is stopped to take observations we make excessive leeway even with very moderate winds and the lines "stray" to such an extent as to render our work quite unreliable.'[27] Furthermore, the occasionally violent motions of the ship and the scientists' forgivable desire to complete their operations as swiftly as possible resulted in the fragile equipment being damaged. Despite his lack of real sympathy with Kemp, Stenhouse could appreciate the conscientiousness of the scientists and their willingness to undergo extreme physical discomfort to obtain their results. 'I do not think it possible for anyone who has not experienced the pendulum like movements of this ship to appreciate the difficulty in working the outboard gear without occasional damage,' he noted.[28]

In departing from South Georgia, the scientists intended to conduct a series of stations en route to the Falkland Islands. From there, they would head again for Cape Town, where Stenhouse hoped to improve the ship's sailing qualities by further modifications to her design. But, once again, the tempests of the South Atlantic took the *Discovery* and shook her as a terrier might shake a rat. 'On the 17th April, on leaving Grytviken, we encountered South East winds with a high confused sea,' he reported. 'The ship laboured, and rolled so heavily that I had to "heave to" in order to ease her. During the whole of the night of the 17th the ship continued to roll with occasional violent lurches. At daybreak it was found that the fore and main topmast caps were working badly and, in the main, the wood of the topmast head was badly splintered.'[29] Despite this damage, on 24 April, the *Discovery* limped into Port Stanley to be welcomed by the Governor and his wife, Sir John and Lady Middleton.

Some on board had looked forward rather gloomily to the prospect of a few weeks' stay in Stanley, believing the tiny township must prove a dreary backwater – but they were pleasantly surprised. Parties, they discovered, were 'a feature and dances incessant. . . . In the Town Hall, a fine building erected by the Colonial Engineer, the dancers were as fashionably dressed and the music as up-to-date as in the ballrooms of any metropolis.'[30] After four weeks of partying, interspersed with trawling, dredging and tow-netting, on 20 May Stenhouse and his companions waved goodbye to their jovial hosts and began their long voyage to Cape Town. It had been decided that the *Discovery* and her crew should spend the worst of the winter in South Africa, where some attempt might be made to remedy the worst of the ship's faults, in particular her tendency to roll. Nothing short of a miracle would convince Kemp that the *Discovery* could ever serve satisfactorily as an oceanographic research vessel, but the fitting of sister keels might give her greater stability and enable his team to achieve better results in the period before a replacement ship could be acquired.

Of course, Kemp planned an extensive series of observations to be conducted during the cruise and the scientists completed a considerable amount of work, including nine full stations and soundings in the vicinity of the Subra and O'Brien shoals. But, inevitably, bad weather and the ship's incessant rolling interfered with the programme and resulted in damage to, and the loss of, a number of valuable tow-nets. More significantly, temperamental and professional differences between Stenhouse and Kemp were becoming more pronounced. While the chief scientist fretted at the continual interruptions to his experiments, the mariner thought longingly of the kind of passages he had made when an apprentice: sailing before the wind and clapping on as much canvas as the masts and rigging would carry:

> Owing to the nature of the work on which we are engaged there are few opportunities for testing the sailing qualities of the ship. Our work is at sea and the daily averages under sail or steam cannot be compared with those of this ship when she is being driven in order to make passages in the shortest possible time. I hope that you will not think that I have no scientific sympathies when I say that I would welcome the opportunity to make a passage such as this one from the Falklands to the Cape with the object only of beating her previous records under sail.[31]

In fact, Stenhouse's scientific sympathies were straining to breaking point. Handling the ship in order to make stations demanded consummate skill, but the pleasure in exercising such skill paled in comparison with the joy of squeezing every ounce of speed from his ship. And, of course, the *Discovery*'s limitations meant that the results of such strenuous labour seldom lived up to Kemp's demanding and deeply conscientious expectations.

Everyone on board now knew that the *Discovery* had been purchased to undertake work for which she was wholly unsuited. Disappointment followed disappointment and, to make matters worse, the ship seldom if ever enjoyed an opportunity to demonstrate her finer qualities. To Stenhouse, whose career at sea had been conspicuous for its success, constant failure must have been galling. Furthermore, no captain, least of all one of his character, likes to hear his ship constantly criticised, no matter how aware he might be of her failings. He also began to detect in Kemp's repeated complaints an implied criticism of his own command. Even John Chaplin, the second officer, and a man who did not always feel obliged to side with his captain, thought that 'It was possible that some of the blame for the shortcomings of the ship's sailing qualities was attributed to Captain Stenhouse.'[32] Such mutual suspicions, no matter how veiled, boded ill for the future of the expedition.

THE FINAL SEASON

The *Discovery* reached Cape Town on 29 June and immediately made her way to the Simonstown Naval Dockyards for her overhaul. For three months the Navy shipwrights crawled all over her, fitting the sister keels, checking for the presence of Teredo worm in her planking and strengthening her badly shaken masts. As Stenhouse and his officers supervised this work, Kemp and his team visited the whaling station at Durban and made repairs to their nets and other equipment ready for next season's labours. They also enjoyed ample opportunities for relaxation: reacquainting themselves with the hospitable residents of Cape Town, exploring the interior, playing football and relishing the unaccustomed luxury of hotel accommodation. And opportunities for social intercourse increased still further when the National Oceanographic Expedition's second vessel, the new-built *William Scoresby*, arrived at the Cape en route to South Georgia. Throughout this period, Stenhouse, of course, spent most of his time consulting with the dockyard staff and reporting progress to the Committee in London but, in addition, he had another altogether more unpleasant duty to perform: the sacking of his first officer, Lieutenant-Commander W.H. O'Connor.

In writing to Gladys on the approach to Simonstown, Stenhouse had told her that 'I have had quite a lot of worry and trouble through breaches of discipline and I get rather tired of it. I wish sometimes that we were under Naval discipline or the old sailing ship rule of law and order, instead of this ladylike shipboard government.'[1] He complained also of 'one or two duds' and O'Connor stood foremost in their ranks, though the chief problem lay not so much in his incompetence as in his total inability to get on with his fellow-officers. Matters came to a head on 15 August, when Horton and Chaplin headed a deputation, requesting that Stenhouse either accept their resignations or dismiss O'Connor. When asked the reasons for such drastic action, they told Stenhouse 'that the only reasons were Mr O'Connor's general behaviour and his disloyalty to me and all members of the expedition'.[2] No matter how unwilling he might be to have his hand forced in this way, Stenhouse had little option but to accede to their terms. No captain could afford to lose all of his officers in order to save one man – particularly a man whom he already believed guilty of causing 'suspicion and general discontent, not only between the officers but also between the officers and ship's company'. After an unpleasant interview, he discharged O'Connor, who then took passage home to England. Painful though it might be, it seemed that the matter had been resolved.

After two brief cruises, which included a series of six full stations in the whaling grounds off Saldanha, the *Discovery* set sail for her second season on 27 October. The trials off the coast of Africa had served to demonstrate that the work completed at Simonstown had been beneficial. 'The sister keels proved effective in reducing the rolling,' Stenhouse reported happily. 'The period of roll has been increased to about 8½ seconds and the general movements of the ship are now much easier and she makes less leeway. In consequence we were able to carry out a programme of long consecutive stations which would have been extremely difficult and almost impracticable before the keels were fitted.'[3] As usual, however, the good omens proved deceptive.

This time their enemy was ice. Stenhouse and Kemp had agreed to head south from the Cape of Good Hope to a latitude of approximately 58° where they hoped to pick up finer weather and easterly winds. Instead, they encountered their first ice at 50° on 9 November, and they entered the pack five days later. 'At first the pack was loose with wide leads of open water,' Kemp noted, 'but, as we went on it became closer; it was clear that if we were ever to make our passage to South Georgia we should have to abandon the route we had planned. . . . Everywhere icebergs were hemmed in by the pack and these, in the high wind that then prevailed, gave cause for some anxiety.'[4] Stenhouse merely noted that 'with the pack driving hard to leeward and many bergs about our position was extremely uncomfortable'.[5] Both men agreed that the ice conditions were abnormal for the time of year and Kemp, in particular, could hardly believe his ill luck.

Hoping to escape the bergs, Stenhouse set a north-westerly course to carry the *Discovery* towards Bouvet Island. But the ice remained ever present, and Hardy rather naively wondered if any man had ever seen more in a single day. The constant presence of the bergs, often hidden in dense banks of fog, made it necessary for Stenhouse to keep to the freezing bridge for hours on end, watching the floes and exhorting the lookouts to remain alert. Hardy thought he overtaxed his strength while Dr Marshall, observing his captain with a professional eye, thought that Stenhouse was becoming 'nervy and shows it. He is extraordinarily irritable: takes food – tea and toast mostly – at all hours, and sleeps in three different places.'[6]

Over the next few worrying days, they continued to work their way through the open pack. 'The ship's hefty stem advances through the slush of floating fragments,' Gunther recorded, 'until it comes across a good solid cake of ice: it often splits it into two or three pieces, and our ship's progress continues unchecked. If, however, the obstruction is too large and too solid – if, for instance, it is a couple of feet higher than the surface of the water – the ship may be stopped altogether and possibly recoil.'[7] And so, from dawn until dusk, the ship echoed and vibrated with thump after thump as the *Discovery's* reinforced bow collided with segments of ice which broke with a dull crack and then scraped noisily down her sides. 'The sea temperature is −1°C', Herdman recorded, 'and the air temperature just on Freezing Point, so we don't loiter about on deck when there's any wind!'[8] Icicles hung from the rigging and, every now and then, fell, to shatter on the deck below, often only narrowly missing the scientists and sailors.

During the afternoon of 16 November, with the yellowish loom of Bouvet Island on the horizon, they drew close to a large berg. As they approached to within a ship's length, the great mass of ice suddenly capsized and rolled over, its bottom unevenly melted and worn away by the sea's motion. 'When we were abeam of the berg,' Stenhouse reported, ' . . . topsails and headsails were set, and under sail and steam we drove past with our stern about ten yards clear. Contemplation of what might have happened if circumstances had not favoured us, serves no useful purpose and in ice-navigation particularly, "a miss is as good as a mile".'[9] Fortunately, this near miss marked the end of this strenuous episode and, within a few hours, the *Discovery* broke through the pack and into open water.

Scientists and crew alike breathed a sigh of relief at their escape but other problems now needed to be addressed. Most serious of all was the shortage of coal. On 17 November, the *Discovery* still lay nearly 1,400 miles from South Georgia. Progress had been painfully slow and navigation through the pack had left the coal reserves seriously depleted. 'It was not likely,' Stenhouse remembered, 'that we could expect fair winds or fine weather in these latitudes and Dr Kemp and I had therefore to consider the unpleasant possibility of returning to the Cape. . . . From the 19th to the 23rd November we steamed on one boiler. As we could at times hardly make steerage way, even with a beam wind, this was not economical and I decided to go all out.'[10] As though to demonstrate that 'fortune favours the brave', this decision saw the weather turn in the *Discovery's* favour: but at a cost. To enjoy any chance of reaching South Georgia, Stenhouse had to order that all scientific work be halted – even the tow-nets were brought inboard to reduce the effects of drag on the ship's progress. Most galling of all, the weather was ideal for working stations and, had it not been for the fuel shortage, a full programme of investigations might have been

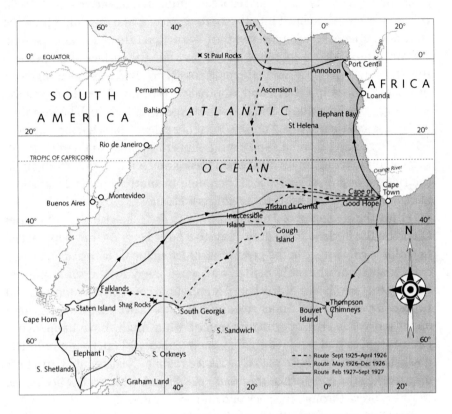

Map 4. The Voyages of the RRS *Discovery*, September 1925–September 1927.

completed. At last, on 5 December, South Georgia loomed on the horizon and that afternoon, with only two days' worth of coal left in her bunkers, the *Discovery*'s anchors struck the floor of Cumberland Bay.

It had been an epic voyage, with ice conditions the worst for a decade; but Stenhouse had brought his ship and crew through it without serious incident. Even Kemp, despite his enormous disappointment at the curtailing of his scientific programme, acknowledged that the passage had been 'much the most anxious that we have had' and paid tribute to Stenhouse who 'so far as human endurance permits has spent every minute on the bridge'.[11] Congratulations might have been reasonably expected but, instead, the letters from the Committee which awaited Stenhouse on his arrival at Grytviken proved anything but complimentary. They revealed that O'Connor's ability to ferment discord on board the *Discovery* had not ended with his departure from the ship.

After being fired, the first officer had sailed to England on board the *Carnarvon Castle* and he had lost no time in putting his case to the *Discovery* Committee. He told them how his dismissal 'came as a severe shock to me and completely unnerved me, for I realised how helpless I was against this very underhand plot'.[12] He went on to explain how his accusers had constantly been 'a source of hindrance to me when I was endeavouring to keep discipline on board' and how 'I had never allowed any order I received from my Captain to be ignored'. The cause of the other officers' dislike of him resulted, therefore, from a mixture of resentment at his own exacting standards, his loyalty to his captain, and their objection to receiving orders from a mere RNR officer. Halfway round the world from the scene of the action and from the other key players, presented on the one hand with an emotive self-defence from the 'victim', and only a month-old official letter from Stenhouse on the other, the Committee members erred on the side of caution. Writing two letters in the carefully couched language of Whitehall, they requested that Stenhouse refer all such matters, including promotions, to them before making his own decisions. They made no explicit reference to his having exceeded his authority, but the implication was clear. To a tired and anxious Stenhouse who, throughout the episode, considered that he had acted fairly and in the best interests of his crew, these letters were like a red rag to a bull.

As captain of the *Discovery*, he believed unequivocally that he possessed the right to discipline his officers. Furthermore, his belief was reinforced by the terms of the crew's contracts; they stated: 'your appointment . . . will be liable to be determined at any time by the Captain of the ship subject to the provisions of the Merchant Shipping Acts'.[13] The Committee's letters of rebuke left him staggered, depressed and furious by turns and he resolved to solicit Kemp's views. No matter what differences of opinion they might have had, Kemp immediately leapt to his colleague's defence:

I can find no words in which to express my feelings about one of these
letters. It makes my blood boil. Has the Committee lost all confidence in
us? Do they not know that we are heart and soul in this show with the
one object of making it a success? Or is there someone in the background
with a private spite against Stenhouse? Even so unworthy a suspicion I
can almost credit ...

Cannot you understand that such things take all the heart out of a man
and that they are utterly destructive of the good relations which have
hitherto existed between us and the Committee. If this had happened in
London you would have had Stenhouse's resignation within a few hours
– he would have resigned by cable if he felt himself a free agent – and I
myself (for the second time in my existence) would have lost my temper in
a Govt. Secretariat.[14]

Kemp then went further, castigating O'Connor as a 'plausible scoundrel'
who, after manipulating his companions on board ship, had then turned
up at the Colonial Office to spread poisonous reports regarding them and
the expedition as a whole. Spurred into action by this vitriolic defence, the
Committee instigated further inquiries. These brought to light the fact that
the first officer had been guilty not merely of disloyalty but also of selling
ship's supplies – a criminal offence – and the matter was closed.

Although the episode left Stenhouse bitter and resentful, Kemp's
angry letters to London wrought a significant change in the tone of the
Committee's correspondence. Aware of just how close they had come to
losing a first-class captain, their next communication, on the subject of
the recently avoided retreat to South Africa, was almost fulsome in its
praise. 'The Committee feel,' they told Stenhouse, 'that the avoidance of
so deplorable a contingency and the safe completion of the voyage was
due to the skilful handling of the vessel, in circumstances of difficulty and
danger, by yourself and the officers and men under your command; and
it is a source of the greatest satisfaction to them to know that the safety
of the enterprise is in such competent hands.'[15] In the circumstances, the
recipient of such a letter must have smiled, albeit grimly.

The *William Scoresby* had arrived at Grytviken before the *Discovery* and
now the two ships worked in unison, surveying the plankton and water
conditions of the whaling grounds. Since the *Scoresby* was by far the faster
vessel, capable of 10 knots, Kemp directed her to undertake the most distant
stations, while the sluggish *Discovery* operated closer to the shore. And,
almost immediately, the good-humoured competition between the two very
different ships added an extra zest to the work of their crews: each wanting
to complete their stations faster and more successfully than their opposite
number. Amazingly, given her reputation for being so ill-suited for the work,

by 21 December the *Discovery* had leapt four stations ahead of the *Scoresby* and her crew felt able to send a mockingly sympathetic message deploring their fellows' ill fortune. The race was on. The *Scoresby* scientists, under Hardy, who had temporarily transferred his flag, were spurred to additional efforts and, by the 23rd, the two ships were level pegging: each with only one station needed to finish their programme. Gunther, working with Hardy on the *Scoresby*, remembered that 'Half-past three soon merged to half-past five, ten, midnight, and so midsummer night was passed – doing stations, bottling catches, pushing forward.'[16] And then, just as it looked as though the *Discovery*, after so many months of failure, might prove the more successful of the two ships, the weather turned against her. While she lay hove to being battered by one of South Georgia's never-ending gales, the *Scoresby* completed her last station – slipping across the finishing line and winning by the merest whisker. In reality, the victory of one ship and the defeat of the other meant very little. The five days leading up to Christmas 1926 had been some of the most successful of the entire expedition. Twenty-nine complete stations had been worked over an area of 10,000 sq. miles of ocean; no fewer than 370 water samples and 307 plankton net hauls had been taken, with each man working to the utmost of his ability. Every member of the expedition could be justifiably proud of his achievements.

Christmas could not have arrived at a better moment. Sailors and scientists had pulled together as a well-ordered professional team; the weather, though seldom kind, had allowed them to do their jobs with only minimal interruptions; and something closely approximating a dead heat in completing the stations had left all the members of the expedition well pleased with themselves and with each other. Now they could afford to celebrate. On Christmas Eve, the whole expedition met at the Marine Station at Grytviken for songs and games, the festivities being lubricated by a generous supply of punch. The ensuing party lived up to the best traditions of heroic age Antarctic exploration, with every member of the team contributing to the makeshift entertainments to the best of his ability. Hardy, in particular, became the star turn when he delivered his own parody of an Edwardian music-hall song, with humorous allusions to each of the crew – including Stenhouse:

> Now Stenhouse our skipper, a hard-case old ripper,
> Since he was a nipper of nine,
> Took command of this barque, 'Cutty Sark' of an ark,
> And sailed her far over the brine.
> He'd coal short and pack-ice, and fog that was not nice,
> Conditions most sure to annoy,
> But when the Chief at the keys, played with such breezy ease,
> He set the wheel spinning with joy![17]

The Christmas Day festivities followed in equally cheerful, though somewhat more staid form. They held a simple church service on board the *Discovery*, followed by a tinned-turkey dinner and present-giving presided over by Dr Marshall as Father Christmas, complete with cotton-wool beard.

A week later, they celebrated New Year's Eve in a truly riotous fashion, the stresses and strains of more than a year of intensely hard work, anxiety and frustration giving way to an explosive, alcohol-fuelled revel. The party began with dinner on board the *Discovery*, with the Norwegian manager of the whaling station, Mr Esbensen, and his daughter, the guests of honour. As dessert was being served, the officers and scientists from the *Scoresby* arrived, already flushed from their own toasts and keen to take full advantage of Stenhouse's and Kemp's hospitality. Bottles circulated with ever-increasing rapidity and soon Esbensen and his daughter departed, excusing themselves on the grounds that they must wish the captains of the whale-catchers a Happy New Year. Unusually sober, Herdman volunteered to take them to shore; when he returned, the bacchanal had entered its liveliest phase. He found his fellows 'well away with the *Discovery* repertoire of vulgar and lewd songs, which, I can assure you, takes some beating! *Scoresby* retired in disorder about 11.30 to get ready their rockets etc and at midnight there was an unholy din – catchers, a transport and our two vessels all whistling in a confined harbour with hills all round made an appalling noise!'[18]

Next, the revellers 'abandoned ship' and made an increasingly uncertain progress round the other vessels in the harbour, drinking additional toasts at every stop. At 3.15 a.m., the party finally staggered to a close, and Herdman again assumed the role of ferryman. 'The skipper was well "away" coming home,' he told a friend, 'and would insist on steaming the launch and trying to incite me to speed – which, knowing him, I wouldn't do – and it was just as well, as he damned nearly wrecked us coming alongside and it was only by going full astern that we managed to avoid a bad crash – as it was, we bumped fairly heavily!'[19] Perhaps Dr Marshall forgot this incident when he later affirmed that Stenhouse was a strict disciplinarian with regards to drink[20] or, perhaps, as a doctor, he identified this unaccustomed over-indulgence as a necessary and timely release of a psychological safety valve.

By the end of 1926, Marshall was observing the signs of intense nervous strain in Stenhouse's behaviour. Incompatible temperaments and their widely differing views on the nature of exploration meant that tensions had always existed between Stenhouse and Kemp and these had been exacerbated by the expedition's split command. Unable to fully sympathise with its goals and *modus operandi*, Stenhouse had perhaps been at fault in accepting such a critical role in the expedition. But Kemp, too, had failed to inculcate an enthusiasm or real understanding of his work in any but the expedition's scientists. Hardy certainly believed that the two men shared the blame. He later stated that 'I have always found that if one tries to understand the difficulties and responsibilities of the captain and at the same time gives him a clear idea of what one is trying to achieve, so as to excite his interest too, there is never any trouble.'[21] Unfortunately, Kemp did not possess this gift of empathy. He was not 'difficult to get on with,' Hardy opined, 'but expected people to realise the importance of the work without being told'.[22] Nor could Kemp fully understand Stenhouse's peculiar difficulties and responsibilities, in particular the fact that, as captain, his ultimate duty was to his ship and to the men on board, with the furtherance of science coming a very poor second.

On top of these problems, the scarcely veiled criticisms of the *Discovery* Committee had rankled deeply. Combined, these irritations served to fray Stenhouse's temper. He became irascible and aloof – even to those, such as Marshall, with whom he had previously been on very friendly terms. Early in the expedition, Gunther had commented in his diary on the harmonious relations that existed between the members of the expedition, on how mealtimes passed in convivial conversation and occasional good-humoured repartee. Now, however, Stenhouse, hitherto a most affable companion, had become 'unapproachable on the ship, morose, and irritable at table',[23] a man whom Worsley would hardly have recognised as his boon companion. Perhaps, in an unconscious attempt to convince himself of his own value to the expedition, Stenhouse also began to push himself forward among the whalers of South Georgia, to seek 'the limelight, to do all the honours and to relegate Dr Kemp to a subordinate position'.[24] Some of these behaviours had shown themselves relatively early in the voyage but many had put them down to the pernicious influence of O'Connor. When the first officer's dismissal failed to remedy them, resentment began to grow, particularly among the officers.

Throughout January 1927, the expedition's two ships continued their detailed plankton survey in the waters surrounding South Georgia. The *Scoresby* concentrated her investigations on the west of the island while the *Discovery* focused on the east, trawling and dredging in Cumberland Bay. During a frenetically busy month, they ascertained the extent of the continental shelf, investigated the strange and previously unexplained patchiness of the krill, and measured the currents. Overall, they subjected the whole eco-system of the whaling grounds to an analysis the depth and comprehensiveness of which had never previously been attempted. In addition, Chaplin, as Surveying Officer, undertook surveys of Larson Harbour, Drygalski Fjord, Leith Harbour and the entrance of Stromness Bay. And, finally, through conversation with the whalers, Stenhouse gathered a wealth of information about the harbours and anchorages of the Dependencies which he submitted for inclusion in the Admiralty's Sailing Directions. For once, all could agree that they had had an immensely productive, if also an immensely exhausting, stay.

At the beginning of February, the crews of the *Scoresby* and the *Discovery* said goodbye to the residents of South Georgia and, for the time being, to each other as well. While the *Scoresby* headed for the Falkland Islands to embark on a campaign of whale marking and trawling, the *Discovery* sailed for the South Orkneys and the South Shetlands. On the 7th, she worked a full station close to the Shag Rocks and, by making a sounding in 97 fathoms, demonstrated that a shoal ridge linked the Rocks and the Wallis Islands. The scientists were delighted to prove the existence of this ridge beneath their keel, but Stenhouse was altogether less pleased at the discovery of a field of twenty-two icebergs some 10 miles distant. He reported to the Committee:

> During the night of the 7th February we had to heave to owing to numerous bergs which loomed all around us. It was now my intention to make westing in order to keep to windward as we expected long and strong gales from the westward in this particularly wild part of the southern ocean. In this expectation we were not wrong and from this time onwards we had a succession of hard westerly gales with high seas. The whole ocean along our track was studded with large bergs. We had sailed on a Friday, a day which has an ill repute as a sailing day amongst sailors and this circumstance was eagerly taken by some of the older members of the ship's company as the reason for the continuous bad weather.[25]

Over the next few days ice remained ever present but the strong winds enabled Stenhouse to set a spread of sail and the *Discovery* soon bowled along at 8½ knots, an almost unheard-of speed for the old ship. He set fore and main topsails, as well as foresail, jib and spankers – all instantly catching the wind and swelling to such an extent that it seemed they must burst with the pressure. Then, on the 10th, as a bright, blustery day drew to a close, the sky began to darken, heavy with the promise of a coming storm. At a word from Stenhouse, the crew swarmed up the rigging and began to take in sail, their active bodies silhouetted against the lowering sky. 'Up aloft go the sailors,' remembered a deeply impressed Hardy, 'as calmly as if the ship had been in port, and out upon the swaying yards which are describing great arcs through the roaring air. . . . Filled with admiration, who cannot wish that he had the nerve to stand on the chains which run below the yards, with nothing else for support, and the strength to pull with all one's might at the wet and heavy sail?'[26]

After a brief stop for coaling at the South Orkneys, where the crew watched the whale factory ships the *Sevilla* and *Orwell* at work, the *Discovery* reached Deception Island on 26 February. Throughout the voyage the ocean had been studded with bergs, all carved and sculpted by wind and sea and some achieving the most extraordinarily contorted shapes. On the 22nd they had passed an enormous example, 35 miles long on its northern side and soaring to a height of 150ft. 'After working stations off the north side of the berg,' Stenhouse noted, 'we rounded its north-west cape from which point it extended beyond our horizon to the south. We were afterwards informed by the whalers that a berg over 100 miles in length was seen by them to the south of Clarence Island.'[27] The following day, the scientists gathered at the rail to catch a distant glimpse of the forbidding outline of Elephant Island, the tiny lump of barren rock that, for four long months, had been home to twenty-two of Stenhouse's friends, as they awaited the return of Shackleton from South Georgia.

Deception Island, with the Antarctic peaks of Graham Land in the far distance, presented the scientists with yet another spectacle. Formed from the sea-filled mouth of an active volcano, the island consists of a ring of snow-capped mountains, rising to nearly 2,000ft, enclosing a deep lagoon which can only be entered through a narrow and dangerous passage, variously called Neptune's Bellows or Hell's Gates. Only three years before the *Discovery*'s arrival the island had demonstrated its latent power. A powerful underwater tremor shook the rocky ring, the black volcanic beaches burst into violent life, giant boulders tumbled and fell and, most terrifying of all, the waters of Port Foster, the inland lake, actually began to boil. Perhaps to the scientists' disappointment, the volcano showed no inclination to further activity during their stay, although the onset of a brief but furious storm showed them that Deception's walls and towers offered only limited protection from the violence of the elements.

Sailing from Deception Island on 2 March, the *Discovery* next skirted the western shore of the Antarctic peninsula. At first, progress was slow, retarded by poor weather, including fog and blizzards, and the continual presence of bergs and pack-ice. Nonetheless, Chaplin managed to complete some valuable surveying work, correcting the charted positions of the Kendall and Austin Rocks, as well as those of the Hoseason, Snow and Smith Islands. They also surveyed the Schhollaert and Neumayer Channels and Gerlache Strait, and Stenhouse took the opportunity to name a newly discovered channel after his ship. The scientists, meanwhile, made hauls with dredge, trawl and tow-net at every opportunity, often with considerable success. In particular, Hardy delighted in the discovery of a curious transparent sea-cucumber and a remarkable and entirely unknown form of bright purple octopus. A few days later, the *Discovery* reached her furthest point south on this expedition: 65° South latitude by dead reckoning. 'These waters are but roughly charted,' Stenhouse told the Committee, 'and during the long nights of March and April when there is 12 hours darkness navigation is extremely difficult.'[28] He added that 'There is much exploration and surveying to be done in this neighbourhood,' but now he possessed neither time nor leisure for such activities.

On 24 March Hardy recorded how the Antarctic sky was 'lit with coloured light, broad sweeps of pure colour passed either by gentle gradations, or sometimes by sharp contrasts, into different hues. In the sun the snow on the steep ranges high above us was a vivid rose pink with the rocks warmed to a rich apricot shade; the sky behind was violet-blue merging lower down to that rich translucent turquoise now so familiar to us. . . . It was if we were steaming in a giant kaleidoscope.'[29] It seemed as if the great and mysterious Antarctic continent was putting on her most beautiful face to welcome back the *Discovery* after her decades of absence: welcoming back, too, Stenhouse, who had seen her in all her varying moods. In remarkably calm and clear weather, the scientists worked line after line of highly profitable stations before returning to Deception Island for coaling.

Now the *Discovery* faced some of the most demanding work of the entire National Oceanographic Expedition. Departing on 14 April, Kemp intended to run a line of stations through Drake's Strait, the 400 miles of notoriously turbulent sea stretching from the South Shetlands to Cape Horn and dividing the Atlantic from the Pacific Ocean. It was these waters that Stenhouse had first encountered nearly a quarter of a century earlier, when the *Springbank* had been tossed like a cork in a bucket en route to San Francisco. In that Christmas of 1904, the young sailor would have laughed to scorn the very idea of keeping a ship in a fixed position in these waters while soundings were taken and nets trawled. And it was true that never before had such a programme been attempted. On the other hand, if they succeeded, their work would yield some of the most eagerly anticipated results of the whole programme and round off the expedition victoriously.

Miraculously, the fine weather continued with hardly an interruption and the crew completed station after station in relative calm. They lost some equipment in the shape of water-bottles and wire cable but, overall, the South Atlantic treated them with remarkable charity. Not until the very end of April did the weather fully turn, as the *Discovery* approached Cape Horn from the south and headed for the Strait of Le Maire to pass back into the waters of the South Atlantic. 'We passed through the strait on the following day,' Stenhouse reported, 'not however without incident, for with a strong north-north-west wind we were set towards the Staten Island shore and in the tide race were unable to make headway. All hands were called and all sail set except top-gallantsails. The ship was labouring heavily in the high confused sea and the main engines raced as I have never known them to do before.'[30] Hardy recorded how 'The old ship battled into this clash of elements and pitched as never before, putting down her head and lifting it as if purposely throwing sheets of white spray over her back.'[31] At last, however, just as it seemed the tides would turn against her, a change of wind gave Stenhouse the opportunity to hoist sail. 'We bore away under steam and a heavy press of canvas,' he noted with relief, 'on a course almost parallel to the north coast of Staten and eventually made a good offing, clear of danger.'

They worked a further set of six stations en route to the Falkland Islands, where the *Discovery* was briefly reunited with the *Scoresby*, and then, on 28 May, the two ships parted again to undertake further observations on the way to Cape Town. The *Scoresby* would sail via South Georgia and Gough Island, while the *Discovery* set a course for Tristan da Cunha. The voyage started well, with a series of stations being worked at 10-mile intervals and horizontal nets being towed every two days or so. On 3 June, however, the wind began to freshen from the south-west and soon reached gale force. It proved impossible to complete a series of stations in the vicinity of Tristan and, rather than revisiting the islanders and stocking up on fresh fish, the *Discovery* was forced to continue her voyage towards the coast of Africa. She spent around a fortnight in dry dock at Simonstown having her hull overhauled and then, on 18 July, she began the last leg of her journey back to England.

At last, on 24 September 1927, after a two-month passage during which a further series of stations were made up the west coast of Africa, the *Discovery* dropped anchor at Falmouth: two years to the day since she had sailed from Dartmouth. Looking back on their endeavours, Stenhouse, Kemp and their companions could be justifiably proud of their achievements. In the twenty-four months since September 1925, despite adverse weather conditions, the prevalence of icebergs, towering seas and serious flaws in their ship's design, they had completed the most comprehensive oceanographic survey since the *Challenger* deep-sea expedition of 1872–6. In fact, while the *Challenger* had completed 362 stations in her three and a half years' voyage, the *Discovery* and the *William Scoresby* between them had worked no fewer than 435 in two years (the *Discovery* working 299 and the *Scoresby* 136). Over 1,000 plankton samples had been taken and an even greater number of physical and chemical observations made, including measurements of temperature, density, salinity and alkalinity, from a range of depths.

'The results of the expedition are of the greatest scientific interest,' asserted L.H. Matthews, one of the South Georgia scientists, 'for never has a fully equipped expedition properly investigated an area such as that of the Dependencies. . . . In responsible quarters it is, and in the most short-sighted ones it will be, agreed that the enterprise and foresight of the Government of the Falkland Islands are of paramount importance not only to the Dependencies but to the whole Empire and indeed to the entire world.'[32] All the scientists knew that, once brought together and analysed, the mass of data they had gathered would create a picture of ocean life of unparalleled complexity and completeness. The creation of this picture would be a difficult and long-winded business but, fortunately, as Hardy later affirmed, 'Just as there is excitement in snatching our samples between the storms so there is another fascination, quieter but no less real, of reconstructing the course of nature from what at first appears to be a flood of data almost equally opaque as the sea itself.'[33] Eventually, this reconstruction would become embodied in thousands of pages of detailed scientific reports. The expedition also laid the groundwork for further investigations which, given the *Discovery*'s very mixed performance as a research ship, would be undertaken in a newly commissioned vessel, the RRS *Discovery II*. This time, however, another captain would take Stenhouse's place at the helm.

The storm that had been gathering for so many months on board the *Discovery* finally broke on the expedition's arrival in England. Within a fortnight of his return to London, Stanley Kemp wrote to the *Discovery* Committee categorically refusing any suggestion that he should ever again serve with Stenhouse. In December 1926, when discussing Stenhouse's decision to dismiss O'Connor, the Chief Scientist had defended his colleague with robust and uncompromising language; he employed a similar tone now, when addressing the Committee's chairman, Rowland Darnley:

> It is with very great regret that I have to inform the Committee that I could not serve on a second commission with Captain Stenhouse. Though we have managed to pull through the past two years, I have come to the conclusion that I could not undertake a second voyage under the same conditions.
>
> In my opinion Captain Stenhouse does not possess the right temperament for the post he holds: he is very nervy, subject to prolonged fits of depression, and being by nature egotistical, the fact that he was not in full command of the expedition has always been very distasteful to him. I do not feel that I have had from him that loyal co-operation which I had a right to expect, and except as a safe navigator I have scarcely a shred of confidence left in him.[34]

Darnley and his colleagues could hardly ignore such a damning indictment. In 1924, the Committee had been at great pains to recruit Kemp's services, entering into protracted negotiations with his previous employer, the government of India, and even going to the lengths of significantly increasing the stipulated wage and guaranteeing his pension rights. Now he offered them an ultimatum which, if they chose to brush it aside, could result in their having to locate another, equally well-qualified Director of Research. And they knew full well that scientists with the requisite experience who were also willing to devote themselves to two or more years of field research in the harshest shipboard conditions were few and far between. But neither could the Committee simply cast Stenhouse aside. He too, had been employed only after they had completed the most exacting recruitment process, he had given four years' exemplary service and he had actually been in the Committee's employ longer even than Kemp.

Eventually, they decided not simply to take Kemp's word regarding Stenhouse's perceived unfitness for the post of captain, nor to give any form of precedence to the higher-paid scientist. Instead, a special meeting would be convened at which both antagonists would be given an opportunity to defend themselves. Perhaps more importantly, other senior members of the expedition would be asked to give their opinions. The meeting was held at the Colonial Office on 2 December 1927 and three members of the expedition, in addition to Stenhouse and Kemp, attended: Chaplin, the first officer, Hardy, the chief zoologist, and Marshall, the ship's surgeon. The meeting began with a recapitulation, in front of the two protagonists, of the difficulties that had been brought to the Committee's attention. With nothing new being added by either side, the Committee asked Stenhouse and Kemp to wait in an anteroom while their shipmates gave evidence, beginning with Hardy.

Of the three witnesses Alister Hardy was perhaps the most reluctant, knowing that his remarks must contribute to one man or the other losing his job. He believed himself to be, he said, the friend of both men and had the greatest respect for each. Fundamentally, he thought the problems encountered had arisen through incompatibility of temperament. 'Kemp was a man,' he stated, 'who did not like any show or fuss and perhaps he might have done more to awaken the interest of the marine staff, who had never had the importance of the work made clear to them.'[35] Stenhouse, on the other hand, 'had not the scientific temperament. He has tried his best, but had sometimes appeared tired and disappointed . . . [Hardy] thought that the ship would be better under a Captain with a scientific interest, rather than under one of the "dashing explorer" type.' Kemp's quiet temperament simply did not fit in with that of the Captain. He also thought that Stenhouse was inclined to 'spend too much time on the bridge and became over-tired'; this exhaustion, in turn, may have contributed to making him increasingly cautious and this propensity retarded the progress of the scientific work.

Chaplin's remarks tended to underpin Hardy's assessment: Stenhouse had, he thought, become cautious though, as a sailor, he saw this more in his reluctance to carry a greater mass of sail than in anything else. He also saw 'the present system of dual control as impossible and that it was essential to have one definite head'.[36] The shared command had perhaps engendered a degree of competitiveness between the two men and 'Dr Kemp occasionally "trod on the Captain's corns" through dealing direct with the latter's subordinates.' Stenhouse, in turn, showed an inclination to 'butt in' and attempted to do everything himself. Overall, however, Dr Marshall's remarks proved the most telling. As ship's surgeon he had become increasingly concerned over Stenhouse's state of mind. On ship and shore the Captain became two different men: hearty and companionable by land, morose, irritable and intensely nervy by sea, and prone to question everybody else's judgement. 'Captain Stenhouse "cried for ice" at South Georgia in 1926,' Marshall told the Committee, 'but when he got it in 1927 was very nervous.'[37] All the symptoms, the surgeon opined, were indicative of an imminent and 'definite breakdown in the Captain's health. . . . Captain Stenhouse's condition was almost pathological and . . . probably he could not change.'

Faced with such a weight of professional opinion, delivered by men whom, it was clear, bore Stenhouse no personal malice, the Committee found that they had little option but to side with Kemp. They would confirm the Director of Research in his post while, albeit with regret, they would cast adrift the Master of the *Discovery*. Although Hardy criticised the Committee for being a machine, its members did make every attempt to mitigate the impact of their final decision on Stenhouse. In particular, they gave him a glowing testimonial, in which they expressed the Committee's 'desire to record their high appreciation of his ability and conduct, and his loyalty to their instructions during the whole period of his service. In particular, the Committee greatly appreciate the safe and successful navigation of the *Discovery* under his command, during her first voyage, under conditions of extreme difficulty. . . . The Committee recall with pleasure their pleasant personal relations with Captain Stenhouse, and they wish him every success in the future.'[38] Generously, they also continued his employment until 30 June 1928, allowing him six months in which to find another job.

Overall, Stenhouse took the blow well, writing to the Committee, without a trace of irony, to thank them for their support and wishing them every success with their future investigations. He may even have accepted that their decision was the right one. His two years in command of the *Discovery* had been demanding ones, certainly not made any easier by the O'Connor episode and by his inability to see eye to eye with Kemp. The constant strain had taken its toll on his temper and had, perhaps, brought to the fore latent, previously suppressed, stresses. His two gruelling years with the Imperial Trans-Antarctic Expedition had been immediately followed by work on Q-ships, one of the most nerve-racking forms of sea-service, and by another year in North Russia. Then had come a period of often profound uncertainty as to his future. Individually, each of these episodes had included moments of high exhilaration and enjoyment; they had brought him into close companionship with men he both liked and respected; and they had been rewarding, if not in terms of financial remuneration, then at least so far as fame and decorations were concerned. But it was inevitable that a decade of often extreme pressure and responsibility for other men's lives must, eventually, exact a physical and mental toll.

In observing Stenhouse, Dr Marshall believed that he had identified a man on the edge of a total mental breakdown: unpredictable, averse to risk, inclined to laziness, intensely nervous and irritable. A character, indeed, wholly at odds with the public image of the highly decorated war hero and bullish man of action known to so many. Marshall had not shared with the Committee his views on the best prescription for Stenhouse's condition, but his report had ensured that he would not, at least, continue to be subjected to the peculiar strains inseparable from command of the *Discovery*. Instead, for a period, Stenhouse might be able to relax in the company of his family. But this sojourn was unlikely to be of long duration since, without a private income, he must quickly find a means by which to support Gladys and the children. Though he didn't yet know it, the next decade would actually prove to be one of the most difficult of his entire life.

PIECES OF EIGHT

With no immediate prospect of employment, Stenhouse's priority was to find a suitable and affordable home in which to consider his future. Fortunately, Gladys's family, the Campbells, proved both sympathetic and generous. Before his departure on the *Discovery* in September 1925, Stenhouse, Gladys and the three girls had spent much of their time on the Isle of Wight with Gladys's older sisters, Helen, Ada and Grace. Now the spinsters offered them a permanent home on the island in the form of Matchells, an ancient smugglers' cottage near Colwell Bay. They had purchased the cottage after the war, with the intention of retiring to it when age and infirmity made their larger house, Kinloch Tay, unmanageable; but, recognising Gladys's pressing need for a suitable home, they immediately made it over to the Stenhouses.

Originally two dwellings which had been converted into one house, Matchells offered comfortable and roomy, if occasionally primitive, accommodation, with eight rooms spread over two floors, and a bathroom housed in a small extension. Nestling in a fold of the hills, the cottage had no sea view, but a beautiful sandy beach lay a mere 5 minutes' walk to the west. A quarter of a mile in the opposite direction the village of Freshwater possessed shops and a church – not that the latter amenity would mean much to Stenhouse, who avoided regular churchgoing by insisting that, as a Scot, he could worship only in Kirk.

At last, after two years of separation, the Stenhouses had a home they could call their own and, with no immediate prospect of another voyage, an abundance of time to spend together, playing with their children and making plans for the future. Their new home also provided ample opportunities for recreation, including horse riding. During his early years with the Weir Line, as an apprentice and young ship's officer, Stenhouse had developed a real taste for exploring on horseback the hinterlands of the ports he visited. Now, he and Gladys borrowed mounts from their neighbours and galloped across the broad expanse of Tennyson Downs close by. The stately Victorian poet, Alfred, Lord Tennyson, had regularly walked here from his home,

Farringford House, and he claimed that the air on the Downs 'was worth sixpence a pint'. Unfortunately, a bolting horse's pell-mell charge towards the cliff edge turned Gladys against riding, and the Stenhouses then moved towards more sedate forms of relaxation, spending hours walking with the children in nearby Victoria Woods.

As time passed, with no hint of long-term employment on the horizon, Stenhouse tried to eke out his slender resources by accepting piecework, sometimes sailing pleasure boats from England to France and Spain for wealthy yachtsmen. As a professional seaman, he had little sympathy with weekend sailors, but their money proved welcome. Then, between 1929 and 1930, he toyed briefly with a new and highly unusual money-making scheme: Antarctic tourism. His first idea was to charter a Dutch liner named the *Volendam*, which he would command on a sightseeing cruise to Antarctica. Hoping to attract wealthy Americans, he sailed to New York to set up a temporary headquarters and to start promoting his scheme but, in September 1929, the Wall Street Crash sent investors reeling, forcing him to abandon his plans and return to England. Undeterred, he decided to work up a new proposal along similar lines. This time he would purchase the Norwegian passenger ship, the *Stella Polaris*, and then sail her via New York, Havana, the Panama Canal, the Galapagos Islands and Tahiti to Auckland and thence south to Antarctica. Having crossed the Antarctic Circle, the ship would penetrate the fringe of floating pack-ice with the intention of entering the Bay of Whales; weather conditions permitting, she would then cruise 400 miles along the Great Ice Barrier to visit Ross Island and McMurdo Sound before returning by way of Australia.

The scheme intentionally combined the pleasures of a holiday cruise with some of the thrills of high adventure and, in advertising his plans, Stenhouse made frequent reference to the fact that his passengers would be given an opportunity to see sites made famous by the exploits of the Heroic Age explorers. Always keen to appeal to the American market, he told *Time* magazine that 'We shall visit Admiral Byrd's old headquarters on the barrier, see Mount Erebus, the steaming volcano, and watch the great whaling fleets in action.'[1] And, in the hope, perhaps, of attracting some wealthy invalids, he also emphasised the salubrity of the Antarctic climate: 'A pure germless atmosphere, 24 hours of sunshine every day of the season at which we will visit it and a cold, dry, invigorating climate with the temperature around 31° Fahrenheit.' But whatever the benefits of Antarctica's germ-free air, Stenhouse's ambitious and innovative plans were brought crashing to the ground by the altogether less benign economic climate. After his failure the year before, he might have hoped that, given time, the world's financial markets would stabilise. Instead, the economic chaos showed no signs of abating. In such circumstances, and no matter how desirable it might be to take part in the first-ever Antarctic pleasure cruise, few would-be holiday-makers could justify spending the

$2,500 that Stenhouse intended to charge for each ticket. With ticket sales dwindling to nothing, he had no option but to abandon his scheme.

His plans in ruins, Stenhouse again found himself at Matchells with time on his hands. He occupied some of his enforced leisure making improvements to the cottage, spending days on his hands and knees, with shirtsleeves rolled up, boarding the earthen floor with wood salvaged from old tea chests. But, while he kept himself busy with whatever paid work materialised, with home improvements and with organising cricket matches and other games on the beach, it was impossible not to be concerned at an increasingly uncertain future. Sometimes, with their supply of funds at an all-time low, the Stenhouses even found themselves obliged to accept vats of home-made soup from the neighbouring Campbell sisters, just to keep the family from hunger. And, at times, Gladys's optimistic assertions that their 'ship would come in' must have sounded distinctly hollow.

Stenhouse's current existence also had an undeniable element of incongruity. Having spent the majority of his life with men of more or less his own stamp, whether working ship or relaxing with a whisky and an uproarious performance of sea shanties, bawdy or otherwise, he now found himself a solitary male in a household of women. It was both a novel and, at times, a frustrating experience. In particular, accustomed to the discipline of shipboard life, the untidiness of some members of his family drove him to distraction. As the worst culprit, Patricia would be subjected to a frequent and increasingly irate repetition of the mantra 'A place for everything and everything in its place!' And, on one occasion, Stenhouse became so incensed by the chaos of her bedroom that he picked up her cluttered bedside cabinet and deliberately upturned it in the middle of the floor: another pile of rubbish, he told her, could make no difference!

Male guests were relatively few and far between but Walter Campbell, Gladys's brother who had served as a regular Army officer until seriously wounded on the Somme, visited occasionally. The two men had become friends when Campbell stayed with his sisters after the death of his first wife and, sharing similar views on a range of subjects, they enjoyed long walks along the cliffs. On other, particularly happy days, the cottage rang with the cry 'Yoicks, tally-ho!' as Worsley burst in upon them, now happily married and bubbling over with jollity and news of his latest exploits. And, not surprisingly, it was Worsley who brought the offer of another adventure that would take Stenhouse away from his family and back to sea: from the Isle of Wight to Treasure Island.

When writing his famous adventure novel at the beginning of the 1880s, Robert Louis Stevenson had been inspired by stories of a real-life treasure island: Cocos Island in the South Pacific. Lying some 550 miles south-west of the Pacific outlet of the Panama Canal, this tiny jungle-covered island had become legendary as the hiding place for the ill-gotten gains of an assortment of pirates, including William Dampier and the picturesquely named Bonito-the-bloody. All of these buccaneers had made themselves wealthy and notorious in equal measure by scouring the Spanish Main and plundering the galleons which every year carried tons of Inca gold from the New World to the Old. Most famously of all, in 1821 as Simon Bolivar prepared to storm Lima, the Spanish dignitaries resident in the city had loaded their gold on to a brig named the *Mary Dier*. The Spaniards intended that the treasure should be returned to them once Bolivar had been defeated but the brig's nefarious captain, an Englishman named Thompson, had other ideas. Once the treasure had been loaded, he cut his cables and ran his ship out to sea. He, too, chose to bury his treasure on Cocos but then died before he could return to reclaim his ill-gotten gains.

By the beginning of the twentieth century, these assorted stashes of treasure carried a collective value of many millions of pounds sterling: a hugely tempting prize for any adventurer, impecunious or otherwise. Innumerable expeditions had visited the island's shores, each convinced that it possessed the knowledge and skill to uproot the bullion which had escaped the prying eyes and spades of so many others. Most importantly for Stenhouse and Worsley, nearly a quarter of a century earlier, the island had been visited by two of their fellow Antarctic veterans and friends, Aeneas Mackintosh and Frank Bickerton.

In April 1911, the two explorers had landed on Cocos Island with a small party which included, unusually, two Edwardian lady philanthropists. The ladies meant to devote any recovered treasure to the founding of a new orphanage in London; the motives of Bickerton and Mackintosh, on the other hand, may have been altogether less altruistic. They had spent a month rowing round the island's rocky shore and hacking their way through the lush rainforest, squinting at the scratches which they found on every rock and which, Mackintosh had admitted, 'we all try to shape into anchors, arrows or such-like shapes!'[2] Of course, the treasure hunters, who were pitifully ill-equipped and wholly dependent upon a treasure map of dubious provenance, eventually left the island disgruntled, disillusioned and empty-handed. But the adventure had at least given them a wonderful story with which to entertain their friends. And it had not been long before they both found themselves in environments where any romantic anecdote was looked upon as a real boon: Bickerton trapped by 300mph winds in the AAE hut at Cape Denison and Mackintosh on board the *Aurora*. A mysterious, uninhabited island in the South Pacific; tales of bloodthirsty and piratical derring-do; and gold and precious stones valued, even by the conservative officials of the Foreign Office, at £5 million: what greater temptation could there possibly be for men of Stenhouse's and Worsley's stamp?

By 1934, Cocos Island belonged to Costa Rica, whose government, over the years, had capitalised on the island's reputation by selling exclusive but time-limited treasure-hunting concessions to a number of expeditions, most recently that funded by a Canadian firm called the Clayton Metalophone Company. The offer to Stenhouse of a cruise to Cocos Island now came from the directors of another company, the optimistically named Treasure Recovery Ltd (TRL), who claimed to have purchased the final years of the Canadian concession. Unusually, Stenhouse and Worsley were to act, in the first instance, not as ship's officers but rather as 'field executives', responsible for the on-the-spot management of the expedition's personnel and the planning of the programme of excavations.

And the management of the personnel in question might prove a difficult and explosive responsibility. In most company, Stenhouse and Worsley could confidently expect to stand out from the crowd, with their breasts covered in medal ribbons and their CVs packed with incident and adventure. But now they found themselves among men whose buccaneering careers vied with their own. Colonel Jack E. Leckie, an associate of the Clayton Metalophone Company, was a Canadian whom Stenhouse had met in North Russia; he had won the DSO during the Boer War and brought to TRL his experience as a mining engineer and gold prospector in British Columbia. Lieutenant-Commander F.C. 'Finnie' Finnis DSO and Captain Charles Polkinghorne were sea officers of long standing, while Stratford Dowker Jolly was perhaps the most experienced treasure hunter. He had taken part in Edgar Sanders's hunt for Jesuit treasure on the Sacambaya river in Bolivia in 1928, the Montezuma Treasure Expedition to Guatemala in 1930 and the Spanish Main Treasure Expedition of 1932–3, but most of the participants had joined at least one treasure hunt in the last decade. Finally, Captain S. MacFarlane Arthur, a cashiered Army officer, out-Heroded Herod in the sheer variety and colour of his career. In a trial which had proved the *cause célèbre* of 1924, Arthur had been heavily implicated in a blackmail ring that had surprised Sir Hari Singh, the Maharaja of Jammu and Kashmir, in *flagrante delicto* with a married woman. Arthur's reputation had been blasted but crime paid and, by 1934, he could boast possession of his own yacht and he had already accompanied at least one expedition to Cocos.

It soon became clear that the directors of TRL had no intention of letting their expedition slip away under a veil of secrecy; instead, they did everything possible to raise public awareness. At the beginning of August, Arthur gave an interview to *The Times*, and expounded the expedition's novel approach: 'This is the first scientific treasure hunt. Our experts will tackle it as an engineering problem. . . . We shall electrify an area and prod the ground with instruments. On getting a reaction we shall send down the core drill, and if there is anything there we shall get a sample of it. We are using an aeroplane for survey purposes. Telephones will link up the camp and the works.'[3] For their expedition vessel, TRL had borrowed the 600-ton luxury yacht, *Queen of Scots*, from the millionaire Anthony J. Drexel, and no one watching the preparations for departure could doubt that the company intended to do the thing on a grand scale. In a flurry of publicity, the directors attempted to sell the story of the expedition to the newspapers; and they ostentatiously waved the records of their field executives under the noses of prospective backers. Nor were they above persuading Stenhouse and Worsley that they, too, should attempt to convince wavering investors by writing suitably enthusiastic letters, despite 'our original pious wish that no-one should put in enough to inconvenience themselves in the event of failure'.[4]

With as much of a fanfare as it could conjure, the expedition finally sailed on the evening of 19 August 1934. Standing not at his accustomed post on the bridge, but at the rail like any common passenger, Stenhouse watched the sun setting in a blaze of glory. The yacht echoed with all the accustomed activity of a vessel just put to sea: the thump and whirr of her reconditioned engines; the flap of the ensign at her stern; and, in response to an order from Captain A.D. Bellingham, the pounding of feet on the teak decks. But intermingled with the well-known hubbub, another familiar but incongruous sound could be discerned: the laughter and conversation of women. A number of the treasure seekers had decided to take their wives with them to the South Pacific and the presence on board the luxury yacht of so many ladies lent to the expedition the atmosphere of a pleasure cruise. Even Worsley had succumbed to the temptation and had brought Jean; suffering the first pangs of seasickness, she could now be heard retching in their cabin below. Gladys, of course, with the children to look after, had waved the yacht off from London's South West India Dock and she would now be travelling back to Matchells by train. If all went according to plan and Cocos Island disgorged its gold, by the time Stenhouse saw her and the children again, their money worries might be over forever.

After a voyage of eight days, trouble-free except for leaking water closets and the prevalence of seasickness among the ladies, the *Queen of Scots* anchored in Tenerife's Santa Cruz Harbour at 3 p.m. on 27 August. Keen to make the most of the fine weather and the holiday atmosphere, Worsley decided to lead a party of twelve on a sightseeing tour of the island. Stenhouse, meanwhile, stayed on board, discussing the forthcoming voyage with Captain Bellingham, poring over the charts of Cocos Island and supervising the ship's carpenter as he sought to address the shortcomings of the yacht's plumbing. The afternoon passed productively but without any incident of special note and he retired to his cot before the return of the sightseers, whose laughter and clatter as they embarked at midnight passed unnoticed. A few short hours later, however, an anxious-looking steward shook him awake with the unwelcome news that, not only had two of Worsley's party not returned, but that they had been arrested for affray, with the authorities threatening to charge one, at least, with attempted murder!

On their arrival at Santa Cruz, the members of the expedition had heard rumours of an impending dock strike but there had been no suggestion that it would directly affect them. Worsley's party had landed without any difficulty at 4 p.m. and, after a pleasant afternoon exploring the Orotava Valley and enjoying the local hospitality and the local wine, they had returned to Santa Cruz to hire boats to ferry them back to the *Queen of Scots*. But the noise made by the happy revellers, as they tumbled into their boats, had attracted the unwelcome attention of some shop stewards who objected to the boatmen accepting fares and thereby breaking the strike. Ten members of Worsley's party had regained the yacht without hindrance, but the last two day-trippers, Howe and Allen, had been intercepted while still negotiating their fare. There had been some attempt at manhandling, which the Englishmen resented, a policeman had been called and a scuffle had ensued. The end result was that Howe and Allen now found themselves languishing among pimps and toughs in the disgustingly squalid local jail.

Pulled from his bed, bleary-eyed and tousled, over the next few hours, Stenhouse managed to engineer the release of Allen, but the local magistrate seemed inclined to take seriously the trumped-up charges against Howe, who now occupied a cell with two jovial murderers. Having ascertained that Howe was unharmed, Stenhouse occupied the rest of the day soliciting the help of the British consul, seeking witnesses to the alleged assault on the policeman; and appealing to the magistrate. The following day, too, was filled with a flurry of similar activities, with Stenhouse and the consul gathering character references for Howe and liaising with the British Embassy in Madrid. Eventually, on the 30th, his campaign met with success: the magistrate decided to drop the charge of assaulting a policeman (fortunately the stories of a charge of attempted murder had proved to be an exaggeration) and he permitted a relieved but sheepish Howe to rejoin his ship. The jailbird received a hero's welcome from his comrades, but the barking of orders soon drowned out their laughter and cheers as the yacht turned towards the harbour entrance. Neither Stenhouse nor Captain Bellingham intended to allow any further opportunity for mischief, or for the magistrate to change his mind. Unfortunately, despite their best endeavours, this would not be the expedition's only brush with the law; nor would Howe remain the only treasure hunter to experience the delights of a foreign prison.

Three weeks later, on 20 September, the *Queen of Scots* reached Colón, prior to passing through the Panama Canal and embarking on the final short leg of the voyage to Cocos Island. While Stenhouse busied himself about the ship's affairs (Captain Bellingham had proved himself more inclined to pick fault with the work of others than to undertake anything himself), Worsley travelled up to Panama, where he visited the British consulate. The consul, Mr Cleugh, whom Worsley had previously met at Montevideo during the

Endurance Expedition, had bad news. Thanks to the publicity so assiduously courted by TRL's directors, newspaper reports regarding the expedition's destination and intentions had reached the Costa Rican authorities and they had lodged a complaint with the British government. The concession granted to the Clayton Metalophone Company was, Cleugh had been warned, exclusive and would run until October 1935. Despite the protestations of Captain Arthur and Colonel Leckie, no transfer of the concession had been agreed by the Canadian company and, even if it had, the transfer had not been sanctioned by the Costa Ricans. This being the case, Costa Rica would not countenance a landing on its sovereign territory by the staff of TRL; furthermore, any such unauthorised landing would be resented and actively resisted. Worsley brazened it out, stating that he had it on good authority that the concession had been transferred and, even if it hadn't, Costa Rica's claim to the island and, therefore, its right to interfere were unproven. And so the interview ended, in a manner satisfactory to none.

Despite his bullishness, Worsley was worried and, as soon as he rejoined the *Queen of Scots* on 22 September, he told Stenhouse of his interview and of his concerns. Stenhouse, whose attention remained focused almost solely on ship-related matters, didn't attach too much weight to the words of the Foreign Office officials, who naturally erred on the side of caution, but he agreed that they should share the news with the other senior expeditionaries. Arthur, who might be viewed as one of the architects of the expedition's current problems, was dismissive; Jolly, whose nature matched his name, seemed largely unconcerned; but Polkinghorne shared Worsley's anxiety over the doubtful transfer of the concession, which everyone on the expedition had been assured was a done deal. Having come so far, however, and with too little money in TRL's coffers to allow of unnecessary delays, they agreed that they should continue with their voyage to Cocos and, once there, with their programme of excavations. If the transfer of the concession had not yet been completed, then negotiations could continue while the treasure hunters got on with their investigations. As for the Costa Rican government, for all its threats, it had taken no real steps to stop the expedition from progressing; indeed, it hadn't even gone so far as to send its own accredited representative to talk to TRL's executives, relying, instead, upon an unofficial representation through the British Foreign Office. Although Worsley believed that 'the British Embassy hadn't warned us for fun',[5] if the Costa Ricans had wanted their warnings to be taken as anything but bluff, surely they would have interfered in a more determined manner? Their decision made, Stenhouse and his companions sailed for 'Treasure Island' on 24 September.

They reached their destination two days later and all agreed that, on first sight, Cocos certainly lived up to its reputation as an inaccessible pirate retreat, the hiding place of millions of pounds' worth of ill-gotten gold and jewels. Between 25 and 30 sq. miles in area, the island possesses a coastline some 5½ miles long. But, despite its ruggedness, the shore has only two bays capable of taking ships, Chatham Bay and Wafer Bay; neither offers a good anchorage close inshore, and their waters teem with sharks, waiting for boats to be overturned in the violent surf. Worsley later told his goddaughter that 'you can hardly haul a fish up before a blackguard of a mouth almighty snaps him off. We never let go anchor without braining a pair of 'em!'[6] The island's interior is dotted with hills, the tallest of which rises to nearly 3,000ft, their sides scored with innumerable precipitous ravines and gullies, all of them draped in dense equatorial jungle. Worsley found that 'The "bush" here is dark and very hard to penetrate but with a strange wild beauty of its own. There are great trees running up 200ft with huge lianas or vines with stems as thick as a man's body creeping up and festooning the trees. . . . Undergrowth, creepers and 7ft high jungle grass that cuts like a fine saw make the boulder strewn slopes terribly difficult to cross.'[7]

In the heat and humidity, cutting a path through this abundant vegetation to then dig and hew excavation shafts into the solid rock would be hugely demanding, but all were anxious to start work. As soon as the stores and equipment had been landed, the latter including a wireless station, a washing machine and a refrigerator as well as the expedition's fêted metal detectors, Stenhouse and Worsley, like two schoolboys, dived into the interior to begin their quest. 'Stennie and I,' Worsley recorded, 'searched under enormous rocks hurled down [the] mountainside, probably by some earthquake or great landslide. Found signs that others had searched there before. . . . We bathed in stream from pirate village where coconut trees are growing. (Davidson says, mischievously, that in front of our ladies the pirates kept their women there so that they couldn't see where the pirates buried the treasure, as they knew they could keep a secret, but not the women).'[8] In fact, the two friends' opportunities for gold-digging would be very limited. At a meeting on 1 October, the expedition's leaders decided that the *Queen of Scots* constituted too great a drain on their funds. They agreed therefore that Stenhouse, Worsley and Arthur should return the yacht to her owner and bring out instead another, cheaper vessel, the 83-ton *Veracity*, owned by Arthur. They would return in two to three months and, in their absence, operations would continue on the island, led by Jolly and Polkinghorne.

Not all of the proposed land party relished the thought of a 3-month sojourn on the remote island, no matter how much gold might lie beneath its surface. But, with funds fast running out, there seemed to be no viable alternative and, on 4 October, the parties separated: the 'islanders' standing among their crates and luggage like so many castaways, while the luxurious pleasure yacht, gleaming in the afternoon sunlight, turned her head towards Panama. 'We all tally-hoed to them,' wrote Worsley, 'dipped ensign, waved towels and blankets to shore party who waved blankets, tally-hoed again, blew whistle and siren, dipped again as the little settlement disappeared round Morgan Point, and then continued waving to boat until it too disappeared.'[9] As the last of the land party faded from sight, Captain Bellingham remarked melodramatically that the sunset looked blood red. 'Yes, but changing to gold,' responded the ever-cheerful Worsley. The captain looked at him dolefully for a moment and then ended the conversation with the gloomy prognostication that 'there'll be blood before the gold'. Worsley thought the lugubrious captain a 'chump' but, even as they spoke, some eighty armed Costa Rican policemen were clambering into launches to liberate their island from the unauthorised foreign invaders. Trouble was definitely in the offing.

Two days later, at just after 4 a.m., Bellingham woke Stenhouse to tell him that the Chief Engineer had collapsed in his cabin, and appeared to be gravely ill. The Chief had been unwell even at the time of sailing from England but he had insisted on accompanying the expedition. His illness had not prevented him from performing his duties but, towards the end of September, a dark purple patch appeared across his stomach. The mark looked much like a large bruise, but the Chief had not had an accident and, over the next few days, the 'bruise' grew darker and darker, instead of fading, as might have been expected. At midnight on 6 October, he retired to his cabin at the end of his watch and managed to change into his pyjamas and remove his false teeth before collapsing on the deck, knocking his head in the process. With the ship's surgeon, Dr Stephenson, still on the island, Stenhouse had to assume the role of medic. But, though he possessed the St John Ambulance certificate for first aid and had, of course, attended to the medical needs of his crew on board the *Aurora*, Stenhouse soon had to admit that the Chief's ailment exceeded his knowledge. Over the next few hours he could only sit in the Chief's stuffy little cabin, applying ice to the patient's head and heart in a desperate attempt to prevent his overheating. All to no avail: at 10.30 a.m., without uttering a word, the Chief died.

Stenhouse knew that, in shark-infested waters, the solemnity of a burial at sea would be swiftly followed by a razor-toothed feeding frenzy. During his early years with the Weir Line he had seen a crewmate's body snapped up in just such a manner in the Gulf of California, so he must have been relieved when favourable weather conditions and the *Queen of Scots'* fast sailing prevented the same fate befalling the unlucky Chief Engineer. Instead, he received a proper burial at Balboa on 8 October, within 48 hours of his death. Standing at his crewmate's graveside, Stenhouse might have felt a twinge of superstitious anxiety at the apparent accuracy of Bellingham's melodramatic omen, but the Chief's untimely demise would soon pale into insignificance when compared with events upon the wider stage.

Treasure Island to the *Cap Pilar*

On 9 October, the *Queen of Scots* passed through the Panama Canal and, at Cristóbal, Stenhouse and Worsley heard for the first time the worrying reports of the Costa Ricans' determination to 'liberate' Cocos Island with armed police. The islanders were well armed, possessing an arsenal that included everything from hunting rifles and shotguns to a Mauser semi-automatic and an assortment of revolvers and pistols. These weapons had been intended for hunting, but some impetuous fool might attempt to put up a struggle rather than be forced from the island. Fearing the worst, Stenhouse telephoned Arthur, who had travelled on to Panama, but the Captain veered between an irritating sang-froid and anger at what he regarded as unwarranted interference. 'If Worsley and you are going to butt in I'll throw in my hand,' he yelled at Stenhouse before slamming down the receiver.' Fortunately, Stenhouse kept his temper and, conferring with Worsley, the two agreed that Arthur was attempting to engineer his own escape from any responsibility for the situation. The following day, in another telephone conversation, they managed to persuade the erstwhile blackmailer that all three of them should meet in Panama and then solicit the assistance of the British Consul.

In Panama, Consul Cleugh gave the delegation a distinctly cool reception. The members of the expedition had been warned of the possible consequences of any unauthorised landing, he reminded them, and yet they had persevered. It also became clear that Arthur's arrogance, coupled with his history, had done nothing to endear him to the British diplomat. Luckily, the placatory and apologetic approach of Stenhouse and Worsley helped to bring Cleugh round and, by the end of the interview, it had been agreed that the two friends would send a suitably worded telegram to no less a person than the President of Costa Rica, Señor Jiménez. After leaving Cleugh's office, they immediately sat down to compose their telegram. They decided that it should be sent in Worsley's name, since he was perhaps the better known in Central and South America, and that they would express their wish to meet the President in person. After much debate and redrafting, they agreed on the following wording: 'Commander F.A. Worsley, DSO, OBE, RD, RNR, representing the directors of Treasure Recovery Ltd, respectfully presents his compliments to His Excellency and tenders deepest regrets for expedition's misunderstanding of situation and hopes His Excellency will grant him an audience at San José in order that this apology may be offered in person.'[2] Having despatched the telegram, they could only wait – and, using their wireless transmitter, break the unwelcome news to their friends on the island.

A rapid exchange of wireless transmissions ensued, with the islanders becoming ever more anxious at the thought of an armed confrontation. 'All here urge you to go personally to San José by plane,' they pleaded, 'and interview the President and if possible arrange everything the safest and quickest way. If you go to San José find out if Costa Rica could hold ship personnel or company's property on arrival at Puntarenas.'[3] At the same time, Stenhouse received from the directors of TRL in London the unwelcome news that 'financial affairs are bad; business at a standstill owing to great upset if we [fail to] obtain a concession . . . imperative to avoid liquidation; situation must be made quite clear to Costa Rica'.[4] If, as the British officials implied, one of Costa Rica's most pressing concerns would be to reclaim all of their expenses from the expedition, this news of the company's financial straits could not have come at a worse time.

The situation became even more fraught when reports began to circulate that the two Costa Rican launches had disappeared en route to Cocos. A Costa Rican government goaded into action by British wilfulness was one thing, a government faced with a public outcry at the drowning of its troops would be quite another. Stenhouse and Worsley were at their wits' end. On the one hand, their fellow adventurers urged them to visit the Costa Rican President but, on the other, Señor Jiménez showed no inclination to receive them; and, while being advised that ready cash would be critical to the solution of their current problems, TRL told them that the company's coffers were empty. Now, to top it all, Costa Rican lives might have been lost. It seemed as though the situation could not possibly get any worse – until, that is, they learned that they were being accused of espionage.

'Ain't it a strange coincidence,' the *Panama American* newspaper asked on 16 October, 'how many Commanders, Colonels, Captains and Lieutenants there are in those Treasure Hunting parties that come out of London to search for treasure on Cocos Island. And ain't it funny how many of 'em happen to arrive in Panama just when the US Fleet is due to show up? And how many excuses they can dig up for getting stranded here and playing around Canal Zone waters?'[5] Stenhouse and Worsley might have laughed at the thought of their current predicament being an excuse for anything – but the editor of the *Panama American* was not the only individual querying the motives of the expedition. A few days after the newspaper published its accusations, the US Consul-General, Mr K. McVitty, visited the British Consulate in Panama. 'Although it was obvious that Mr McVitty placed no credence in this rumour,' a harassed Cleugh reported to the Foreign Office, 'it appeared more than mere coincidence that he should call upon me immediately following the weekly meeting of the US staff officer in charge of war plans and military intelligence, himself and other naval and Canal Zone officials engaged in the same branch of work.'[6] Unfortunately, even the claim that the expedition's only interest was in Cocos Island would not necessarily allay all suspicion. Earlier in the year, the US government had entered into top secret negotiations with Costa Rica over the purchase of Cocos Island, which it hoped to fortify in order to protect the Pacific entrance of the Panama Canal – the quickest route for its fleet to pass between the Pacific and Atlantic oceans. The presence on the island of a party of heavily armed British war veterans accorded very ill with the United States' ambitions.

From the very outset of the expedition, the British government had signalled its profound reluctance to become embroiled in the affairs of TRL. But now, in order to smooth the ruffled feathers of both the Costa Rican and US governments, it had little choice but to intervene. It quickly decided that, if at all possible, everyone associated with the expedition should be removed from the scene. Questions might be left unanswered and doubts, no matter how ill-founded, might remain in the minds of the suspicious, but it seemed unlikely that answers would be actively sought once the expeditionaries had vacated not merely the island but Central America as a whole.

There was great relief when the two missing launches turned up unharmed and the islanders showed enough good sense not to offer any form of resistance to the Costa Rican police. Instead, they gave their visitors a cordial welcome and, when the time came for them to be herded on to the steamer, the *Nuevo Panama*, they submitted to their fate without argument. Reassured that his troops were safe, the President seemed more inclined to amused forbearance than retribution, later admitting that 'he did not consider that any of the people on the Island were really responsible for the many foolish blunders that had been made. . . . He rather dryly added that he thought the real leaders had shown more common sense than he had given them credit for, by not venturing within Costa Rican territory, after the many blunders that they had made.'[7] Jiménez and his Minister for Foreign Affairs desired the reimbursement of the $1,500 that had been spent in evacuating Cocos Island, but a further cable from Stenhouse in which he assured the President that TRL's 'financial condition [is] bad and if company must cease operations [on] Cocos, liquidation inevitable' went a long way to convincing them that any cash payment was improbable.

The expeditionaries that had been left on the island finally arrived in Puntarenas on 28 October, bedraggled and angry, but otherwise unharmed. Their tempers became even more frayed when they discovered that, to all intents and purposes, they would remain under house arrest until the local authorities decided their fate. In practice, this meant being confined in the office of the Port Captain. Jolly and Polkinghorne requested that they be allowed to meet with the President to place their case before him but, since the President was not in the habit of receiving malefactors, of whatever nationality, the request was, of course, refused. Instead, on 29 October, they received a summons to appear before the local magistrate. As usual, Jolly and Polkinghorne acted as spokesmen and they painted a sorry picture of the expedition's attempts to locate the pirate gold. 'No excavation work was done before the arrival of the police,' Jolly claimed, 'as the prospecting apparatus was sent out from England incomplete for operating purposes.' Despite this rather pitiful admission, indicative of an embarrassing degree of ill-preparedness and incompetence, he went on to state, rather lamely, that 'We all sincerely trust that arrangements may still be made which would be beneficial both to Costa Rica and ourselves, who possess the latest equipment and very definite knowledge of the location of the treasure.'[8]

Behind the scenes, meanwhile, the British diplomats in both Costa Rica and Panama continued to work towards the release of their countrymen in a manner that, had they known of it, would have made the reporters of the *Panama American* deeply suspicious. While Jolly delivered his deposition in court, Frank Cox, the British Consul in San José, had succeeded in obtaining an audience with President Jiménez. He managed to persuade the President that the island expeditionaries were merely dupes of TRL's directors and that, since Costa Rican territory had been 'liberated' and most of the costs of this liberation could be recovered by the confiscation of the company's equipment, there could be little benefit in holding the miscreants. Keen to avoid an embarrassing international incident, Jiménez agreed. But the Costa Rican executive could not be seen directly to influence the judiciary, so an 'escape' would have to be carefully stage-managed.

With the connivance of the President, Cox spoke with the captain of the *Nuevo Panama*, the vessel that had brought the islanders to Puntarenas, and agreed a fee for the transfer of the prisoners from Puntarenas to Panama. Next, with the assistance of his opposite number in Panama, he obtained the necessary permit for the vessel to pass through the canal at short notice. Now, all that remained was to sneak the prisoners aboard. 'I nearly had heart failure about 3 p.m.,' Cox later told the Foreign Office mandarins, 'as I rang up the Presidencia for news of the departure and was told that the Judge in Puntarenas, who had been taking their depositions, had first of all ordered them to be placed at liberty and later had cancelled the order and had instructed the police to arrest the party. . . . I am trying to find out whatever made the Judge change his mind, but knowing the local idiots fairly well, the whole thing may have been a subterfuge to "save his face".'[9] The judge's fickleness came close to scuttling the operation but, fortunately, the President again intervened and asked the local police to take their time in carrying out their orders. As a result, by the time the police arrived at the dockside, the bewildered treasure hunters had been bundled aboard and the *Nuevo Panama* had dwindled to a smudge on the horizon. It had been a close-run thing.

A fortnight later, after an exchange of telegrams in which TRL told the jaded and disbelieving expeditionaries that a transfer of the Canadian concession had belatedly been negotiated and that the directors expected their 'loyal co-operation', the *Queen of Scots* sailed for home. In writing to his superiors in London, Frederick Adam, the senior British diplomat in Panama, summarised his views of the expedition. 'It seems', he wrote, 'that many of the party entered this expedition in a light-hearted spirit of adventure and without sufficient means to carry it out, while others, including almost certainly Captain Arthur, who disappeared as quickly as possible from the scene . . . took advantage of the adventurous spirit of the others for their own ends. . . . The general effect of this adventure in Panama and Costa Rica has not been such as to bring credit to our country, and I trust that it will not be renewed.'[10] Frank Cox was altogether more scathing. 'As a good instance of the casualness of the Cocos Island party . . . practically none of them had their passports in proper order; Mrs Jolly's passport was still in her maiden name . . . most of the others either required renewing or were clean out-of-date, while two or three had left their passports behind them in Balboa; one, the wireless man, had a certificate or licence from the GPO, with his photograph on it. Of course none of them had a Costa Rican visa, but what can one expect of a set of people who set out without seeing that their passports are up-to-date, at least; no wonder that they fell into traps.'[11]

Despite the hopes of officialdom that TRL would not attempt a renewal of the expedition, many of the same crew, including Worsley, set out again the following year – this time with the appropriate concession agreed in advance. But Stenhouse refused to take part. Throughout the whole sorry episode, he had done everything possible to further the interests of TRL. En route to Cocos Island, he had taken from the recalcitrant Bellingham much of the responsibility for the day-to-day running of the yacht; once they found themselves in trouble, he had done all he could to achieve the release of his companions; he had liaised continually with the directors in London, with the representatives of the Foreign Office and with the Costa Rican authorities. He had even offered to place his own head in the noose by flying to the Costa

Rican capital. And yet, despite all of this effort, he had been described by the directors as a 'dissatisfied element' that should be 'eliminated'. By the time he reached England again on 18 December, he had spent exactly four months on the abortive and unprofitable treasure hunt. The irrepressible Worsley might remain sanguine about their chances of discovering the treasure, but Stenhouse had had enough. And so, while Worsley continued to seek his fortune with dynamite and pickaxe, Stenhouse decided to toil in a very different field of endeavour: that of literary composition.

Throughout much of his life Stenhouse had kept a diary and, fully aware that his career contained far more of incident and adventure than that of most men, he decided to commit it to paper with a view to eventual publication. Worsley had already shown that he could at least supplement his income with writing and lecturing: over the last decade he had written a handful of books about his part in the *Endurance* and, more recently, the *Island* expeditions and he had become a veteran public speaker. But, while Worsley concentrated almost exclusively on his polar exploits, Stenhouse decided to begin his tale not with the *Endurance* Expedition but with his apprenticeship at sea; he could move on to his adventures in the Antarctic and elsewhere in due course. The Antarctic might be the linchpin of his career, but the sea itself, and the great sailing ships which had fascinated him as a boy, and which had now all but disappeared, formed the lodestone of his very soul.

He took as his starting point his first day aboard the *Springbank*. That autumn morning, three decades ago, upon which he voluntarily sundered himself from all that he had hitherto known, exchanging the comforts and precedence of an only son for hard labour, danger and occasional brutality. And, in weaving his tale, Stenhouse made no attempt to disguise the physical and mental hardships experienced by the apprentices: the loneliness and bullying, the exhaustion and the physical effects of saltwater and exposure upon soft skin. He described with realism and humour the temptations faced by young men when, after months on board ship, they found themselves catapulted into the seedy underworld of the old waterfront towns: of the publicans, whores and opium dealers all plying their trade. But his writing reached its greatest heights of poetry and lyricism when he discoursed on the sea itself, in all its moods, and on the sailing ships which he had known and loved so well.

Despite his enthusiasm for his subject, he found the act of sustained writing difficult: the ordering of his thoughts, the selection of anecdotes and the polishing and retouching of his prose, all of which demanded entirely new skills. But he stuck to his chosen task with all his accustomed tenacity. He wrote not just about the ships in which he had served, but also about those he had seen scudding before a gale with every yard of cordage vibrating and every inch of canvas straining: ships like the 5,000-

ton *Preussen*, which had made the passage from the Lizard to Iquique in fifty-seven days. 'Imagine her tearing along with a bone in her teeth,' he enthused, 'a fresh breeze just abaft the beam, and all her square sails ramping full! What a joy it would be to be on the royal yard, over two hundred feet above the deck, and watch her long lean hull racing through blue water.'[12] At times, writing became an almost cathartic experience and, as he gave full vent to the nostalgia he felt for the age of sail, his prose became heavy with regret for a lost existence:

> It was a life apart, linked with the past in unbroken line from the days of the early sea rovers. Through the centuries mariners had plied their sea craft with little change in custom or conditions; ships differed in appearance, build and qualities, but their motive power was the same. The galleons of the Dons, standing across in the north-east Trades to the Spanish Main, the lumbering East Indiamen beating up the Bay of Bengal and the New Bedford whaler becalmed on the Line, were all white-winged sisters; their companies, separated by time and tongue, yet spoke the same language of the sea.
>
> That is all changed now. The end of the sailing ships came suddenly and, in their passing, they took with them much beauty, romance, old traditions and the rich sea idiom of men who spent their lives upon the waters, men who knew the sea in all its moods as no others ever will. And if, as many will say, this loss is of little importance to our modern world, I would ask them then – what is?[13]

With memories of his own youthful love of the sea so vivid, Stenhouse was perhaps unusually responsive to the approach of a sea-going romantic of the up-and-coming generation: Adrian Seligman. Like Stenhouse, Seligman had been born into a comfortable middle-class family and had learned to sail when holidaying with his family on the coast of Brittany. Later, having experienced three almost simultaneous disappointments – failure in his second-year examinations at Cambridge, the desertion of his girlfriend, and the receipt of a 'charmingly courteous threatening letter' from his bank – in a fit of pique he had signed on as a mess-boy on a small freighter in London's docks. The event had marked the beginning of an altogether more enduring love affair – with the sea. He had spent three years sailing before the mast in a number of ships including the Weir Line's *Olivebank*, in which he had raced from Australia to Queensferry in a remarkable passage of only 104 days – an exploit sure to quicken Stenhouse's pulse. More recently, the 26-year-old adventurer had been left £3,500 by an indulgent grandfather and, rather than buy a house or invest his new-found wealth in stocks and shares, he had decided to purchase a 250-ton veteran French fishing barquentine in which to undertake a round-the-world cruise. Now he needed someone to advise him on refitting the distinctly malodorous and down-at-heel *Cap Pilar*.

How could Stenhouse resist the appeal of a young man whose predilections so closely matched his own? Nostalgia aside, however, the challenge of preparing the *Cap Pilar* for sea was a daunting one. Time and neglect had reduced the ship to little more than a floating hulk. 'Decay had so changed the very shape of things,' Seligman later wrote, 'that much of her gear was barely recognisable. Rust, inches thick, bulged all over her prehistoric-looking windlass, and over every square inch of ironwork on deck and aloft. . . . At first sight we found it impossible to believe that this reeking ill-lit prison had ever supported human life, far less that it had been the cosy home of twenty healthy men.'[14] When Stenhouse first clapped eyes on this mildewed wreck in July 1936, she lay in dry dock in the historic Breton port of St Malo. Already, the local shipwrights, chandlers and riggers were hard at work making her seaworthy, but a huge amount remained to be done and it would be some two months before he returned home to Matchells and to his family.

Supervising the refit, chivvying along the local contractors and haggling over their bills was just the kind of work that Stenhouse excelled in. Every morning, he and his happy, carefree companions clattered down the town's picturesque cobbled streets en route to the harbour for another long day of scraping, polishing, varnishing, caulking and rigging. The work was hard but the hands proved willing, though largely unskilled. In fact, Seligman's crew of eighteen consisted almost entirely of novices and, as he tried to teach them the rudiments of seamanship, Stenhouse may have looked upon their prospective voyage with more than a tinge of trepidation. But he carefully hid his reservations and instead gave out advice and encouragement unstintingly; then, each evening, as they regaled themselves with cheap red wine and succulent joints of veal and mutton, he entertained his companions with tales of his exploits in the Antarctic and elsewhere.

The *Cap Pilar* sailed for London on 9 September and then spent a fortnight taking on stores. Stenhouse's original intention had been to leave the ship at London but, when the time came for the vessel to sail on 30 September, he couldn't tear himself away and, instead, with Seligman's hearty approval, decided to stay on board until she reached Plymouth. The youthful crewmen and women were all cheerful but nervous and clearly glad to have so experienced a sailor with them for the first short leg of their journey. The weather had turned cold and miserable, but the wind set fair and the *Cap Pilar* made a respectable 9 knots as she passed Prawl Point on 2 October. A couple of hours later, she hove to off Plymouth and waited for a boat to ferry Stenhouse and Seligman's father back to dry land. 'The wind had freshened a little,' Seligman remembered. 'The boat came up like a cork alongside. My father jumped. Up came the boat again. The Commander jumped. The boat sheered away.'[15] And then, as the *Cap Pilar* stood away for the open sea, Stenhouse let loose three hearty cheers and waved his cap in farewell – in Adrian Seligman, he might almost have been waving off his own youthful self on his first great adventure.

After Seligman's sailing, Stenhouse could at last concentrate on the final edit of his book. He decided to call it *Cracker Hash* after the compound of ship's biscuit and tinned beef which formed a staple of the sea apprentices' shipboard diet. But, when he finally laid down his pen early in 1937, he discovered that his own compound of anecdote and lyricism was unpalatable to publishers. 'You have told (in excellent English),' one editor wrote to him, 'a plain story of your life afloat in sailing ships; but something more than a plain tale is necessary to-day if a book of this nature is to be acclaimed by the Press and demanded by the Public.'[16] *Cracker Hash* would eventually be published, but not until after Stenhouse's death. On its appearance, the acclamations of the press were not widespread, being restricted to specialist shipping journals, but they were generous. 'The lot of the apprentice in sail around the turn of the century is a familiar enough theme in sea literature,' wrote a reviewer for the *Shipbuilding & Shipping Record*, 'but it has seldom been so vividly described or entertainingly written, as in this lively account of the author's early voyages.'[17] Overall, however, Stenhouse would probably have been most satisfied with the affirmation in *Lloyd's List* that 'Every page tastes strongly of salt water, of the romance of the sea that departed with the sailing ship.'[18]

Fortunately, 1937, the year of *Cracker Hash*'s rejection, offered Stenhouse a number of distractions – the first being an opportunity to make a film with fellow Antarctic veteran, Frank Bickerton. After an astonishingly varied and adventurous career as an explorer and fighter pilot, Bickerton had spent some years in California mixing with the glitterati of America's sporting and movie worlds. After a disastrous love affair, he had returned to England in the early 1930s where he used his contacts in the film industry to secure a job at one of the smaller British studios, working as a screenplay writer and editor. Over the last few years, he had made a number of eminently forgettable B movies for the Associated British Picture Company, mostly of a sentimental or musical nature. Early in 1937, however, Bickerton started work on a very different kind of project: an adaptation of Jack London's bloodthirsty tale of nautical derring-do, *The Mutiny of the Elsinore*.

Starring the future Oscar-winning Hungarian-American actor, Paul Lukas, and the beautiful English actress, Kathleen Kelly, *The Mutiny of the Elsinore* was to be set almost entirely on board a four-masted ship sailing from England to America. Although much of the action would be filmed on a specially constructed set in Welwyn Garden City, the director, Roy Lockwood, wanted to achieve as much realism as possible and, when he expressed his wish to employ a nautical adviser, Bickerton suggested Stenhouse.

In fact, though Bickerton might not have known it when he put his friend's name forward, Stenhouse already possessed some experience of filmmaking. As well as featuring in the newsreels shot to celebrate the return of the ITAE in 1917, more recently he had appeared in a documentary made by the conservationist Harold Noice. A veteran of Vilhjalmur Stefansson's Canadian Arctic Expedition of 1913–18, Noice wanted to make a wider audience aware of the plight of many endangered species and in his 1931 film, *Explorers of the World*, he publicised the horrors of the whaling industry. Sympathetic to his aims, the *Discovery* Committee allowed him to include footage shot during the National Oceanographic Expedition and, sharing Noice's abhorrence of the barbaric slaughter, Stenhouse, too, had agreed to work with the Canadian, giving a brief account of the expedition in front of the camera.

Despite this experience, Stenhouse viewed the cinema with distrust. It was, he claimed in *Cracker Hash*, a 'universal mis-educator',[19] wilful in its misrepresentation of the life of the sea. During his work on *The Mutiny of the Elsinore*, however, he managed to put his reservations firmly to one side. Whether because London's novel possessed some of the 'saltwater tang' that he so admired in the writings of Frederick Marryat and Clark Russell, or because Lockwood seemed so genuine in his wish to achieve realism, Stenhouse threw himself wholeheartedly into the task at hand. When production began in June, he even agreed to be filmed hauling on ropes and dancing a hornpipe. This quest for authenticity paid dividends and, on its release at the box office, the film attracted praise from critics on both sides of the Atlantic. With the English *Kine Weekly* reporting that 'the maritime atmosphere is always realistic and convincing',[20] and the New York *Daily Film Renter* calling it 'convincingly staged',[21] Stenhouse would have been delighted to learn that he had made a small contribution to the creation of a genuine portrait of the sea and of professional seamanship.

By the time that Bickerton and his fellow technicians were adding the finishing touches to *The Mutiny of the Elsinore*, Stenhouse had returned to sea. Worsley had become a director of a ship and yacht delivery business, Imray Laurie Norie & Wilson Ltd, and on 26 August 1937 the two friends joined together in a short commission sailing the Steam Yacht *Calamara* from Ramsgate to Piraeus for its owners. Then, in early October, Stenhouse returned from the heat of Greece to embrace the prospect of a return to southern latitudes: with Ernest Walker's British Antarctic Expedition.

Walker, who had taken part in the James Bay Geological Expedition of 1930–1, had spent a couple of years toying with the idea of a British Empire Photographic Expedition, but funding had proved elusive. Having been persuaded that an Antarctic expedition would be far more likely to appeal to prospective backers, with disarming sang-froid he had dropped his original idea and now proposed an expedition that would undertake a geological survey of South Victoria Land, conduct a pioneering aerial survey of Oates Land, and investigate the area's marine biology and meteorology. In addition, the expedition's support vessel would survey the islands of the South Pacific to ascertain their value as air bases for future Trans-Pacific air services. It was an ambitious programme: too ambitious. In response to an appeal for support, Frank Debenham, geologist on Scott's *Terra Nova* Expedition, Director of the Scott Polar Research Institute and one of the grand old men of Polar exploration, opined that 'both the cost and the difficulties in the operations are seriously underestimated'.[22] Walker tried to wave aside such reservations, but Debenham's views were shared by all of the official and semi-official bodies connected with exploration and the public purse remained tightly closed.

As a result of the establishment's reluctance to support the expedition, funding continued to be Walker's single greatest obstacle. In a manner reminiscent of practically every hard-pressed explorer of the Heroic Age, he moaned that 'These financial difficulties are really beyond a joke. I had simply no idea that they could be so hard to overcome. . . . It seems that everyone and everything makes it a point of stopping you if they possibly can and of putting as many difficulties in the way as possible.'[23] Recruiting suitable staff for the expedition also proved something of a nightmare: 'I have had dozens of letters asking positions from all kinds of men,' he told Leonard Hussey, ' – mostly from young undergraduates – Cissies in Oxford bags and brown sports jackets – who have a science degree, and not one single one of them has proved an atom of use. They have all been spineless, long-haired, ascetic-looking miseries, who have never done an honest day's work in their miserable lives.'[24] If Walker felt little inclination to choose even the scientists from such inexperienced candidates, the safety of the expedition demanded that his sailors and navigators must be men of proven character and experience: men like Worsley and Stenhouse.

Always alert to such opportunities and an unerring champion of his own abilities, Worsley stood first in the queue. But when the two met, Walker left with the strong impression that they would be unlikely to work well together and, besides, Worsley refused to sail without Jean. Next, Walker wrote to Stenhouse, who would have been gratified to hear that 'Doctor Hussey (Chairman of our Committee) and quite a number of people have pointed out to me that you are practically the only man with the necessary qualifications.' In his present impecunious circumstances, he would have been even happier to learn that Walker was 'prepared to offer what I believe to be very fair terms. . . . We are very short of money, but I do not propose economising at the expense of the personnel of the Expedition.'[25]

Stenhouse's particular role would be to command the expedition's support vessel, the motor-yacht *Westward*, and in so doing he would become responsible for a highly novel money-making scheme. Built in 1920, the *Westward* was a 2,000-ton, four-masted schooner with accommodation that included twelve bathrooms, a luxurious dining saloon, a lounge, a smoking room, a fully equipped surgery and a barber's shop. Her primary function would be to carry the expedition's staff and heavy equipment to the fringes of the Ross Sea, where they would transfer to the expedition ship proper, the *Shackleton* (this opportunistic naming of the expedition ship was a propaganda coup of which the 'Boss' himself would have been proud). But with the expedition staff numbering only twenty-one, and with so much high-class accommodation going spare, why, thought Walker, should the *Westward* not carry some fare-paying passengers, whose guinea-a-day would help to defray the expedition's expenses? Once the expedition staff had transferred to the *Shackleton*, she would be free to continue on a 35,000-mile world cruise and her passengers, in addition to enjoying all the more prosaic pleasures of such a voyage, would be able to boast that they had taken part in the early stages of a real Antarctic expedition.

The scheme bore obvious similarities to Stenhouse's own plans for the *Volendam* and *Stella Polaris* a few years earlier, and it clearly appealed to him. Having agreed a remuneration package that brought him £40 per month during fitting out, and £80 per month during the voyage, he quickly accepted Walker's offer and immediately threw himself into the task of preparing the *Westward* for sea. Of course, he brought all his usual enthusiasm and energy to the work and Walker was soon waxing lyrical: 'Everyone on board is working like a hero and for practically no pay. It sometimes brings a lump into my throat – not one of them has a shred of decent clothing left and seldom can anyone afford to go ashore. And yet they are all cheerful and tell me they don't care two hoots as long as they are helping the Expedition.'[26]

For a while, it looked as though the British Antarctic Expedition might actually sail for the south and, by the spring of 1938, the *Westward* had been brought to a state of readiness. But, on the other side of Europe, events were unfolding which would scupper, once and for all, Walker's grand plans. In ordinary circumstances, Stenhouse would have fought tooth and nail to retain command of an Antarctic expedition vessel; but war loomed on the horizon and war would place him in the position that he loved above all others: command of one of His Majesty's Ships.

THAMES PATROL

Despite its horrors, for Stenhouse, as for many of his friends, war remained an adventure – moreover, an adventure which gave definite purpose and direction to his life. For most of the 1920s, command of the *Discovery* had given him some stability, a steady income and, most importantly, an occupation commensurate with his peculiar experience and temperament. But the 1930s had proved a wilderness: financial need and his own irrepressible zest for employment had driven him from one berth to another, some adventurous, others relatively mundane, some bizarre and some on the cusp of illegality. But none could ever have been viewed as anything more than a stopgap and many, despite Stenhouse's natural ebullience and the energy which he brought to every task, reeked of desperation. In contrast, war brought with it clearly defined goals and a common enemy.

Promoted to Commander, Stenhouse had been placed on the Royal Navy's 'Retired List' in December 1931. But, observing the inability of international diplomacy to curb the rise of Fascism in Italy, Spain and Germany, towards the end of the decade he again volunteered for service – this time with the Observer Corps, which he knew would form an essential part of Britain's aerial defences in the event of war. When war finally came, however, he and most members of his inner circle virtually tumbled over each other in their urgent desire to take on more active roles with the Armed Forces. After months of pestering, Frank Worsley managed to persuade the War Office to employ his services as an 'Advance Agent' in Norway – though he lied about his age to gain the appointment. Frank Bickerton, at 50 the youngest of the group, abandoned his film career at the first whiff of cordite and accompanied the Air Component of the British Expeditionary Force to France – where he would soon find himself caught up in the pell-mell retreat towards Dunkirk. Even Walter Campbell, still suffering the after-effects of having his skull torn open by a shell splinter on the Somme, stepped forward – though his disability left him with little option but to accept a post with the newly formed Home Guard. No obstacles stood in

Stenhouse's path. Still only 51 years of age, an experienced mariner whose skills had not been allowed to rust during the interwar years, and a highly decorated officer of the Royal Naval Reserve, he immediately received a command, albeit in Home Waters.

In fact, the post of Senior Officer Afloat of the Thames & Medway Examination Service had been offered to him as early as 1938 and his enthusiasm in accepting the post had waned only when he discovered that the Admiralty did not expect him to take up his duties until the outbreak of war. When, at last, the call came, he answered at once, reporting for duty to the Port of London River Superintendent, the man responsible for finding suitable recruits for commissions in the new service.

In his long career under sail, Stenhouse had never been closely associated with the Thames and its administrative bodies, but even he must have been aware of the current process of transformation all along the river. Everywhere great comical barrage balloons floated into the sky, key public buildings became cocooned in sandbags, and parks and other public spaces added huge arc lights and anti-aircraft batteries to their furniture. Military engineers installed high-angle guns at locks and other vital positions and stevedores, river pilots and merchant sailors of all nations found themselves rubbing shoulders with officers and men of the Royal Navy. Some of the latter, from beardless sub-lieutenants to gnarled flag officers, had never previously been seen among the crates and cables, grease, dirt and packing cases of the civilian port. Others, made self-conscious and embarrassed by their suddenly acquired gold braid and polish, were quickly identified as old Port of London hands, pressed into naval service. Stenhouse became just one among thousands thronging the Thames: reporting to newly commandeered offices belonging to the Port of London Authority (PLA) or to ships and smaller vessels attached to the host of organisations tasked with protecting the river and the ships upon her broad back.

The job of Senior Officer Afloat might not have been one that Stenhouse would have chosen for himself, being primarily a defensive role, but he would soon discover that it was anything but a sinecure. In 1939, London was one of the world's three greatest ports and its protection was absolutely crucial to the nation's survival. Out of sight of both the day-trippers and the office-dwellers, down below London Bridge and Southwark Cathedral, beyond the frowning mass of the Tower of London and the bizarre gothic fantasy of Tower Bridge, lay the Lower Pool and the docklands: a vast, complicated, interconnected and seemingly endless maze of waterways, jetties and colossal red-brick storehouses. Handling around 60 million tons of cargo and 90 million net registered tons of shipping each year, the Port of London's wharves and warehouses, particularly those in Wapping and Limehouse, served as the primary storage centre for goods flowing into and out of the capital. Here all the commercial wealth of the empire could be found: commodities brought from every corner of the globe. Most of the country's supply of sugar, rum, grain and hardwood passed through the India and Millwall Docks, while the Royal Docks at North Woolwich possessed no fewer than 11 miles of deep-water quays for berthing cargo liners. Taken all together, this vast storage facility formed one of the richest and most concentrated targets any raider could hope for. And there would be no shortage of raiders. No one doubted that Germany would rapidly resume the U-boat war that she had waged with such ferocity between 1914 and 1918 and which had come to within an ace of bringing Britain to her knees. But, in addition to the submarine threat, the country could expect to be subjected to aerial bombardment on a scale that would dwarf the Zeppelin and Gotha raids of the First World War. With Germany intent on strangling Britain's trade, the Port must inevitably become the principal target. Worst of all, the Tideway's distinctive serpentine form, glistening on a moonlit night, would make an unmistakable landmark for the Luftwaffe's aerial navigators as they steered their bomb-laden aeroplanes towards the wharves and enclosed docks, piled high with the food and raw materials critical to Britain's continued war effort.

On 2 September 1939, Stenhouse took command of a motley flotilla of five hitherto peaceable sea-going and lighterage tugs, now commandeered to patrol the Thames Estuary and operating out of Sheerness. With her rust-streaked steel hull transformed by a coat of Navy-issue grey paint and her name aggrandised with the prefix of 'His Majesty's Ship', his flagship would be the *Danube III*. Launched in 1924, with a displacement of 234 tons and coal-fired boilers, prior to being pressed into military service this large tug had spent fifteen years quietly plying her trade up and down the Thames, mostly towing self-emptying hoppers loaded with spoil dredged from the river bed out into deep water. Although she was one of the biggest of her kind in the Port, being 112ft long and 28ft across the beam, conditions on board were unusually cramped. Len Bates, a long-time employee of the PLA and now one of Stenhouse's officers, described how twenty-two Royal Navy officers and ratings tried 'with the shoehorn of cheerful ingenuity, to insert themselves into accommodation designed for a civilian crew of half that number. The extra suitors for her favour . . . necessitated by adornments in the way of armament, searchlight, semaphore, etc.'[1]

In peacetime ship-tugs escorted vessels along the more congested river reaches, helping them to swing to anchor and to manoeuvre into and out of the enclosed docks or to and from berths at riverside wharves and jetties. In wartime, their job was not dissimilar. Day and night, the river swarmed with barges ferrying goods between ship and shore and any blockage in this artery – a sunken or stranded ship, an enemy mine or floating wreckage –

could cause chaos. Working with the Royal Naval Auxiliary Patrol and with the Minesweeping Service, the role of the Thames & Medway Examination Flotilla was to patrol and protect the Port of London from mines, bombers, sabotage and submarines; to board and examine ships seeking to enter the Port; and to offer assistance to stranded, damaged or distressed vessels. Brought together, these activities formed a considerable body of work and the sphere in which they were to be conducted included the whole of the tidal Thames, from Teddington to the sea: 69 miles of waterway, five enclosed dock groups and in excess of 150 independent riverside wharves. The Examination Service's particular responsibility would be to cooperate with Naval Intelligence in pursuit of contraband and enemy spies and to halt and search any suspicious-looking vessel. Beyond the seaward limit of the Port, the Royal Naval Examination Service took over the role.

In the following months, Stenhouse's flotilla received call after call: sometimes to seek out a particular vessel – one looming shadow among dozens at anchor – to examine papers or interview a captain; or to make their laborious way through the crowded waterways, to take a spell as guard-ship or to act as escort to a vessel whose pilot had become disoriented. If the job of maintaining some form of order in this seeming chaos was difficult by day, by night it became all but impossible. The usual hazards of the Thames, its crowded anchorage, clinging mists and fast-running tides were made doubly dangerous by the introduction of blackout regulations (a vain effort at obfuscation given the broad, reflective surface of the undulant Thames). Well-known leading lights, such as the lamps of a jetty or wharf, the welcoming glow of a waterside pub or an illuminated warehouse clock were either extinguished or veiled. With sinister irony, only when the Blitz began in earnest did the lot of bemused watermen become somewhat alleviated, when their attempts at navigating the river were rendered easier by the sight of well-known buildings being silhouetted against the flickering light of a burning city.

In the First World War, the Admiralty had been painfully slow to adopt the convoy system, but it did not make the same mistake twice and, day by day, the frequency of convoys increased. Having spent days crossing the Atlantic, playing the deadly and nerve-racking game of cat-and-mouse with marauding U-boats, the forty or more ships in each convoy often steamed into the Estuary at full speed, caring little for the attentions of the Examination Flotilla in their anxiety to reach safe harbour. On each occasion, Stenhouse ordered *Danube III* and her escorts to form a line at one mile intervals, stern on to the approaching convoy and with their engines at slow-ahead. As the huge ships rushed past, streaming black banners of smoke from their funnels, the tugs would increase their speed and, carefully observing the newcomers, latch on to any that looked in any way untoward or suspicious. In constant danger of a collision – and, in the event of an accident, the tugs would inevitably fare far worse than the larger, fast-moving convoy ships – Stenhouse used all his skill to manoeuvre his vessel close in to his chosen target. He conducted his initial investigation with the aid of a megaphone, bawling questions regarding their passage and cargo, while one of his junior officers made notes in the deck log. If dissatisfied with the replies he received, he ordered the ship to the Examination Anchorage where she would undergo a more detailed scrutiny, undertaken by an officer and a party of heavily armed Royal Marines. At night, when the Port was closed and convoys could not enter, the tugs of the Examination Flotilla anchored in strategic positions, and those on watch strained eyes and ears, listening for the hum and throb of an enemy vessel's engine or looking for the phosphorescent stream left by a raised periscope.

Determined to make the weekend sailors among his crew into something as closely approximating an efficient fighting unit as time and circumstances would allow, Stenhouse drilled his officers and men day and night. On first joining the service he had been appalled at the inexperience of many of his officers; now he ordered them to take the wheel, and to steer compass courses to his orders; coded flag signals were practised until the men attained a satisfactory level of proficiency; and the Aldis lamp flickered ever faster in rhythmic sequences of Morse code. He drove the ordinary seamen equally hard, allowing them no latitude, and with a stern face and a stentorian voice, he revealed his impatience at mistakes and incompetence. As a young apprentice, over thirty years before, he had been disappointed to discover that the ship's officers positively frowned upon any exercise of free will on his part. Now, though he might not recognise the trait in himself, he showed his own men that he had taken the lesson deeply to heart. He expected initiative from his officers; but from his men, no more and no less than unquestioning and immediate obedience. Even Sub-Lieutenant Bates, who admired his captain greatly, thought him inclined to be a martinet.

Not that Stenhouse was averse to displaying the more amiable side of his nature. From his earliest days under sail, when carrying coal from Cardiff to Antofagasta or timber from Vancouver to Melbourne, he had enjoyed 'yarning' during the evening watches – walking and talking 'of days past and days to come, recounting and reminding each other of pranks, larks and happy times'.[2] Night watches on the Thames were no exception, and he whiled away the hours with his officers, telling them stories of his exploits in Antarctica and North Russia. Bates, in particular, became spellbound by these tales of high adventure, and found that 'every yarn betrays the fascination which the land and the life held for him'.[3] On the few occasions when he managed to meet up with his chosen friends, all of whom wore uniforms bedecked with medal ribbons, Stenhouse could laugh and joke and enjoy the adventures and the occasional comedy of war. He also exercised his humour among his officers: he relished the absurd, so long as the absurd did not endanger the efficient working of his ship, and on one occasion even relaxed so far as to dance the hornpipe on the bridge of the *Danube*. In the 12 hours shore leave which the crew enjoyed every five or six days, he usually dashed up to Bedford, where the family had relocated during the early days of the war. If the uncertainty of the rail network made a flying visit home impossible, however, he might instead join his officers for a whisky at the Fountain Hotel or at the officers' club in Sheerness.

With the evacuation of the British Army from Dunkirk at the beginning of June 1940, enemy air raids intensified. Stenhouse implored his superiors to allow the *Danube III* and her consorts to take part in Operation Dynamo but, with every available warship crossing and re-crossing the Channel, crammed with exhausted and demoralised troops, the Thames and the Port of London could not be left undefended. Unwilling spectators, Stenhouse and his men offered what succour they could to the bullet-riddled vessels limping back to England, knowing that they were witnessing a miracle of survival. Some expressed the conviction that they were present at the birth of an enduring legend, but Stenhouse remained unconvinced: 'It'll all be forgotten when the war is over,' he told them.[4]

The resentment and frustration caused by enforced inaction soon dissipated when the all-conquering German forces turned their attention towards England. At first, the beleaguered RAF bore the brunt of the attack but, as Reichsmarschall Goering's confidence in the imminent collapse of Britain's air defences swelled, the Luftwaffe switched its attention to London and to England's out-ports and coastal areas. Raids on the Thames became more frequent and soon Stenhouse's patrol area in the outer estuary became one of the most dangerous corners of the country's sea-lanes with his small armada frequently under direct assault. On 5 September, bombs struck the Thameshaven oil tanks and the leaping flames could be seen several miles out to sea. Two days later, thousands of Luftwaffe bombers made a concentrated attack on the docks and warehouses, causing widespread devastation. Between 7 September and 2 November, London and the Thames endured constant attack – though RAF successes resulted in the enemy switching to night-time raids to reduce their losses in men and aircraft.

On the night of 12 October, as usual, Stenhouse was on board the *Danube III*, anchored some 2 miles east of the Nore lightship. For a little over a year his little ship had been in constant service. She had dodged bombs and mines and even the great flaming wrecks of barrage balloons, which occasionally combusted spontaneously during particularly hot and humid nights; she had also narrowly escaped collision with low-flying aircraft and, through Stenhouse's superb seamanship, avoided a hundred near misses with convoy ships. For weeks now, every night had been marked by an air raid of varying duration and intensity. England seemed to teeter on the brink of the first full-scale invasion by foreign troops since 1066 and, swinging at anchor in the outer Estuary, *Danube III* and her sisters might be the first to meet the invaders. Her armament was light, consisting of a single antique 12-pounder that had seen service in both the Boer War and the First World War, twin Lewis-guns and a handful of rifles. Now, with ammunition at an all-time premium, Stenhouse suggested that his crew be issued with cutlasses to repel boarders; his officers thought he was joking, until, that is, they saw his completed requisition form.

The night of the 12th offered no exception to the routine of attack: 'It was a moonlight night,' Stenhouse reported, 'and three 'planes came over about 9 o'clock at night and dropped a bomb. . . . That bomb, I think, was about 4 or 5 cables from us and it went off immediately and shook us but did not put our lights out. Immediately afterwards we heard the roar of a 'plane's engines and opened fire with a Lewis-gun and hit him at about 400ft. He came down, we think, because one of the [mine-] sweepers fired at him with a pom-pom. We could not make out what he was but he was close enough to see the size.'[5] For 2 hours there was relative calm but then, at 11 p.m., the crew heard the sound of an engine running, which they mistakenly believed to be a motor-boat approaching. 'Suddenly he must have taken off,' Stenhouse remembered, 'because he came right over us, so that it was a mine-laying seaplane. Then he flew all round by the Nore Light Vessel. We did not lose his sound and he came round in a direct line from the Outer Cant Buoy and went back to the Eastward from direction of Outer Bar Buoy towards the East Cant Buoy, so he appears to have spent some time laying mines.'[6]

By 8.30 a.m. the *Danube III* had resumed work. Stenhouse had received orders to fix the position of the wreck of a ship named the *Resolvo* and, with a strong breeze whistling among her halliards, the tug headed away from the South Thames Gate towards the Outer Bar Buoy: in just the area where the mine-layer had been operating the night before. In the distance could be seen His Majesty's Yacht *Janetha IV* and, in the Medway Channel, an outward-bound destroyer. After the excitement of the previous night, the normal routine of shipboard life had quickly resumed: Stenhouse and his officers gathered on the bridge, the forenoon watch busied itself about its duties, and the dingy after-mess deck rang with the laughter of men enjoying their breakfast. At 8.40, and at a distance of about 2 cables from the Outer Bar Buoy, the peace came to an abrupt end. The *Danube*'s captain, Lieutenant Richard Sullivan, described how 'a prolonged, muffled, rumbling explosion and terrific concussion'[7] struck the ship. The vibration of her propeller had detonated an acoustic mine, just under her port quarter: 'the bow went under and the stern went up,' Stenhouse reported. 'By the time I picked myself up the whole of the aft was covered with froth and the stern had gone down again. She was awash aft then.'[8]

The explosion wrought fatal damage: 'All officers on [the] bridge were flung off the deck and across the bridge; quartermaster thrown from wheel inside wheelhouse and jammed under interior wreckage. Carley Floats aft were blown off and not seen again. . . . Starboard boat, swung overboard in davits, smashed, davits bent. Port boat hanging on davits inboard smashed, davits bent and useless.'[9] Flames leapt upward from the funnel's port side and large volumes of steam gushed from the engine-room and stoke hold. Bates, who had been thrown bodily   into the air by the explosion and whose leg had been smashed in his descent, also recollected seeing a 'great rent running across her main deck'.[10] With no watertight bulkheads, with her back broken and her stern already sinking beneath the waves, Stenhouse had no option but to abandon ship.

Even as he gave the command, the stricken ship heeled over and disappeared beneath the waves: 'vessel listed to port, bow was hove clear out of water with quarter deck submerged; vessel again settled fore and aft, listed quickly to port and sank'.[11] Less than 5 minutes had passed since the explosion.

Both Stenhouse and Bates now found themselves fighting for their lives as the fast-sinking wreckage pulled them down towards the seabed. Bates recalled how 'a tangle of signal halliards and the foremast stays trapped me and bore me down steadily. I tried to keep cool while extricating myself, but I was soon fighting madly.'[12] At last he freed himself and his old-fashioned cork life jacket brought him bobbing to the surface, gasping for air. As for Stenhouse, 'Having gone down with the ship and been foul of the funnel and gear I was partly dazed on coming to the surface. Two other explosions occurred; I saw the columns of water, not far distant, felt concussion, went under and on coming to the surface saw *Janetha IV* coming towards us.'[13] He found himself 'amongst a lot of black oil. My face and clothes were black and oily' but, fortunately, since the *Danube III* had been coal-fired, he and the other survivors had none of the horrors of ignited oil-fuel to contend with. Despite the pain from a badly twisted back and the disorientation resulting from the explosion and his submersion, he refused the grating gallantly offered to him by the ashen-faced Bates. Instead, while his fellows shouted and waved at the approaching yacht, he concentrated on supporting one of his injured crewmen, until willing hands plucked them from the water.

In the *Janetha*'s wardroom, somewhat revived by the rum offered by their rescuers, the survivors looked about them, and began to count the cost of their collision with the mine. Out of a crew of twenty-two, only thirteen now huddled round the red-hot stove of the wardroom. All those in the *Danube*'s engine-room, stoke hold and mess deck were dead: either killed by the explosion, which had detonated just beneath their feet, or drowned as the cold, brown waters of the Estuary rushed in upon them. Traditionally, seamen are superstitious; but on this occasion, superstition seemed more than justified by the chilling repetition of the number thirteen: the *Danube III* had been destroyed on the thirteenth day of the thirteenth month of the war, and she had sunk almost precisely 13 miles from land. But any contemplation of this bizarre coincidence was soon interrupted by more pressing concerns.

Shortly after being pulled from the water, Stenhouse and the other survivors felt a sudden jar as the *Janetha* struck a submerged object – almost certainly the wreckage of the *Danube III*. Reassuringly, the ship's engines continued to hum and she proceeded on her journey towards the shore. But, as the minutes passed, the ship began to heel over, her list becoming more pronounced with each passing second. Doubts about the seriousness of the damage she had sustained were confirmed when an officer put his head round the wardroom door and advised the survivors to don their life vests again: it looked as though they would be needing them for the second time in a matter of minutes. Tired and subdued, Stenhouse led his depleted crew out into the light: if the ship must go down, no one would be trapped below decks this time. As they gathered on deck, the steering engine gave a prolonged death rattle, the helm went hard over and the ship's precarious progress came to an abrupt halt as she grounded on a mud bank just outside the harbour mouth. Shortly afterwards, Stenhouse clambered down into an RAF launch which then sped towards Cornwallis Pier, where ambulances and medics waited to tend the wounded.

Fortunately, his injuries proved relatively minor: the worst being his strained back, almost certainly caused when he was felled by the concussion from the first explosion. His officers had not fared so well. The Chief Engineer had suffered a fatal head wound and had gone down with the ship; Sullivan had been so badly shaken that he was eventually invalided out of the service; while Bates, besides his broken leg, had a fractured heel and a number of cracked ribs – the latter caused by a collision with floating wreckage when he separated himself from the rapidly sinking vessel. Bates and the others were admitted to hospital, but Stenhouse, swathed in bandages, made his way home to surprise his family in Bedford, and to be nursed by them.

He submitted his initial report on the loss of his ship immediately after the event; by 27 November, his strength restored by a diet of fresh eggs procured with great difficulty by his stepdaughter, Elisabeth,[14] he was able to attend the full Board of Inquiry. It proved to be an open and shut case: the *Danube III* had not been properly protected against mines but the necessary work had been scheduled; quite simply, the crew had been unlucky in that the dockyard had been too busy to complete the job sooner. No one levelled any criticism at Stenhouse or his crew, all of whom had conducted themselves in an exemplary fashion. In his own report, Stenhouse stated that he found it 'difficult to single out any individual for special praise amongst the survivors. Before abandoning ship all who were able did all they could to clear away the port boat, help the injured and provide lifebelts for those without.'[15] Were it not for the tragedy attached to the loss of so many men, his summary of their behaviour would have been almost comical in its demonstration of the power of discipline and custom: 'P.O. Curley, Coxswain, although badly shaken up got off his grating in the water and offered it to Lieutenant Mitchell who would not take it. Lieutenant Bates RNR, with [broken] leg offered me his grating. The Captain, Lieutenant R. Sullivan RN, although badly shaken, rallied his men cheerily.'[16] He went on to assert that 'I am very proud to have been shipmates with these men' and, remembering those whose corpses lay trapped in the wreckage of the *Danube III*, he expressed his hope that 'all will be done to alleviate the distress and suffering of their dependants'. In its own summing up, the Board commended Stenhouse for his 'gallant conduct which was reported on by several observers'.

For Stenhouse, a man almost pathologically compelled to action, the next three months would prove particularly frustrating. When he was an apprentice on the *Springbank*, a swinging sheet block had once smashed into his face and broken his nose but, despite the pain, the gory handkerchief tied round his face and his blood-spattered shirt, he had insisted on continuing with his duties. Three decades later, his attitude hadn't changed and he remained as restless as ever when on the beach. Desperate to re-enter the fray, he besieged his superiors with requests for a new command but, despite his importunities, three months dragged by before the Royal Navy's medical officer finally declared him fit for duty. When, in the early spring of 1941, news of his next posting finally came through, he could hardly contain his excitement. 'I am in a tearing hurry,' he told Worsley, 'as I am sailing on Saturday morning and have much to do; what a pity we cannot meet before I sail but what a reunion after the war is over and the foul Boche licked . . . oh Boy oh Boy!'[17] His orders directed him to the Red Sea port of Massawa: a theatre of war about as far removed from the grey skies and cold waters of the Thames Estuary as it was possible to imagine.

16

WITH HIS BOOTS ON

Massawa lies on the Abd-El-Kader Peninsula, approximately two-thirds of the way down the Red Sea from Suez. In 1881, sixty years before Stenhouse's arrival, the Italian government had purchased a strip of the Eritrean coast, including Massawa, from the Ottoman Empire. Dreaming of an overseas empire to rival those of Britain and France, the Italians planned to strike into Abyssinia, capturing huge swathes of territory from an unprepared and unprotected native population, thereby linking their colonies in Eritrea and Somalia. These grandiose plans ended in disaster when, at the Battle of Adowa on 1 March 1896, the Abyssinian forces of Emperor Menelik II routed the better-armed Italian invaders. Despite this defeat, however, the strip of Eritrean coast remained in Italian hands and, thirty-nine years later, Mussolini, obsessed with the idea of his own Fascist empire, had decided to use Massawa as the point from which to launch a full-scale invasion of Haile Selassie's Abyssinia.

To make such an invasion possible, it had been necessary to invest huge sums in transforming Massawa from an insignificant Arab slave-trading settlement into a modern port capable of supporting submarines, destroyers, and motor torpedo boats. The work had been done on a grand scale. The port was gradually equipped with enormous stone quays, warehouses, offices, barracks, airfields and all the paraphernalia of a state-of-the-art naval base, designed not only to act as the jumping-off point for an inland invasion but also to dominate the whole of the Red Sea. Under the hands of the Italian engineers Massawa became the greatest harbour in the region, far superior to Port Sudan to the north, and perfectly positioned to threaten Britain's shipping lanes to India. This last factor also meant that when Mussolini's troops crossed the Abyssinian frontier in 1935, Britain, for all her protests, refused to interfere directly. But, with Italy's declaration of war against Britain and France five years later, in June 1940, the roles played by the British and Italians were effectively reversed. The British controlled the Suez Canal and this meant that, to all intents and purposes, Italian troops in Abyssinia and Eritrea became totally isolated from their homeland and vulnerable to attacks from Britain's African colonies, as well as from the most powerful navy in the world.

While German forces in Europe chalked up victory after victory, the Italians in Europe and in Africa suffered a humiliating series of defeats. In November 1940, antiquated British aeroplanes crippled the Italian fleet in Taranto and the Greeks routed the Italian Ninth Army in the Balkans. Then, in December, General Sir Archibald Wavell, British Commander-in-Chief in the Middle East, began his inexorable offensive in the Western Desert, inflicting total defeat on the Italians at Bardia, Tobruk and Benghazi. In January 1941, the Fourth and Fifth Indian Divisions attacked in East Africa, crossing the border from Sudan into Eritrea, to threaten Abyssinia from the north. In the face of the British advance, the Italians fell back towards the Red Sea coast and Massawa. Vainglorious to the last, Mussolini had ordered his commander there, Admiral Bonetti, to hold the port or die – but Bonetti had other ideas. As the men of the Fifth Indian Division approached, supported by the Highland Light Infantry and the Free French, he ordered his men to embark on the systematic destruction of the port's facilities: everything that could be of the slightest use to the Allies must be totally dismantled.

Explosion after explosion rent the air as the Italian engineers reduced Massawa to a mass of twisted steel and shattered concrete, and the harbour echoed to the clang and thump of sledgehammers as the erstwhile empire-builders beat their invaluable machinery to scrap. Then came the *coup de grâce*: sappers detonated a series of carefully placed charges, wrecking the floating dry docks and tearing the bottoms out of some forty Italian and German vessels, effectively blocking both the harbour entrance and the quays. By the time the British forces entered Massawa, on 8 April 1941, the port and all its facilities lay in ruins. Now, if the British wanted to utilise this crucial base for operations in the Red Sea and the eastern Mediterranean, they would first have to undertake the biggest salvage operation of all time. With his experience of salvage work at Chanak in the 1920s, the man appointed to undertake this daunting task was Stenhouse.

Having tried unsuccessfully to recruit both Len Bates and Worsley to join in this new adventure, Stenhouse finally left England in the last week of April. In writing to his sister, Nell, shortly after his arrival in Eritrea, he stated that 'I cannot tell you any news of what I am doing nor what job I had coming out but it was full of thrills and excitement; we were with the fleet!'[1] From Alexandria, where he arrived in the middle of May, he had proceeded to Port Tewfik, via Cairo, by train. The journey had comprised, he told Gladys, 'about 100 miles or so over the desert with nothing to see but long stretches of sand, dunes, and distant sun-scorched hills; the only signs of life a few Egyptian railway people at the halts and here and there an Arab camp with an occasional camel padding along through the desert.'² From Port Tewfik he joined a ship bound for Aden but was diverted to Port Sudan and then on in a man-o'-war to Massawa.

Commander Edward Ellsberg, an American naval officer who arrived at the port about a year after Stenhouse, believed that the 'next stop beyond Massawa was Hades'³ and, undoubtedly, the one-time pride of Mussolini's African Empire presented a grim spectacle. Approaching from the sea, Stenhouse beheld a long, low, sandy coastline stretching as far as the eye could see in either direction. A few bald, grey boulders bleached in the sun, occasionally surmounted by depressed, dusty-looking seabirds. There was very little vegetation, and those plants that had displayed sufficient temerity to lift their heads above the baking sand appeared parched and fragile, easy prey to the next breeze that might waft in from the sea. The sun dominated everything, beating down mercilessly on rocks, birds and sea, and nailed so high in the sky that it deprived the landscape of the least shadow. It seemed impossible that the heat and the constant glare could have left the slightest drop of water in the ground and yet here and there a thin film of moisture might be seen, rising like marsh mist from the sand. Practically every building in Massawa had been constructed – and, in many cases, subsequently deconstructed – by the Italians; most aped the colonial style: single-storeyed, with wooden, slatted shutters instead of glass in the windows and with wide eaves or verandas designed to provide as much shade as possible. Originally painted white, all the buildings had been stained yellow by the fine, coral dust which blew in from the coast and covered everything and everyone, giving Massawa and its inhabitants a jaundiced appearance. No trees broke the monotony of the scene and the only visible colour, other than the uniform yellow, was provided by the White Ensign hanging limply from the base's flagstaff and by the bougainvillaea that wilted on the trellises screwed to the buildings' walls.

Even more depressing for a naval man like Stenhouse was the view seawards. Massawa possessed three harbours: to the north lay the main naval harbour, beautifully landlocked, with another, similar harbour to the south. Separating them, and protected on the one hand by the island of Massawa itself and, on the other, by the Abd-El-Kader Peninsula, lay the smaller, hoop-shaped commercial harbour. But, where one might expect to see and hear the vibrant life of a busy port, silence and stillness reigned supreme. On the superbly engineered quays, crazy, broken-backed cranes bent over the water, as though peering down curiously at the scuttled ships that strewed the harbour. These could be spotted all around: vessels of every size, their superstructures jutting out from the water, their hulks blocking the entrances to the three harbours and rendering the state-of-the-art port quite useless. Some sat on their keels, still upright; others had heeled over when the explosive charges had torn out their steel plates, and now rested on their sides, wallowing in the silt. And from each wreck seeped oil and diesel fuel, mixing with the rust and creating clouds of discoloration in the water, making it look unhealthy, diseased under the glare of the unblinking Red Sea sun.

More than the yellow dust, the shattered port and the twisted wrecks beneath the stained water, it was the sun that defined Massawa. During the long summer months, temperatures soared and the humidity meant that fresh clothes and bedding became sodden rags in a matter of seconds. Stenhouse described it to his sister as 'the hottest place on the shores of the Red Sea. In the summer (there are two summers here) it is a poisonous dump with occasional outbreaks of dengue fever. . . . The temperature in Massawa last week averaged about 110°F with almost maximum humidity. It is a good place to avoid in the hot season!'[4] Indeed, the Royal Navy considered the climate so debilitating that it had adopted a policy of, whenever possible, sending only men below the age of 50 to Massawa. In 1941, Stenhouse was 53 years old but the rarity of his particular skills and experience meant that the usual rule had to be waived.

Although he managed to avoid the scourge of dengue fever, however, the conditions in which he worked as he attempted to identify salvageable equipment in the furnace-like buildings around the port did bring on a severe bout of prickly heat. With his condition complicated by heat exhaustion, Massawa's medical officer decided that Stenhouse should be moved to a military hospital that benefited from the cooler mountain air of Asmara, the bizarrely Italianate capital of Eritrea, some 75 miles to the west. As usual, his ox-like constitution enabled him to overcome the irritation, but a month dragged by before Stenhouse could resume his duties. Unable to remain idle, and feeling confident in his returning strength, he took the opportunity to make a trip to Keren, where British troops had engaged in bitter fighting with the retreating Italian army. The view of the fortress-like escarpment that had been stormed in March 1941 impressed him immensely: 'our troops did a wonderful show there,' he enthused, 'and scaled steep ridges (that are difficult even to climb) with full equipment, under continuous fire.'[5]

Believing his recuperation complete, Stenhouse returned to Massawa only to be told that his doctors advised repatriation. He was, they thought, simply too old for duty in the Red Sea theatre of war. In the face of his impassioned resistance to such a move, and no doubt swayed by the shortage of suitably qualified and readily available officers to take his place, the Navy agreed a compromise. Stenhouse would be allowed to continue his work at Massawa, but he must live and sleep in the mountains, where the cooler temperatures would help to preserve his health. The next

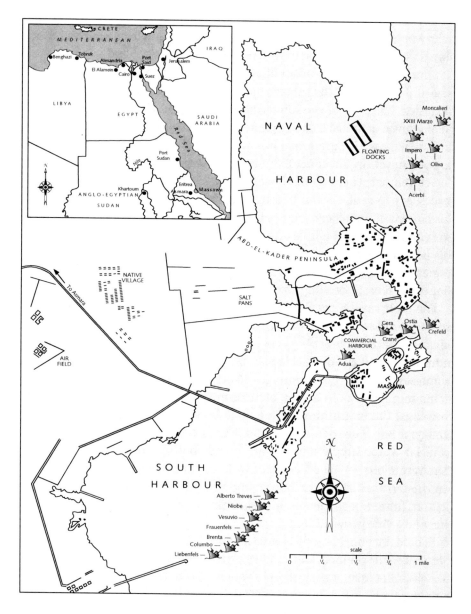

Map 5. Massawa, 1941.

problems to be overcome were the identification of a suitable residence and, given Stenhouse's reluctance to drive, the recruitment of a chauffeur who would be willing and able to transport him to and from Massawa every day. Fortunately, a solution to both problems lay close at hand.

Shortly before being taken ill, Stenhouse had suggested that, given its size and complexity, the salvage operation at Massawa should be properly recorded. The crew of the submarine depot ship HMS *Lucia*, now stationed at Massawa, included a young photography enthusiast named John Cutten and, when asked, Cutten had jumped at the chance to practise his hobby in such novel circumstances. But the process of developing film demanded lower temperatures than those at sea level and Cutten had found it necessary to rent a room in a hotel at Asmara. Now, since both he and his commanding officer required coolness, it made sense for the two men to rent a house in the hills and, since he must drive himself to and from his laboratory, for Lieutenant Cutten to drive Stenhouse as well. 'Thus,' remembered Cutten, a quarter of a century later, 'I became associated with one of the most interesting men I have ever met.'[6]

For their residence, Cutten selected a large bungalow at Embakalla, some 50 miles from Massawa and 4,000ft up in the hills. The distance meant that, each morning and evening, the two men must make a 90-minute drive in a ramshackle Fiat motor car that Cutten had managed to commandeer, but the advantages clearly outweighed the inconvenience. 'This bungalow is in a very picturesque setting,' Stenhouse told Nell, 'amongst the mountains, with a view from the veranda away down the valley; it has four rooms, stone-built with corrugated iron roof to catch rain for water supply and has an outside bathroom etc with a shower. The veranda is 34' by 14', shaded by bougainvillaea; we have coffee trees on the terraces above the house, and around it are wild olives, fig trees, lemon, lime, tangerine and pomegranate trees with fruit now ripening, etc. and a vine pergola.'[7]

Behind the bungalow, there lived a native woman, a one-eyed crone whom Stenhouse nicknamed 'Lily Langtry', whose job was to watch the house for the absent owners, rather than to wait on the new residents. Instead, they employed a talented Italian cook from one of the scuttled vessels. In fact, despite their having been warring enemies so recently, relations between the British victors and the defeated and imprisoned Italians remained quite cordial. Some of the POWs refused to undertake any work for their captors, but others proved quite willing and some even became engaged in repairing the damage which, only a few months previously, they had themselves wrought. And there could be no doubt that Stenhouse would need all the help he could get if he was to succeed in clearing the harbours of Massawa and returning at least some of the sunken ships to usefulness.

The partnership between Stenhouse and Cutten, too, proved a happy one. With his fathomless fund of stories and anecdotes, Stenhouse had the ability to capture the hearts and imaginations of a younger audience and soon Cutten, who had spent months kicking his heels in boredom and frustration on board the *Lucia*, was in thrall. During the evenings, the two men, dressed in their Navy whites, would sit on the veranda while their cook prepared dinner and Stenhouse regaled the younger man, like Bates before him, with stories of his service in the Arctic and Antarctic and on board the Q-ships. They could also talk during their daily rides to and from Massawa, as they admired the magnificent mountain scenery with its vertiginous precipices and the grand vistas which opened before them every time they swung round one of the innumerable hairpin bends. Whenever an opportunity presented itself, they explored inland, sending the old Fiat bounding and bumping across the desert roads which, for mile after mile, showed no sign of life beyond an occasional camel or donkey tottering along under a burden many times its own size. Cutten remembered:

One incident that typified the man occurred while driving over the mountains into Abyssinia. He was fond of singing, particularly hymn music, though he would break off in the middle of a hymn to let out a curse at an army truck driver encountered on a hairpin bend. Sometimes we would sing together in harmony while going along and on this occasion he suddenly asked me to stop; we got out of the car and he said 'Let's sing "Abide with Me"'. We stood at the edge of the road overlooking a vast valley and filled the air with our efforts. Then he said 'That will be the first time "Abide with Me" has been heard across these valleys'.[8]

Despite such invigorating and occasionally surreal outings, Stenhouse's mood veered between happiness and frustration. Sometimes, Cutten felt the sharp side of his tongue, usually when Stenhouse considered that, in the heat of debate, the junior officer had forgotten their difference in rank. He also missed his family generally, and Gladys in particular. 'I am so longing to hear your news,' he told her, 'you are in my thoughts all the time. . . . I do wish I could tell you about my adventures since I left home but that must wait till our reunion – what a time we will have.'[9]

Stenhouse found Massawa's remoteness from the front-line particularly depressing. Anyone could appreciate the port's strategic importance but, once the Italian resistance had been put down, in terms of active combat, it had become a backwater. 'This seems out of the picture altogether after the Thames Estuary and North Sea,' he complained to his sister. And to rub salt into the wound, recent British successes made him think that victory might be just around the corner, depriving him of any further opportunity to make the kind of contribution to the war effort that he valued and enjoyed the most. 'I think the Huns will be licked by us before Christmas,' he noted half-wistfully, 'but it will take a year or two to clean up the mess.'[10] But, with his usual resignation and energy, he turned to the task in hand: that of trying to make some impression on the thousands of tons of rusting wreckage in the harbour. Some of the ships would almost certainly be salvageable – given the availability of suitable equipment and skilled men, such as divers. But these were in chronically short supply.

Distance from the front-line did not render the work at Massawa devoid of danger: far from it. As well as demonstrating zeal and imagination in the task of destruction, the Italian sappers had rigged booby-traps both in the wrecks and on land; they had scuttled many of the sunken vessels with their full complement of munitions; and the waters around Massawa abounded with floating mines. In describing his passage out to the Red Sea, Stenhouse had asked Nell whether 'You remember what happened to me last October? Well, the same thing happened at midnight to the ship astern of us on the passage out and we also got one, but got in without any trouble; I thought I was going to have another swim.'[11] The thought proved to be prophetic.

In early September, Stenhouse and his team enjoyed their first victory: the salvaging of the scuttled Italian oil tanker, the *Giove*. Now, buoyed up by this success, he wanted to turn his attention to one of Massawa's greatest challenges: the raising of one of the two sabotaged floating docks. The larger of the docks lay in 40 or 50ft of water, on the bottom of the north harbour. Just under 600ft in length and 100ft wide, the U-shaped structure would be an enormously valuable asset to the Allies if they could raise it. In particular, it would enable them to clean the bottoms of the cruisers of the Mediterranean Fleet which currently formed long queues at Alexandria. The dock looked forlorn indeed, with only 2 or 3ft of its rusty sides showing above the discoloured water and with a lopsided crane still attached to the superstructure. With several large holes blown in its hull, raising the wreck would be an immensely difficult task even with the best equipment; with the limited tools available to Stenhouse, it looked all but impossible. But its probable usefulness to the Allies meant that an attempt must be made. To improve his chances, Stenhouse decided to make a voyage to HMS *Sheba*, the large British naval shore base at Aden, in order to scrounge additional equipment and, if possible, skilled men. He would make the trip in His Majesty's Tug, *Taikoo*, a small ship with a Chinese crew and a veteran English master. At the same time, Cutten received orders to rejoin the *Lucia*, which was heading to Colombo for a refit.

The two men exchanged their parting words on the quayside at Massawa, Stenhouse expressing the wish that Cutten could be released from his duties to continue their work together. But it was not to be and, though the two ships both sailed towards Aden, the two men would not meet again. The faster *Lucia* reached Aden first and Cutten then transferred to another vessel which transported him home to England for further training. The much slower *Taikoo* took another day to reach Aden, having wound her way laboriously through the extensive Italian minefields still festooning the approaches to Massawa. Having begged, borrowed and stolen all the equipment that he could find at Aden, Stenhouse once again embarked on the tug on 10 September and she sailed late that night.

He had hoped that the return voyage might present him with the opportunity to investigate reports of a wrecked submarine near Ghabbihu, one of the islands of the Dahlak Archipelago, some 40 miles out from Massawa, but Admiral Hallifax, Commander-in-Chief of the East Indies Station, vetoed the diversion. Instead, he passed his time talking with Philip Fairbairn, a serious-minded RNR lieutenant who had been posted to Massawa to serve as the port's Pilot. Neither man felt much confidence in the abilities of the *Taikoo*'s master, Captain Thirwell, who seemed intent on ignoring his orders. Even as they were leaving Aden, Fairbairn observed the captain diverging from his prescribed course and thereby putting his ship at risk of striking one of the many Italian mines that still bestrewed the waters of the Red Sea. The lieutenant tried, tactfully, to draw the correct courses to Thirwell's attention, but the stubborn old man rebuffed him with the remark 'Oh, those! I don't take much notice of those. I have my own courses.'[12] He also declined to accept Stenhouse's and Fairbairn's offers to keep a watch, despite the fact that his tug had too few officers, and made it abundantly clear to both of them that Royal Navy personnel would not be welcomed on his bridge.

Banned from the bridge, as mere passengers, Stenhouse and Fairbairn had little option but to spend much of their time in the ship's small saloon and, after dinner on the evening of 12 September, they met there with Peter Shaw, the *Taikoo*'s Chief Engineer. By 7 o'clock, the night was pitch black but still hot, with a slight sea causing the old tug to roll gently as she pursued her course. Then, at precisely 5 minutes past the hour, for the second time in under a year, the ship beneath Stenhouse's feet rocked with the impact of a submarine explosion. 'The saloon was plunged into darkness,' Fairbairn reported, 'and immediately became full of steam.'[13] Shaw remembered being 'lifted bodily from the deck and I could then hear objects falling on the deck above'.[14] On the bridge, the force of the explosion blew Chief Officer Gordon Clouston through the wheelhouse door into the chartroom and practically into the captain's cabin. 'We've found a mine,' he shouted as he staggered to his feet. 'To my mind,' he told the subsequent enquiry, 'the vessel shuddered, rolled heavily to starboard, then to port and commenced to dive.'[15]

In 1941, the most commonly used type of mine for blocking port entrances and deep water channels was the simple contact mine, and it was probably one of these that tore open the hull of the *Taikoo*. The little vessel suffered colossal damage. She possessed no watertight doors and only two watertight bulkheads. Exploding between the after part of the lower hold and the forward part of the boiler room, the mine utterly destroyed one of the two bulkheads and thereby rendered it highly improbable that the ship could live for more than a few minutes. The concussion also smashed the wireless transmitter, making it impossible for the operator to send out a distress call.

Pandemonium reigned in the saloon. Fairbairn sprang to his feet and dashed out on to the wildly tilting deck which he found to be so hot that it blistered his feet through his light shoes. Shaw, meanwhile, disorientated and unable to find the door, escaped through the forward porthole. Neither saw what became of Stenhouse, though the engineer thought that he had followed Fairbairn. On the bridge deck, Clouston fought to release the lifeboats: 'On reaching the after-part of the bridge deck, I sang out, "Clear away the sampans", but seeing it was hopeless to get the boats away owing to the list to port, I ran back to the starboard side of the bridge deck . . . climbed to the bridge sundeck, cut two raft lashings and then climbed down to the bridge and went to look for the Master. . . . The vessel was then diving under rapidly, with an increasing list to port and the Master and I simultaneously climbed over the starboard side bridge deck rail and stood on a plate landing. The vessel then took the final plunge, by the head.'[16]

Having been sucked down with the ship, Fairbairn eventually bobbed back up to the surface. In the intense darkness, he sensed rather than saw that there were many others floundering in the water or clinging desperately to pieces of wreckage. Now they must keep themselves alive and pray that the sharks did not find them. Throughout the night many men slipped quietly below the surface, too exhausted or too badly wounded to resist any longer, and, as the sky lightened in the east, the sight of a corpse in white shirt and shorts revealed that Captain Thirwell had paid a heavy price for his own wilfulness. Eventually, the bedraggled, salt-stained survivors managed to swim or paddle their way to Harmil Island where, with neither food nor water, they sweltered under the remorseless sun and waited to be rescued by a passing Arab dhow. No one had seen Stenhouse since the explosion put out the ship's lights.

The Admiralty telegram announcing that Stenhouse was missing, presumed killed, arrived at 48 Spenser Road, Bedford, on 18 September 1941. Gladys and Patricia were out but Elisabeth, who worked as a balloon-inspector at nearby Cardington, accepted the telegram and, fearing the worst, cycled out to find her mother and sister. For Gladys, who had shown great stoicism in the face of her first husband's death and in the difficult, nearly penurious years that followed, the news proved too much to bear. Staggering and weeping and supported by her two daughters, she reached home to await confirmation of her second widowhood.

It took a long time to arrive. Over half of the *Taikoo*'s seventy-strong complement had been lost and none of the survivors could give any absolute statement regarding Stenhouse's fate. Two of the ship's Chinese firemen, Wong Tse Hai and Lau Ching Foo, believed that they had spotted his corpse washed up on the northern point of Harmil Island, but the search parties found nothing. The letter from the Admiralty confirming his death did not arrive until a month after the first telegram and, even then, the letter could be based only upon reasonable assumptions. In the intervening period, Gladys clung desperately to the hope that her husband might only have been wounded and that he would still be found in a military or civilian hospital. She was sustained in this belief by Walter Campbell's conviction that his brother-in-law had survived the explosion, though he based his certainty upon nothing more substantial than a dream in which he had seen Stenhouse clinging to floating wreckage.

With the confirmation of his death, tributes flooded in. Foremost among his obituary writers stood Frank Worsley, his closest friend, his partner in so many adventurous and occasionally crack-brained schemes, and the man, above all others, who came closest to his own views on life. Asked to prepare an obituary for the *Polar Record*, Worsley willingly complied, writing of his friend:

> Two-thirds of his fifty-four years were spent in sail, on war service, or on polar work. With a wide and varied sea experience and a high sense of duty, he became one of the most efficient seamen of this century. He had sailing ships in his blood. . . . With his enthusiasm and his retentive memory, it was only natural that his knowledge of sailing ships should be practically unique . . .
>
> 'Duty' was Stenhouse's watchword. His epitaph should be – 'A seaman – he served his country well.' I feel it a privilege, after many years of close friendship, to write a few words on my old shipmate.[17]

To Gladys, Worsley revealed the true impact of Stenhouse's untimely death: 'whatever happens,' he told her, 'we must keep his memory fresh and living and bright, rather than sad. . . . I also said how marvellous it would be if one day he was to step in amongst us with a shout of laughter at our expense for having thought he was gone. I don't know if I wasn't wrong to give an illusion of hope, but just think how wild Stennie would be with me if I was the one to cut her off from all hope.'[18] To his wife, Jean, he admitted to feeling 'sadder now for myself at the loss of my Stennie. . . . It is the greatest loss – bar my father – that I have ever had – even more than Shackleton.'[19]

Although *Lloyd's List* acknowledged that 'his experiences were so widely varied that he was well named "a modern Elizabethan",'[20] as might be expected, most of the obituaries focused on Stenhouse's Antarctic service, most particularly his work with Shackleton's Imperial Trans-Antarctic Expedition. *The Times* paid particular tribute to the brilliant seamanship which enabled him to bring 'the *Aurora* safely through 1,000 miles of perilous drift in the pack ice and then, with her rudder torn off and a jury rudder rigged, through the gales of the Southern Ocean to New Zealand'.[21]

Worsley spoke truly when he stated that 'Duty' had been his friend's watchword, particularly when that duty placed him in command of a full-rigged sailing ship – the one place, above all others, where he felt most at home. He embraced the harshness of life at sea, in peace and war, and had little patience with those unwilling or unable to withstand it. But the rough-and-tumble, the moments of intense, adrenaline-pumping excitement, were secondary to his love of the sea itself and of old-fashioned sailing ships. Stenhouse had taken his master's certificates in sail and steam, and had commanded both types of vessel. But the magnificent spectacle of a sailing ship, dashing across the ocean under topsails, headsails, mid-ship staysails and spanker – a great dazzling pyramid of canvas – was all in all to him.

Describing one of his elderly shipmates on the *Springbank*, he had said that, 'He liked life; to him it was still an adventure and a bit of a lark.' Even at 53, the same could be said of Stenhouse himself. He had been fortunate enough to see sailing ships in what, though they could not compare with 50 or 100 years earlier, were still sufficiently large numbers. He had visited ports reminiscent of the waterfronts of the golden age of piracy. And, in volunteering for Shackleton's *Endurance*, he had been able to make a major contribution to the last of the Heroic Age expeditions to Antarctica. His services had also been recognised by his country with the award of the OBE, as well as the Polar Medal, and with the command of the *Discovery* in the 1920s. His military service had been rewarded, too, with the DSO, the DSC and the French Croix de Guerre, making him one of the most highly decorated of all Heroic Age explorers.

But he was a man born out of his time. Each of the things he loved most he saw in their last days: things of tremendous beauty still, but irrevocably doomed. Sail, once the mainstay of ocean-going trade, would soon become the preserve of weekend yachtsmen – a breed that Stenhouse despised. And the kind of muscular exploration that so stirred his blood – and which Shackleton epitomised – was fast being replaced by purely scientific investigation, pioneered by individuals like Erich von Drygalski and Douglas Mawson and championed by their successors, men like Stanley Kemp, with whom Stenhouse had little or no sympathy.

In a shabby postwar world, an old-fashioned sea dog like Stenhouse would find it increasingly difficult to obtain employment commensurate with his age and experience. In the lean periods of his life – the early 1920s and throughout the 1930s – he had shown tremendous resilience, sharing Gladys's optimistic belief that something must, inevitably, 'turn up'. On the other hand, he had seen many of his peers lose their way in life once they had been denied their raison d'être. Shackleton had burst his heart chasing a dream with sad, despairing tenacity. Frank Wild, the veteran of more Antarctic expeditions than any man of his generation, had ended his life as a drunk. Frank Bickerton, now a wing commander with the RAF, would wander from job to job after the war, directionless. A similar fate might well have lain in wait for Stenhouse. If he had any inkling of this possibility, then perhaps, as the warm, dark waters of the Red Sea closed over his head, still in the full vigour of his maturity, and dying for his country, he would not have had it otherwise.

NOTES AND SOURCES

CHAPTER 1: THE APPRENTICE IN SAIL

1. Andrew Weir & Company to J.R. Stenhouse, 30 August 1904. Courtesy of Patricia and Sarah Mantell.
2. Later the Grammar School.
3. Andrew Stenhouse sailed on a round voyage to Australia in 1877–8 on board the *Stirlingshire*.
4. Andrew Stenhouse's first wife, Janet, mother of Joseph, died on 19 March 1899. Andrew remarried in 1901 to Prudence Wallhead.
5. J.R. Stenhouse, *Cracker Hash: The Story of an Apprentice in Sail* (London, Percival Marshall, 1955), p. 3.
6. J.R. Stenhouse diary, 11 February 1905. All diary entries courtesy of Patricia and Sarah Mantell.
7. *Ibid.*
8. Stenhouse diary, 19 November 1904.
9. *Ibid.*
10. Stenhouse, *Cracker Hash*, p. 78.
11. *Ibid.*, p. 25.
12. Stenhouse diary, *c.*12 December 1904.
13. Stenhouse diary, 25 December 1904.
14. Stenhouse diary, 9 February 1905.
15. Stenhouse, *Cracker Hash*, pp. 40–1.
16. J.R. Stenhouse to Andrew Stenhouse, 13 June 1905. Courtesy of Charles Stenhouse Martin.
17. *Vancouver Daily Province*, 13 June 1905.
18. Stenhouse to Andrew Stenhouse, 13 June 1905.
19. Stenhouse, *Cracker Hash*, p. 100.
20. Stenhouse to Andrew Stenhouse, 13 June 1905.
21. Stenhouse diary, 13 August 1906.
22. *Ibid.*
23. Stenhouse diary, 19 September 1906.
24. Stenhouse, *Cracker Hash*, p. 209.

CHAPTER 2: SOUTH WITH SHACKLETON

1. Testimonial for J.R. Stenhouse from Captain D. Royal, 26 July 1909. Courtesy of Patricia and Sarah Mantell.
2. Stenhouse, *Cracker Hash*, p. 25.
3. SPRI, MS 1453/179, J. Foster Stackhouse to Kathleen Scott, 17 September 1913.

4. SPRI, MS 1453/46/5, Dr E.L. Atkinson to Kathleen Scott, 14 November 1913.
5. Douglas Mawson, *The Home of the Blizzard* (Edinburgh, Berlinn, 2000), p. xvii.
6. SPRI, MS 1456/38, Fisher papers: Report of a Conference of the RGS with Sir Ernest Shackleton, 4 March 1914.
7. *Daily Mail*, 7 April 1930.
8. J.R. Stenhouse to Andrew Stenhouse, 18 August 1914. Courtesy of Charles Stenhouse Martin.
9. *Ibid.*
10. SPRI, MS 1456/38, Fisher papers: Report of a Conference of the RGS with Sir Ernest Shackleton, 4 March 1914.
11. Stenhouse to Andrew Stenhouse, 26 August 1914.
12. Stenhouse diary, 16 September 1914.
13. Stenhouse diary, 18 September 1914.
14. Stenhouse diary, 19 September 1914.
15. SPRI, MS 100/136, Alexander Stevens's Report on the Ross Sea Party, 1914–17.
16. Stenhouse diary, 31 October 1914.
17. Aeneas Mackintosh to E. White, 4 December *c.* 1914. Courtesy of Patricia and Sarah Mantell.
18. SPRI, MS 100/136, Report on the Ross Sea Party.
19. Stenhouse to Andrew Stenhouse, 21 November 1914.
20. Stenhouse diary, 15–19 December 1914.
21. SPRI, MS 1456/33, diary of Leslie Thomson, 23 December 1914.

CHAPTER 3: ARRIVALS AND DEPARTURES

1. Stenhouse diary, 30 December 1914.
2. SPRI, MS 1590/9/1, diary of Alfred Larkman, 26–9 December 1914.
3. Aeneas Mackintosh diary, 31 December 1914. Courtesy of Patricia and Sarah Mantell.
4. Stenhouse diary, 1 January 1915.
5. SPRI, MS 1456/33, diary of Leslie Thomson, 2 January 1915.
6. SPRI, MS 100/136, Report on the Ross Sea Party.
7. SPRI, MS 1456/33, diary of Leslie Thomson, 4 January 1915.
8. Stenhouse, *Cracker Hash*, p. 144.
9. Stenhouse diary, 13 January 1915.
10. Stenhouse diary, 7 January 1915.
11. Lionel Hooke diary, 9 January 1915. Courtesy of John Hooke.
12. Mackintosh diary, 9 January 1915.
13. Stenhouse diary, 9 January 1915.
14. Ernest Shackleton, *South* (London, Robinson, 1999), p. 246.
15. Mackintosh diary, 13 January 1915.
16. Mackintosh diary, 15 January 1915.
17. This particular machine is the only survivor of those built for the ITAE. It can be seen at the Canterbury Museum, Christchurch, New Zealand.
18. Mackintosh diary, 19 January 1915.
19. SPRI, MS 1456/33, diary of Leslie Thomson, 21 January 1915.
20. SPRI, MS 100/136, Report on the Ross Sea Party.
21. Mackintosh diary, 24 January 1915.
22. SPRI, MS 1456/33, diary of Leslie Thomson, 24 January 1915.
23. Aeneas Mackintosh to J.R. Stenhouse, 24 January 1915. Courtesy of Patricia and Sarah Mantell.

CHAPTER 4: ADRIFT IN McMURDO SOUND

1. SPRI, MS 1537/4/4/20, J.R. Stenhouse to Ernest Shackleton, 15 February 1917.
2. Stenhouse diary, 7 June 1915.
3. SPRI, MS 1456/33, diary of Leslie Thomson, 31 January 1915.
4. Hooke diary, 8 January 1915.
5. SPRI, MS 1537/4/4/16, J.R. Stenhouse to Aeneas Mackintosh, 3 February 1915.
6. SPRI, MS 1456/33, diary of Leslie Thomson, 18 February 1915.
7. SPRI, MS 1537/4/4/15, J.R. Stenhouse to Aeneas Mackintosh, 8 March 1915.
8. Stenhouse diary, 5 July 1915.
9. SPRI, MS 1590/9/1, diary of Alfred Larkman, 2 March 1915.
10. SPRI, MS 1537/4/4/15, J.R. Stenhouse to Aeneas Mackintosh, 8 March 1915.
11. Aeneas Mackintosh to J.R. Stenhouse, 26 February 1915 [*sic*]. Courtesy of Patricia and Sarah Mantell.
12. John Lachlan Cope to J.R. Stenhouse, 7 February 1915. Courtesy of Patricia and Sarah Mantell.
13. Alexander Stevens to J.R. Stenhouse, 7 February 1915. Courtesy of Patricia and Sarah Mantell.
14. Hooke diary, 12 March 1915.
15. Log of the SY *Aurora*, 12 March 1915. Courtesy of Patricia and Sarah Mantell.
16. Lionel Hooke to J.R. Stenhouse, 30 January 1915. Courtesy of Patricia and Sarah Mantell.
17. J.R. Stenhouse to A.H. Ninnis, 15 April 1915. Courtesy of Patricia and Sarah Mantell.
18. A.H. Ninnis to J.R. Stenhouse, 14 April 1915. Courtesy of Patricia and Sarah Mantell.
19. Stenhouse diary, 6 May 1915.
20. Stenhouse diary, 7 May 1915.

CHAPTER 5: PRISONERS OF THE PACK

1. Stenhouse diary, 9 May 1915.
2. SPRI, MS 1456/33, diary of Leslie Thomson, 17 May 1915.
3. Stenhouse diary, 31 May 1915.
4. Stenhouse diary, 28 May 1915.
5. Stenhouse diary, 23 May 1915.
6. Stenhouse diary, 8 September 1915.
7. Stenhouse diary, 7 November 1915.
8. Stenhouse diary, 13 July 1915.
9. Hooke diary, 21 July 1915.
10. SPRI, MS 1590/9/1, diary of Alfred Larkman, 21 July 1915.
11. Stenhouse diary, 25 July 1915.
12. Stenhouse diary, 7 January 1916.
13. Stenhouse diary, 21 January 1916.
14. Stenhouse diary, 1 February 1916.
15. SPRI, MS 1590/9/1, diary of Alfred Larkman, 22 February 1916.
16. Stenhouse diary, 8 March 1916.

CHAPTER 6: AURORA REDUX

1. Telegram, J.R. Stenhouse to Andrew Stenhouse, 27 March 1916. Courtesy of Patricia and Sarah Mantell.
2. Shackleton, *South*, p. 339.

3. *Otago Daily Times*, 4 April 1916.
4. F.W. White to J.R. Stenhouse, March 1916. Courtesy of Patricia and Sarah Mantell.
5. J.R. Stenhouse to Sir Ernest Shackleton, 18 November 1916. Courtesy of Patricia and Sarah Mantell.
6. *Ibid.*
7. Alexander Turnbull Library, L.O.H. Tripp Papers, MS 95, Folder 5, L.O.H. Tripp, Statement on Stenhouse and his position re *Aurora*, March 1917.
8. J.R. Stenhouse to L.O.H. Tripp, 15 November 1916. Courtesy of Patricia and Sarah Mantell.
9. J.R. Stenhouse to J.K. Davis, 17 October 1916. Courtesy of Patricia and Sarah Mantell.
10. J.K. Davis to J.R. Stenhouse, 17 October 1916. Courtesy of Patricia and Sarah Mantell.
11. Alexander Turnbull Library, L.O.H. Tripp Papers.
12. *Ibid.*
13. SPRI, MS 1456/43, Ernest Shackleton to Ernest Perris, 30 November 1914.

CHAPTER 7: THE MYSTERY SHIPS

1. In a curious coincidence, one of the passengers killed was Joseph Foster Stackhouse, the man who had offered Stenhouse his first opportunity to join an expedition to Antarctica.
2. E. Keble Chatterton, *Q-ships and Their Story* (London, Sidgwick & Jackson, 1922), p. 3.
3. IWM, Captain F.H. Grenfell diary, 18 December 1915.
4. IWM, Grenfell diary, 29 December 1915.
5. Alexander Turnbull Library, L.O.H. Tripp Papers, MS 95, Folder 4, J.R. Stenhouse to Leonard Tripp, 19 June 1917.
6. TNA, ADM240/60, Officer's Record of Service, 8 July 1917.
7. Frank Worsley, *Endurance: An Epic of Polar Adventure* (New York, Norton & Co., 2000), p. 218.
8. *Ibid.*, p. 220.
9. *Ibid.*, p. 221.
10. Chatterton, *Q-ships and Their Story*, p. 60.
11. *Barrier Miner*, 17 March 1918.

CHAPTER 8: WAR IN THE ARCTIC

1. C.M. Maynard, *The Murmansk Venture* (London, Hodder & Stoughton, *c.* 1928), p. vii.
2. Alexander Turnbull Library, Frank Worsley to Leonard Tripp, 26 October 1918.
3. SPRI, MS 1537/2/41/11, Sir Ernest Shackleton to Emily Shackleton, 26 October 1918.
4. *The Times*, 15 April 1919, p. 11.
5. IWM, MS 83/50/1, letter of an unknown correspondent to Audrey White, 31 May 1919.
6. IWM, MS 86/2/1, E. Davey, diary, 19 October 1918.
7. Alexander Turnbull Library, Frank Worsley to Leonard Tripp, 26 October 1918.
8. J.R. Stenhouse to Helen Martin, 20 July 1941. Courtesy of Charles Stenhouse Martin.
9. SPRI, MS 1537/2/41/12, Sir Ernest Shackleton to Emily Shackleton, 1 November 1918.

10. *The Times*, 25 February 1919, p. 9.
11. *Ibid.*
12. Stenhouse, *Cracker Hash*, p. 5.
13. Maynard, Testimonial for J.R. Stenhouse, 22 October 1919.
14. SPRI, MS 1537/2/41/14, Sir Ernest Shackleton to Emily Shackleton, 17 November 1918.
15. IWM, MS 86/2/1, E. Davey diary, 22 October 1918.
16. SPRI, MS 1529/1/25, Frank Worsley to 'Ted', 9 July 1919.
17. TNA, WO32/5698, Maynard, Despatch on Operations, 1 March 1919.
18. IWM, MS 86/2/1, E. Davey, diary, 14 January 1919.
19. TNA, WO32/5698, Maynard, Despatch on Operations, 1 March 1919.
20. Stenhouse diary, 4 January 1919.
21. *Ibid.*
22. TNA, WO32/5698, Maynard, Despatch on Operations, 1 March 1919.
23. Stenhouse diary, 4 January 1919.
24. Stenhouse diary, 7 January 1919.
25. Stenhouse diary, 5 January 1919.
26. L.M. Bates, *The Spirit of London's River* (Old Woking, Gresham Books, 1980), p. 34.
27. Stenhouse diary, 18 January 1919.
28. *The Times*, 5 April 1919, p. 12.
29. Stenhouse diary, 9 January 1919.
30. *The Times*, 4 April 1919.
31. Stenhouse diary, 17 January 1919.
32. SPRI, MS 1529/1/25, Frank Worsley to 'Ted', 9 July 1919.
33. *Ibid.*
34. Stenhouse diary, 5 February 1919.

Chapter 9: The Syren Flotilla

1. TNA, WO158/720, Robert Curteis, *History of the Syren Lake Flotilla*.
2. TNA, WO158/720, Robert Curteis, *History of the Syren Lake Flotilla*.
3. SPRI, MS 1537/2/43/4, Ernest Shackleton to Emily Shackleton, 16 January 1919.
4. Stenhouse diary, 7 January 1919.
5. SPRI, MS 1529/1/25, Frank Worsley to 'Ted', 9 July 1919.
6. Stenhouse diary, 8 January 1919.
7. TNA, WO160/19, J.H. Mather, Report on operations against enemy craft on 5 June 1919.
8. *Ibid.*
9. *Ibid.*
10. TNA, WO158/720, Robert Curteis, *History of the Syren Lake Flotilla*.
11. SPRI, MS 1529/1/25, Frank Worsley to 'Ted', 9 July 1919.
12. Worsley, *Endurance*, p. 230.
13. Maynard, *The Murmansk Venture*, p. 311.

Chapter 10: Discovery

1. Frank Worsley to Jean Cumming, 18 February 1921. Courtesy of John Thomson and Pat Bamford.
2. Worsley to Jean Cumming, 6 December 1920.
3. Worsley to Jean Cumming, 19 September 1921. Courtesy of Pat Bamford.

4. SPRI, MS 1284/4/1, *Nature*, Vol. III, p. 645, 12 May 1923.

5. SPRI, MS 1284/4/1, Meeting of Executive Committee, 8 June 1923.

6. From an unidentified newspaper cutting in the Stenhouse scrapbooks, 1923. Courtesy of Patricia and Sarah Mantell.

7. SPRI, MS 1284/4/1, Meeting of Executive Committee, 8 June 1923.

8. SPRI, MS 1284/4/1, Macklin to J.N. Wordie, quoted by Wordie, 27 June 1923.

9. Alexander Turnbull Library, L.O.H. Tripp Papers, MS 95, Folder 7, J.R. Stenhouse to L.O.H. Tripp, 18 November 1923.

10. SPRI, MS 1284/4/1, Meeting of the Executive Committee, 3 December 1923.

11. 'Aunt Lizzie' to J.R. Stenhouse, 3 May 1915. Courtesy of Patricia and Sarah Mantell.

12. Frank Worsley to Jean Worsley, 26 September 1941. Courtesy of Mr Pat Bamford.

13. *The Gentlewoman*, 13 October 1923.

14. Stenhouse diary, 19 November 1915.

15. SPRI, MS 1284/4/3, H.T. Allen to E.R. Darnley, 29 August 1924.

16. SPRI, MS 1284/4/3, E.R. Darnley to Sidney Harmer, 4 September 1924.

17. G. Grindle to J.R. Stenhouse, 16 December 1924. Courtesy of Patricia and Sarah Mantell.

18. *The Times*, Obituary for Stanley Kemp, 18 May 1945.

19. From an unidentified newspaper cutting in the Stenhouse scrapbooks, 1923. Courtesy of Patricia and Sarah Mantell.

20. SPRI, MS 100/57/1, Stanley Kemp to H.R. Mill, 18 October 1924.

21. SPRI, MS 1284/4/4, J.R. Stenhouse to E. Baynes, 30 July 1925.

22. E.R. Gunther, *Notes and Sketches Made During Two Years on the 'Discovery' Expedition* (Oxford, Holywell Press, 1928), p. 3.

23. SPRI, MS 911/1, H.F.P. Herdman to D.D. Henderson, 1 November 1925.

24. SPRI, MS 1284/4/4, J.R. Stenhouse to E. Baynes, 30 July 1925.

CHAPTER 11: OCEANS DEEP

1. Stenhouse, *Cracker Hash*, p. 72.

2. SPRI, MS 1284/4/1 Professor E.S. Goodrich to the *Discovery* Committee, 21 October 1923.

3. A. Hardy, *Great Waters* (London, Collins, 1967), p. 56.

4. NOC, J.R. Stenhouse to the *Discovery* Committee, 17 October 1925.

5. SPRI, MS 911/1, H.F.P. Herdman to D.D. Henderson, 1 November 1925.

6. NOC, Stenhouse to the *Discovery* Committee, 24 December 1925.

7. SPRI, MS 911/1, H.F.P. Herdman to D.D. Henderson, 1 November 1925.

8. NOC, Stenhouse to the *Discovery* Committee, 22 February 1926.

9. Gunther, *Notes and Sketches*, pp. 6–7.

10. NOC, Dr E.H. Marshall, Report on a Visit to Tristan da Cunha, 1 March 1926.

11. NOC, Stenhouse to the *Discovery* Committee, 22 February 1926.

12. Shackleton, *South*, p. 159.

13. NOC, Stenhouse to the *Discovery* Committee, 22 February 1926.

14. Gunther, *Notes and Sketches*, p. 8.

15. NOC, Stenhouse to the *Discovery* Committee, 22 February 1926.

16. Hardy, *Great Waters*, p. 159.

17. *Ibid.*, p. 161.

18. NOC, Stenhouse to the *Discovery* Committee, 29 April 1926.

19. Stanley Kemp, Fourth Report on the Scientific Work of the RRS *Discovery*, p. 1. Courtesy of Patricia and Sarah Mantell.

20. Hardy, *Great Waters*, p. 168.
21. Kemp, Fourth Report on the Scientific Work of the RRS *Discovery*, p. 3.
22. Gunther, *Notes and Sketches*, p. 11.
23. Kemp, Fourth Report on the Scientific Work of the RRS *Discovery*, p. 1.
24. NOC, Stenhouse to the *Discovery* Committee, 29 April 1926.
25. J.R. Stenhouse to E.W. Baynes, 7 April 1926. Courtesy of Patricia and Sarah Mantell.
26. Gunther, *Notes and Sketches*, p. 12.
27. Kemp, Fourth Report on the Scientific Work of the RRS *Discovery*, p. 2.
28. NOC, Stenhouse to the *Discovery* Committee, 17 July 1926.
29. NOC, Stenhouse to the *Discovery* Committee, 29 April 1926.
30. Gunther, *Notes and Sketches*, p. 14.
31. NOC, Stenhouse to the *Discovery* Committee, 17 July 1926.
32. SPRI, MS 1284/4/8, John Chaplin interviewed at a special meeting of the *Discovery* Committee, 2 December 1927.

CHAPTER *12: THE FINAL SEASON*

1. J.R. Stenhouse to Gladys Stenhouse, June 1926. Courtesy of Patricia and Sarah Mantell.
2. SPRI, MS 1284/4/6, Stenhouse to the *Discovery* Committee, 19 August 1926.
3. NOC, J.R. Stenhouse to E.W. Baynes, 23 October 1926.
4. Stanley Kemp, Seventh Report on the Scientific Work of the RRS *Discovery*. Courtesy of Patricia and Sarah Mantell.
5. NOC, J.R. Stenhouse to E.W. Baynes, 14 December 1926.
6. SPRI, MS 1284/4/8, Dr E.H. Marshall, interviewed at a special meeting of the *Discovery* Committee, 2 December 1927.
7. Gunther, *Notes and Sketches*, p. 24.
8. SPRI, MS 911/3, H.F.P. Herdman to D.D. Henderson, 11 November 1926.
9. NOC, J.R. Stenhouse to E.W. Baynes, 14 December 1926.
10. *Ibid.*
11. Stanley Kemp to H.T. Allen, 7 December 1926. Courtesy of Patricia and Sarah Mantell.
12. SPRI, MS 1284/4/6, W.H. O'Connor to the *Discovery* Committee, 6 September 1926.
13. Quoted by Stanley Kemp in a letter to H.T. Allen, 7 December 1926. Courtesy of Patricia and Sarah Mantell.
14. Stanley Kemp in a letter to H.T. Allen, 7 December 1926.
15. *Discovery* Committee to Stenhouse, 5 March 1927. Courtesy of Patricia and Sarah Mantell.
16. Gunther, *Notes and Sketches*, p. 29.
17. Hardy, *Great Waters*, p. 290.
18. SPRI, MS 911/4, H.F.P. Herdman to D.D. Henderson, 19 June 1927.
19. *Ibid.*
20. Mrs Margaret Marshall in a letter to the author, 29 January 2006.
21. Hardy, *Great Waters*, p. 283.
22. SPRI, MS 1284/4/8, Alister Hardy interviewed at a special meeting of the *Discovery* Committee, 2 December 1927.
23. SPRI, MS 1284/4/8, Dr E.H. Marshall interviewed at a special meeting of the *Discovery* Committee, 2 December 1927.
24. *Ibid.*

25. NOC, Stenhouse to the *Discovery* Committee, 17 May 1927.
26. Hardy, *Great Waters*, p. 375.
27. NOC, Stenhouse to the *Discovery* Committee, 17 May 1927.
28. *Ibid.*
29. Hardy, *Great Waters*, pp. 404–5.
30. NOC, Stenhouse to the *Discovery* Committee, 17 May 1927.
31. Hardy, *Great Waters*, p. 428.
32. L. Harrison Matthews, *South Georgia: The British Empire's Subantarctic Outpost* (Bristol, John Wright, 1931), pp. 150–1.
33. Hardy, *Great Waters*, p. 313.
34. SPRI, MS 1284/4/7, Stanley Kemp to E.R. Darnley, 10 October 1927.
35. SPRI, MS 1284/4/8, Alister Hardy interviewed at a special meeting of the *Discovery* Committee, 2 December 1927.
36. SPRI, MS 1284/4/8, Lieutenant-Commander John Chaplin interviewed at a special meeting of the *Discovery* Committee, 2 December 1927.
37. SPRI, MS 1284/4/8, Dr E.H. Marshall interviewed at a special meeting of the *Discovery* Committee, 2 December 1927.
38. E.R. Darnley to Stenhouse, 15 June 1928. Courtesy of Patricia and Sarah Mantell.

CHAPTER 13: PIECES OF EIGHT

1. *Time* magazine, 4 August 1930.
2. Aeneas Mackintosh, 'Diary of Events on Treasure Seeking Expedition to Cocos Island', 22 April 1911. Courtesy of Mrs Elisabeth Dowler and Mrs Anne Phillips.
3. *The Times*, 20 August 1934.
4. Frank Worsley, Cocos Island Diary, 17 August 1934. Courtesy of Mr Pat Bamford.
5. Worsley, Cocos Island Diary, 22 September 1934.
6. Canterbury Museum, MS455, Frank Worsley to Madeline Meares, 12 August 1935.
7. *Ibid.*
8. Worsley, Cocos Island Diary, 30 September 1934.
9. Worsley, Cocos Island Diary, 4 October 1934.

CHAPTER 14: TREASURE ISLAND TO THE CAP PILAR

1. Worsley, Cocos Island Diary, 12 October 1934.
2. Worsley, Cocos Island Diary, 14 October 1934.
3. TNA, FO288/205, wireless transmission from Cocos Island to Stenhouse and Worsley, October 1934.
4. TNA, FO288/205, telegram from TRL to Stenhouse and Worsley, October 1934.
5. *Panama American*, 16 October 1934.
6. TNA, FO288/205, Vice Consul, Panama, to Her Majesty's Minister, 20 October 1934.
7. TNA, FO288/205, F.N. Cox, British Consulate, San José, to Frederick Adam, British Minister, Panama, 23 October 1934.
8. TNA, FO288/205, Statement made to the judge at Puntarenas by Stratford D. Jolly and C.O. Polkinghorne, 29 October 1934.
9. TNA, FO288/205, F.N. Cox, British Consulate, San José, to Frederick Adam, British Minister, Panama, 30 October 1934.
10. TNA, FO288/205, Frederick Adam to Sir John Simon, 2 November 1934.
11. TNA, FO288/205, Frank Cox to Frederick Adam, 2 November 1934.
12. Stenhouse, *Cracker Hash*, p. 22.

13. *Ibid.*, pp. 239–40.
14. Adrian Seligman, *The Voyage of the Cap Pilar* (London, Seafarer Books, 1993), p. 24.
15. *Ibid.*, p. 52.
16. Philip Allan (of Philip Allan & Co. Ltd) to J.R. Stenhouse, 8 June 1937. Courtesy of Patricia and Sarah Mantell.
17. *Shipbuilding & Shipping Record*, 15 December 1955.
18. *Lloyd's List & Shipping Gazette*, 18 October 1955.
19. Stenhouse, *Cracker Hash*, p. 30.
20. *Kine Weekly*, 9 November 1937.
21. *Daily Film Renter*, 6 September 1937.
22. SPRI, MS 1512/2/39, Frank Debenham to Dr Leonard Hussey, 25 February 1937.
23. SPRI, MS 1512/2/177, Ernest Walker to Leonard Hussey, 17 December 1937.
24. SPRI, MS 1512/2/146, Walker to Hussey, 24 April 1936.
25. Ernest Walker to J.R. Stenhouse, 6 July 1937. Courtesy of Patricia and Sarah Mantell.
26. SPRI, MS 1512/2/177, Walker to Hussey, 17 December 1937.

CHAPTER 15: THAMES PATROL

1. L.M. Bates, *Tideway Tactics* (London, Frederick Muller, 1947), p. 133.
2. Stenhouse, *Cracker Hash*, p. 145.
3. Bates, *The Spirit of London's River*, p. 34.
4. Quoted in Bates, *The Spirit of London's River*, p. 110.
5. TNA, ADM1/11209, J.R. Stenhouse, interviewed during 'Board of Enquiry into the Loss of HMS *Danube III*'.
6. *Idem.*
7. TNA, ADM1/11209, Lieutenant R. Sullivan, interviewed during 'Board of Enquiry into the Loss of HMS *Danube III*'.
8. TNA, ADM1/11209, Stenhouse, interviewed during 'Board of Enquiry into the Loss of HMS *Danube III*'.
9. TNA, ADM1/11209, Stenhouse, written account submitted to the 'Board of Enquiry into the Loss of HMS *Danube III*'.
10. Bates, *Tideway Tactics*, p. 139.
11. TNA, ADM1/11209, Stenhouse, written account submitted to the 'Board of Enquiry into the Loss of HMS *Danube III*'.
12. Bates, *Tideway Tactics*, p. 140.
13. TNA, ADM1/11209, Stenhouse, written account submitted to the 'Board of Enquiry into the Loss of HMS *Danube III*'.
14. Conversation between Mrs Elisabeth Dowler and the author, 6 July 2005.
15. TNA, ADM1/11209, Stenhouse, written account submitted to the 'Board of Enquiry into the Loss of HMS *Danube III*'.
16. *Ibid.*
17. Canterbury Museum, MS539/46, Stenhouse to Frank Worsley, 23 April 1941

CHAPTER 16: WITH HIS BOOTS ON

1. Stenhouse to Helen Martin, 20 July 1941. Courtesy of Charles Stenhouse Martin.
2. Stenhouse to Gladys Stenhouse, 16 May 1941. Courtesy of Patricia and Sarah Mantell.
3. Edward Ellsberg, *Under the Red Sea Sun* (New York, Dodd, Mead & Company), p. 112.

4. Stenhouse to Helen Martin, 20 July 1941.
5. *Ibid.*
6. BL, NCUACS 5/4/88/B.47, John Cutten to Alister Hardy, 17 October 1965.
7. Stenhouse to Helen Martin, 20 July 1941.
8. BL, NCUACS 5/4/88/B.47, Cutten to Hardy, 17 October 1965.
9. Stenhouse to Gladys Stenhouse, 16 May 1941.
10. Stenhouse to Helen Martin, 20 July 1941.
11. *Ibid.*
12. TNA, ADM1/12022, Board of Enquiry into the Sinking of HMT *Taikoo*, 21 September 1941.
13. TNA, ADM1/12022, Statement of Lieutenant P.C. Fairbairn, 18 September 1941.
14. TNA, ADM1/12022, Statement of Peter Shaw, Chief Engineer of HMT *Taikoo*, 18 September 1941.
15. TNA, ADM1/12022, Statement of Gordon Clouston, Chief Officer of HMT *Taikoo*, 18 September 1941.
16. *Ibid.*
17. F.A. Worsley in *Polar Record*, Cambridge University Press, Vol. 3, No. 24, 1942, pp. 581–2.
18. F.A. Worsley to Jean Worsley, 26 September 1941. Courtesy of Mr Pat Bamford.
19. *Ibid.*
20. *Lloyd's List*, 17 November 1941.
21. *The Times*, 19 March 1942.

Select Bibliography

Bates, L.M., *The Thames on Fire: The Battle of London River*, Lavenham, Terence Dalton, 1985

——, *Tideway Tactics*, London, Frederick Muller, 1947

——, *The Spirit of London's River*, Old Woking, Gresham Books, 1980

Bernacchi, Louis, *Saga of the Discovery*, Royston, Rooster Books, 2003

Bickel, Lennard, *Shackleton's Forgotten Men*, London, Pimlico, 2000

Campbell, Gordon, *My Mystery Ships*, Penzance, Periscope Publishing, 2002

——, *The Life of a Q-Ship Captain*, Penzance, Periscope Publishing, 2002

Chatterton, E. Keble, *Q-Ships and Their Story*, London, Sidgwick & Jackson, 1923

Crane, Jonathan, *Submarine*, London, BBC, 1984

Ellsberg, Edward, *Under the Red Sea Sun*, New York, Dodd, Mead & Co., 1946

Fisher, Margery and James, *Shackleton*, London, Barrie, 1957

Gunther, E.R., *Notes and Sketches: Made During Two Years on the 'Discovery' Expedition*, Oxford, Holywell Press, 1928

Haddelsey, Stephen, *Born Adventurer: The Life of Frank Bickerton, Antarctic Pioneer*, Stroud, Sutton, 2005

Hardy, A., *Great Waters*, London, Collins, 1967

Harrison Matthews, L., *South Georgia: The British Empire's Subantarctic Outpost*, Bristol, John Wright & Sons, 1931

Ironside, Edmund, *Archangel, 1918–1919*, London, Constable, 1953

Keeble, Peter, *Ordeal by Water*, London, Pan, 1957

Livesey, Roger, *Atlas of World War I*, London, Viking, 1994

Lockhart, Robert Bruce, *Memoirs of a British Agent*, London, Putnam, 1935

Maynard, C.M., *The Murmansk Venture*, London, Hodder & Stoughton, *c.* 1928

McElrea, Richard and Harrowfield, David, *Polar Castaways*, Montreal, McGill-Queen's University Press, 2004

Morton, H.V., *In Search of London*, London, Methuen, 1951

Savours, Ann, *The Voyages of the Discovery*, London, Virgin, 1992

Seligman, Adrian, *The Voyage of the Cap Pilar*, London, Seafarer Books, 1993

Shackleton, Ernest, *South*, London, Robinson, 1999

Stenhouse, Denis, *A History of the Stenhouse Family*, Edinburgh, Scottish Genealogical Society

Stenhouse, J.R., *Cracker Hash: The Story of an Apprentice in Sail*, London, Percival Marshall, 1955

Tapprell Dorling ('Taffrail'), *Endless Story*, London, Hodder & Stoughton, 1932

Thomson, John, *Shackleton's Captain: A Biography of Frank Worsley*, Ontario, Mosaic Press, 1999

Tyler-Lewis, Kelly, *The Lost Men*, London, Viking, 2006

Worsley, Frank, *Endurance: An Epic of Polar Adventure*, New York, Norton & Co., 2000

INDEX

Index

Lightning Source UK Ltd.
Milton Keynes UK
UKOW05f1428090714

234839UK00004B/36/P